M000300367

Four Guardians

FOUR GUARDIANS

A Principled Agent View of American
Civil-Military Relations

JEFFREY W. DONNITHORNE

Johns Hopkins University Press
Baltimore

Opinions, conclusions, and recommendations expressed or implied within are solely those of the author and do not represent the views of Air University, the United States Air Force, the Department of Defense, or any other US government agency.

© 2018 Johns Hopkins University Press
All rights reserved. Published 2018
Printed in the United States of America on acid-free paper

Johns Hopkins Paperback edition, 2021
2   4   6   8   9   7   5   3   1

Johns Hopkins University Press
2715 North Charles Street
Baltimore, Maryland 21218-4363
www.press.jhu.edu

The Library of Congress has cataloged the hardcover edition of this book as follows:

Names: Donnithorne, Jeffrey W., author.
Title: Four guardians : a principled agent view of American civil-military relations / Jeffrey W. Donnithorne.
Description: Baltimore : Johns Hopkins University Press, 2018 | Includes bibliographical references and index.
Identifiers: LCCN 2017039403 | ISBN 9781421425429 (hardcover : alk. paper) | ISBN 9781421425436 (electronic) | ISBN 1421425424 (hardcover : alk. paper) | ISBN 1421425432 (electronic)
Subjects: LCSH: Civil-military relations—United States. | United States. Air Force. | United States. Army. | United States. Marine Corps. | United States. Navy. | United States. Rapid Deployment Joint Task Force.
Classification: LCC JK330 .D66 2018 | DDC 322/.50973—dc23
LC record available at https://lccn.loc.gov/2017039403

A catalog record for this book is available from the British Library.

ISBN-13: 978-1-4214-3992-1
ISBN-10: 1-4214-3992-1

Special discounts are available for bulk purchases of this book. For more information, please contact Special Sales at specialsales@press.jhu.edu.

Johns Hopkins University Press uses environmentally friendly book materials, including recycled text paper that is composed of at least 30 percent post-consumer waste, whenever possible.

For Katherine, Jackson, and Charlotte

contents

acknowledgments

I have been informally researching the ideas in this book for over 30 years. Experiencing the different military cultures has been one of the narrative threads woven throughout my life. I grew up in an Army family and spent much of my childhood in West Point, New York, home of the United States Military Academy. My first two years as an Air Force officer were spent at Naval Air Station Pensacola, Florida. There I learned to fly jets in a joint-service, Navy-led training program, commanded by officers in the Navy and Marine Corps. The rest of my years with the Air Force have been filled with opportunities to reflect on why airmen tend to think and act as they do. The animating thesis of the book emerges from personal experience, so the list of counselors who have informed these ideas is practically limitless. Thank you to the cast of thousands who have shaped my character and that of this book.

The more formal work on this project developed in stages across multiple academic seasons. First, I am grateful for my time at George Washington University, where my focused thinking about civil-military relations and organizational culture began. I thank my cohort of intern classmates whose reflections on Air Force life have sharpened my own—both then and now. Next, my year at the School of Advanced Air and Space Studies (SAASS) grounded my thinking in the broader context of military history, political science, and grand strategy. I thank the SAASS network—faculty and students alike—for the opportunity to join the "life of the mind" for the second half of my military career. Lastly, my years at Georgetown University forced me to discipline my ideas with a rigorous methodology and more careful habits of inquiry. I am grateful to my Georgetown cohort, professors, and advisers for their committed collegiality and wise counsel. I particularly thank Andy Bennett, Dan Byman, Tom McNaugher, and Liz Stanley—world-class scholars and wonderful people—whose incisive feedback strongly shaped the earlier form of this project.

The original research for the book required the kind assistance of many experts. I am very grateful to the many distinguished national servants who agreed to speak with me and share their perspective on history: David Chu, Seth Cropsey, John Lehman, Jim Locher, Robert Murray, General (Ret.) P. X. Kelley, General (Ret.) Carl Stiner, General (Ret.) Volney Warner, Lieutenant General (Ret.) Dale Vesser, Brigadier General (Ret.) Daniel Kaufman, Colonel (Ret.) Raoul Alcala, Colonel (Ret.) Arch Barrett, Captain (Ret.) William Cohen, Colonel (Ret.) Powell Hutton, Colonel (Ret.) James Stefan, Colonel (Ret.) Jack Wood, Dr. Fred Harrod, and Dr. Edgar Raines. I also benefited greatly from friends and colleagues, who helped to shape earlier versions of the service chapters; my sincerest thanks to Nate Bailey, Thane Clare, Mike Gallagher, and Bryan Groves.

Transforming these seasons of research into a book has been a long journey aided by many companions. My colleagues Harry Foster, Grant Hammond, and Blake McMahon cheered me on and supported me at every step. A distinguished group of military historians generously reviewed the manuscript: Steve Chiabotti, Grant Hammond, Tom Hughes, and Rich Muller all improved my drafts significantly with their perceptive observations. Friend Janet Kurtz read the early chapters and offered superb feedback that launched the book on the right trajectory. I especially thank my parents, Larry and Fran Donnithorne, who read every word of every draft with far more enthusiasm than the text deserved. Their thoughtful suggestions and frequent attaboys fueled my forward progress.

Finally, I thank my wife, Katherine, and our children, Jackson and Charlotte, to whom I dedicate this book. You graciously abided the invasion of this project into our family life. You generously gave me the two-hour blocks of evening and weekend time I needed to chip away at the task. And you faithfully supplied the steady diet of encouragement, coffee, love, and laughs that I needed to do my best while keeping it in perspective. Thank you. *SDG*.

Four Guardians

Introduction

Why *do* the soldiers think one way, and the sailors another, and the airmen still a third?
      —Admiral J. C. Wylie, "Why a Sailor Thinks Like a Sailor"

Old hands at the Pentagon tell a familiar story. One day, the story goes, the four service chiefs report to the secretary of defense for an urgent mission—they are directed to *secure the building*. Having clearly heard their boss, the four services hurry to carry out the secretary's order. The Army establishes a defensive perimeter around the building, rolls out concertina wire, sets up checkpoints, and controls all access to the structure. The Navy interprets the order differently. The sailors go inside, turn off the lights and coffee pots, make an entry in the logbook, lock the doors, and leave. Building secured. When it is their turn, the Marines find the nearest body of water, execute a textbook amphibious landing, assault the building, and plant an American flag on the roof. Finally, the Air Force secures the building by negotiating a five-year lease with an option to buy, and then signs a long-term service contract on the air-conditioning.

This common caricature of the four services reveals a surprising truth about American civil-military relations. Each service interpreted the order differently, so their responses varied wildly. Which of the services, if any, did the right thing? By moving in four different directions to secure the building, the services no doubt frustrated the intent of the secretary of defense—whatever it might have been. Should this be considered disobedience or a compromise of civilian control over the military? Or are there times when the four services comply with civilian direction in different ways, interpreting a policy in a manner that reflects the unique cultures of their organizations?

The fictional world of securing a building shares unsettling traits with the real world of securing the nation. In this crucial business of national security, misunderstandings can cost lives and threaten vital interests. Clarity of language and intent helps to ensure that smart decisions are made and carried out faithfully. But today's civil-military environment appears ripe for more misunderstanding than clarity. Facing complex security challenges in a time of rapid technological change, the US defense community is staring at profound uncertainty when it looks to the future. Inside the Pentagon, this pervasive strategic ambiguity creates a fierce internal competition—not just for resources but for ideas and clarity. What is the real threat to American interests? Which technological investments will give the United States continuing advantage? What do power and leverage even look like in the hyper-networked world of the future? The four services offer provisional answers to these kinds of questions each year as they spend hundreds of billions of dollars, placing bets on the best ways to buy down future risk.

As they place these bets, each of the four military services brings a distinctive style, lexicon, wish list, and worldview to its task. Each has its own culture, a way of thinking conditioned by its operational environment and unique political history. As the US military confronts a new era of security challenges, the services tacitly invoke their cultural beliefs to make sense of the ambiguity, most likely moving in different directions as they advise and execute civilian policies. Certainly, some of the services' actions will flow from routine jockeying for prestige, mission turf, and budget share—the well-documented world of interservice rivalry. But bureaucratic self-interest and rivalry do not tell the whole story. As the mission to secure the building suggests, a military service's response to civilian direction may be a culturally conditioned interpretation of what a task requires.

These varying cultural interpretations can ultimately affect civil-military relations and the health of American democracy. Duke University professor Peter Feaver, a leading scholar in the field, describes a "civil-military empathy gap" as one of the primary challenges in American civil-military relations.[1] Senior civilian and military leaders often fail to understand each other's incentives, equities, and culture. In her analysis of current civil-military paradoxes, Georgetown University law professor Rosa Brooks agrees. Brooks finds the "gap of knowledge" and "gap of trust" between senior civilians and senior military officers to be a particularly troubling condition for the nation.[2] This "mixture of mistrust and almost willful ignorance" can lead directly to damaging policy decisions, she argues, doing "genuine harm both to the military and to US interests."[3] As each side struggles to appreciate the concerns of the other, the result is friction, distrust, and less effective policies in this most critical arena of national security.

This lack of understanding is not limited to political elites. The American people also appear to have little knowledge about their military, despite widespread esteem and frequent offerings of "thank you for your service." A recent study found an increasing proportion of public survey respondents offering "don't know" or "no opinion" answers to questions about the military. Compared with a similar survey in the late 1990s, the recent crop of responses comprised a "large and significant shift" toward general ignorance or apathy about basic military issues.[4] Ironically, the past 16 years of continuous military operations have seen an increase in esteem for the military with a commensurate decrease in knowledge about who the military is, what it does, or how it tends to think.

The goal of this book is to start closing these empathy and knowledge gaps with a new approach to understanding and evaluating US civil-military relations. Civilian leaders, military members, and interested citizens should find this book helpful for understanding more about the cultural beliefs and political incentives in the American civil-military system. It blends theoretical innovation, sociological insights about the four services, and new case studies of civil-military relations in action. In the end, it offers a novel perspective on the four military services, the dynamics of civilian control, and the principled ways in which the services fulfill their role as "armed servants" of the nation.[5]

The Civil-Military Puzzle: Explaining Military Compliance

With its focus on civilian control of the military, this book confronts an enduring dilemma of organized politics: who guards the guardians—and how? How can an elite force with dominant coercive power be sharpened as the tool of the state, without becoming a threat to the state? Since Plato, scholars have pondered the paradox of armed delegation. Plato asked, how could a city's guardians be made "fierce to their enemies but gentle to their friends?"[6] In the United States, the threat of a military coup is indeed remote; but this does not mean that American civil-military relations are thoroughly stable or uninteresting. The lack of coups, in fact, makes the American case all the more intriguing. In his classic work on the military and politics, Samuel Finer insightfully questioned why the military *ever* submits to civilian control: "Instead of asking why the military engage in politics, we ought surely to ask why they ever do otherwise . . . The military possess vastly superior organization. And they possess *arms*."[7] Finer reframed a nineteenth-century insight from Alexis de Tocqueville, who warned, "There is nothing more dangerous than an army amid an unwarlike nation. The citizens' excessive love of quiet puts the constitution every day at the mercy of the soldiers."[8] How, then, do elected civilian leaders—on behalf of the American people—ensure that military behavior remains conformed to the expressed will of the state? What explains the puzzling subordination of the most powerful guardian class in history, fighting foreign threats without becoming a domestic menace?

Samuel Huntington, the founding father of American civil-military relations theory, offered a seminal answer to the question of civilian control. As I explain in greater detail in chapter 1, Huntington's 1957 work *The Soldier and the State* argued that civilian leaders should establish a pattern of "objective control" that gives the military autonomy in exchange for voluntary subordination. Huntington suggested a sort of grand bargain, a division of labor in which civilians made the political decisions and insulated uniformed leaders to focus on military matters. By distancing military leaders from political calculations, civilians could cultivate an apolitical military professionalism that willingly submitted to civilian direction.

Huntington's answer intuitively appealed to many readers, particularly active military officers who craved the autonomy he prescribed. For a theoretical explanation of military subordination, however, Huntington relied on a particular definition of military professionalism—a definition that necessarily included willing submission to civilian control. Peter Feaver, who studied under Huntington at Harvard, recognized the weakness in the objective control thesis. Huntington's causal logic—whereby autonomy leads to professionalism, which leads to willing subordination—required a specific definition of professionalism to animate the theory. "In emphasizing the role of professionalism," Feaver argued, Huntington was "vulnerable to charges of defining away the problem of civilian control."[9] Huntington's normative theory outlined what professional military officers *should* do, but stopped short of identifying the political incentives that channel actual behaviors.

Building on Huntington's normative work, Feaver articulated a materialist principal-agent theory to explain the puzzle of civilian control.[10] Adapting insights from a robust economic literature, Feaver posited the civil-military relationship as a unique case of principal-agent delegation. When a principal delegates a task to an agent, he tries to incentivize the agent to perform the job exactly as requested, at a minimum cost of oversight. Classic principal-agent theory describes the variables that give rise to better or worse outcomes in these agency relationships. Feaver imports this principal-agent framework into the world of civil-military relations, as civilian principals delegate to military agents the mission of providing security for the state. To encourage the military to carry out policies in good faith, civilians shape key variables such as the degree of oversight, the gap between civilian and military policy preferences, and the expectations of meaningful rewards and punishments. Together, these incentives shape the conditions under which military behavior moves closer to or farther from the civilians' ideal point.

A Principled Agent Theory

Feaver's agency model provides the strongest and most flexible point of departure for further study. Building on that foundation, this book presents a new *principled agent* approach to explain finer-grained civil-military outcomes. Civil-military dynamics include not only principal-agent dynamics but also the deeply *principled* decisions made by the four military agents. While Feaver's model offered the first critical step in identifying the major variables that shape civil-military behavior, this analysis goes further by suggesting ways in which the agency model varies across different political conditions.

A principled agent approach stretches the baseline agency model in three directions. First, it expands the temporal scope of agency theory to focus more attention on the advisory or policymaking stage. A great deal of important civil-military dialogue occurs during this advisory period, and civil-military friction is probably higher while a debate is still alive. A military agent's approach to civil-military dialogue differs qualitatively on either side of a final decision. As expert advisors, military agents are expected to provide candid and even contentious input into a policy debate. Once the final decision is made, however, military agents are expected to cease advocacy and carry out the policy in good faith. Military culture esteems those who speak truth to power during the debate, then salute smartly and carry out the final decision to the best of their ability. The importance of this practical distinction motivates an expansion of the theory to give focused attention to both sides of a decision.

Furthermore, during the advisory phase, the agency framework still applies, but it does so in the "shadow of the future."[11] Before a decision is made, a civil-military policy debate involves not only the substantive issues in play but also the contractual parameters of future implementation. *How* a policy gets implemented can be as important as *what* gets decided. How specific is the policy language? How enduring is the policy instrument—is it a verbal order, an executive memo, or formal legislation? How soon does the policy take effect? Is there time to re-litigate the debate? Can the pending policy be monitored effectively? These principal-agent enforcement questions are as much a part of a civil-military debate as is the substance of the policy itself.

This insight can yield counterintuitive outcomes. If a military service opposes a given policy, but the proposal appears unenforceable in the future, the policy debate may be quite tepid—the military agent could anticipate a lax future compliance regime, making the debate unnecessary. On the other hand, a civilian proposal that the military favors might spark heated debate, as the military agent negotiates more rigid parameters to lock in long-term gains from the favorable policy. Such cases of violent agreement may surprise those who focus only on the substantive issues at hand. In some cases, the desired degree of maneuver room could matter as much as the letter of the law.

A second key expansion in the principled agent framework focuses on the relative coherence of the policy in question, as suggested by its clarity, consistency, and feasibility. Policies that are highly ambiguous in language or intent, internally inconsistent, at odds with existing policies, or essentially unattainable create inherent problems for a principal-agent relationship. Traditional agency theory views military behavior largely as a material cost-benefit calculation of whether or not to comply, informed by the monitoring environment, the magnitude of the gap between military and civilian preferences, and the likelihood of meaningful rewards (or punishments) for good (or poor) compliance. For simplicity, the baseline model generally assumes that the principal's policy is known, understood, clear, and attainable; the agent's decision hinges on *whether* to comply. But this is frequently not the case.

For a large number of policies, the environment teems with ambiguity, inconsistency, and infeasibility that render compliance problematic, even with the best of intentions. In such cases, the military agent's decision may be about *how* to comply, not whether to do so. Such a calculation differs qualitatively from a material cost-benefit analysis and requires some kind of default script for sense-making and action. For a military service wrangling with an ambiguous policy, the service might not be trying to go its own way—it might be trying to figure out which way to go. In American civil-military relations, the distinct culture of each service helps provide a ready answer in the midst of policy ambiguity.

Consequently, the third expansion in the principled agent framework moves the agency focus from a single military actor to the four military services. The American military services dominate the defense landscape, with enormous power over what the Defense Department buys, how it fights, what its members wear, how they think, and who is in charge. Treating the American military as a unitary actor ignores the great diversity of thought and action, rooted in the strength, vitality, and power in each service's culture. Culture conditions the preferences each service brings to a policy debate and offers a baseline repertoire for action in ambiguous environments.[12] Understanding American civil-military relations requires a deft understanding of who the four services are and how they think. A major ambition of this book includes painting a meaningful portrait of the four services, explaining what the services tend to believe and why.

How do these three expansions come together in a single framework? Chapter 1 explains this model in richer detail, but figure I.1 previews the essential ideas. It synthesizes the interaction of these newly introduced variables, depicting four unique condition sets where civil-military dynamics are likely to differ. The first two expansions described above—expanding the timeline and evaluating the relative policy coherence—establish the 2 × 2 matrix,

Principled Agent Framework

	Preparatory Agency	Traditional Principal–Agent Theory
High Policy Coherence	• Agents anticipate the slack in the proposed future compliance environment • Civil–military debate covers both the policy substance and the parameters of implementation slack • Military agents seek to lock in favored policies or create slack for disfavored ones **II**	**I** • Civilian principals adjust the monitoring regime, preference gaps, rewards, and punishments to encourage military compliance • Military decision is largely *whether* or *how much* to comply with the stated policy
Low Policy Coherence	**III** Principled Diagnosis • In ambiguous, complex, or cluttered policy environments, military agents diagnose the situation, aided by the lens of service culture • Civil–military interaction is marked by culturally conditioned problem definition	**IV** Principled Agency • Military behavior is marked by culturally conditioned interpretation of what compliance requires in a given context • Military decision may be more about *how* to comply, not a material cost–benefit calculation of whether to do so
	Advising	Executing

Figure I.1. Summary of principled agent hypotheses as the timeline and coherence of the policy vary.

while the third key variable of service culture animates the analysis *within* the matrix.

Traditional agency theory helps explain the figure's top right square, only one-fourth of the rendered policy space. In the other three regimes, where policies are being debated and policy coherence is low, different dynamics require a different framework. Principled agent theory suggests that before arriving at the top right square of traditional agency theory, most civil-military matters migrate through at least two of the other three squares. When policy issues achieve reasonable coherence before getting executed, they move up the left side of the figure. Conversely, when issues move from advising to execution while remaining largely incoherent, the civil-military debate churns across the bottom of the figure. Either pathway challenges existing theory and requires a new way to think about American civil-military relations.

Understanding the American Military

A new approach to understanding civil-military relations invites a new understanding of the American military itself. Despite 15 years of continuous and costly war, public fascination with and respect for the military continue to rise. But survey data suggest that the American people, leaders and laypersons alike, understand few of the elemental differences between the four major services.[13] The opening caricature of the services, securing the building in wildly different ways, reflects more truth than fiction. Consequently, this book takes seriously the core differences in nature and nurture that give rise to very different patterns of belief.

In this approach to civil-military relations, I define service culture as a prevailing belief system about ends, ways, and means. What does each service tend to believe about why it exists, what it exists to do, and with what resources? Many definitions or approaches to culture could be used; I choose to focus on the elements of belief most likely to affect civil-military policymaking. A service's self-conception of its ends, ways, and means is the strategic heart of the service, the kind of beliefs that are most likely to reverberate in civil-military dialogue and practice.

This approach to service culture mirrors the operational code analysis pioneered by Alexander George. Building on earlier work by Nathan Leites, George argued that decision-makers work from an integrated set of beliefs about how the world works—a belief system he called an operational code.[14] These beliefs "provide the basic framework within which the actor approaches the task of attempting to process available information and to engage in rational calculation in pursuit of his values and interests."[15] In other words, operational codes affect both "diagnostic and choice propensities"—the information one tends to notice and the choices one tends to make.[16] As George noted, these codes of belief operate not like a deterministic algorithm but rather as a heuristic guide to perception and judgment.

For the four military services, service culture works much like George's operational code. Cultural beliefs about ends, ways, and means guide the services through ambiguous policy spaces. Such beliefs affect what the services pay attention to and the preferences they have about particular policies. Furthermore, following George's methodological lead, these service cultures can be researched systematically through "structured focused comparison" and then assessed for causal impact on policy preferences through deductive analysis.[17] The case studies in chapters 6 and 7 reveal these cultures at work, as unique cultural beliefs prompt the services to respond differently in various policy debates.

To substantiate these core beliefs, I devote a chapter to each service. In building these chapters, I canvased each service's own narratives in search of its founding context, cherished role models, notable events, and unique operating environment. What messages or stories does each service tend to tell about its own ends, ways, and means? For each service, I distill these insights into a slate of five or six elemental beliefs that provide an empirical shorthand for analytic application in the case studies. These service portraits attempt to convey not only what each service tends to think, but why. The analysis seeks to be empathetic, explaining how both operational nature and political nurture have interacted to create an organizationally rational pattern of beliefs for each service. For example, what are the essential characteristics of life at sea that give Navy sailors a particular view of leadership and command? Or, what contextual factors surrounding the birth of the Air Force in 1947 confer strong service beliefs about the proper way to employ airpower?

My approach takes a broad and historical view in defining the contours of the services. When this book speaks generally of "the Navy" or "the Air Force," for example, it invokes an abstract, anthropomorphic conception. It describes a collective impression, not the concrete beliefs of each and every member of the service. In a sense, this view of each service is a useful fiction—a methodological choice to aggregate each service's history, organization, and personnel into an overall persona.[18] Cultural scholar Edgar Schein describes culture as an "empirically based abstraction." There is clearly something *there*, but it cannot be poked with a stick or held in one's hand.[19] My approach to thinking about the services and their cultures aligns with Schein's description. By targeting the analysis at the service level, I knowingly subsume intra-service and individual-level variation. Subcultures certainly exist within each service, and these service-level beliefs do not inform the mindset of every service member. But as a simplifying assumption, I argue that these within-service variations do more to affect internal service politics than the externally focused civil-military dynamics at issue in this study.

In many respects, this approach follows the course charted by Admiral J. C. Wylie's 1957 essay, "Why a Sailor Thinks Like a Sailor."[20] Wylie believed that the mission of the Navy at sea and the service's unique experiences as an organization gave sailors a worldview quite distinct from that of their ground- or air-centric brethren. "Strangely enough," he observed, "the one aspect of the situation that has never really been publicly aired, nor even examined with enough perception and depth to make it worth the effort, is the underlying basis of the disagreement. Why *do* the soldiers think one way, and the sailors another, and the airmen still a third?"[21] The principled agent approach takes seriously Wylie's challenge, attempting to bring perception and depth to this fundamental question of *why*, while exploring the vital implications for civil-military theory and practice.

What do some of these service-level differences look like? Here I offer a brief preview of the Navy, Marine Corps, Army, and Air Force; chapters 2 through 5 provide the historical background and rationale that explain how these beliefs came to be. The case studies, in chapters 6 and 7, show these beliefs at work by illustrating the deductive linkages between the services' beliefs and their policy preferences in civil-military exchanges.

The Navy

The US Navy boasts a long history and proud tradition of service at sea. It remains securely lashed to its ancient traditions, reflecting the regal sensibilities of its British forebears. Having provided many of our nation's first ambassadors, the Navy continues to believe strongly in its unique capacity to serve as an independent instrument of national power, navigating the border waters between diplomacy and war. Accustomed to operating over the horizon with minimal scrutiny, the service believes it wields power in ways logically alien to those who fight only on land or in the sky. The Navy's fiercely independent culture conditions a preference for autonomy, with minimal oversight and maximum access.

Navy culture, on ship and ashore, breathes salty air—no matter how close to or far away from the ocean the sailors may be. A ship underway requires a choreographed pattern of life to stay alive and do its job. Those rhythms and rhymes of nautical life define the Navy's standard practice on land as well. Sailors in land-locked buildings still stand watch through the night and climb ladderwells (stairs) up to the third deck (floor) to use the head (restroom). In spirit, if not in fact, the whole Navy remains ever at sea. While underway, a ship's crew is always in harm's way—if not from an enemy, then from the corrosive and unpredictable power of the sea itself. To survive and win in a harsh maritime environment, the entire ship's crew must work together, remain vigilant, perform its drills, and obey orders. Enlisted sailors must perform their jobs with dispatch and total obedience, while officers—particularly the ship's captain—are expected to operate not from checklists, but from a deep reservoir of judgment filled through years at sea. The commanding officer (CO) occupies a revered place in naval society. The ethos of command in the Navy emphasizes the unbreakable triad of authority, responsibility, and accountability. Compared with the other services, the Navy offers more trust and swifter accountability to its commanding officers.

Finally, the Navy holds fast to its requirement for a permanent fleet of ships and a professional complement of capable crew. Unlike the Army, which relies on swelling to full strength in wartime, the Navy operates by deploying forward and projecting power. This operational philosophy requires the peacetime infrastructure and resources to have a ready fleet at all times.

The Marine Corps

The US Marine Corps guards its culture closely and reproduces it religiously. Being a Marine is fundamentally an identity, not a job. You do not join the Marine Corps; you *become* a Marine. Together, Marines comprise an elite warrior fraternity; they run toward the sound of the guns, never retreat, and take care of their own. Marines boast a hybrid nature as soldiers of the sea, with one foot on shore and the other afloat. Deployed with the Navy's fleet, the Marines provide a quick-reaction force for seemingly any crisis in nearly any location.

Organized within the Department of the Navy, the Marine Corps sits in a precarious institutional position as the smallest of the services whose tasks span the domains of warfare dominated by the other three services. This uncertain position confers a constructive paranoia on the Corps, which remains ever mindful that the Marine Corps exists only because the American people want it to exist. "In terms of cold, mechanical logic," observed Lieutenant General Victor Krulak, "the United States does not *need* a Marine Corps. However, for good reasons which completely transcend cold logic, the United States *wants* a Marine Corps."[22] As a service, the Marine Corps stays focused on being useful and remaining wanted.

Marines foster a proud culture of frugal ingenuity, emphasizing the importance of stewarding the national trust and taxpayer dollar with care. Throughout their famous history, Marines have made do with what they were given, cared for it faithfully, and transformed meager means into battlefield victories. In fact, the embodiment of Marine culture is the ultimate Marine Corps no-frills weapon system: the enlisted Marine with his rifle. Every Marine is a rifleman, and nearly all efforts in Marine Corps life coalesce around the purpose of supporting the rifle-shooting Marine engaged with the enemy.

The Army

The US Army serves as a microcosm of the nation itself, charting its organizational history in close correlation with the highs and lows of American history. It sees itself as a faithful extension of the American people and as a steward of the historical profession of arms. The Army tends to have the highest civil-military awareness, rooted in colonial-era fears of standing armies. This awareness makes the Army the most compliant and faithful to the executive branch chain of command, and the most leery of engaging with Congress and advocating for its needs. The Army believes strongly in serving as an apolitical and obedient junior partner to the nation's civilian leadership.

The Army understands its role as an indispensable last line of defense. The Army offers the nation an organized and skilled body of servants that must accept glorious and menial tasks alike, serving as a labor force of last resort to do the nation's messiest jobs, prepared to take more blame than credit. On the battlefield, the service's massive size and diversity of functions create a belief in the imperative to coordinate, centralize, and synchronize operations. While tactical flexibility is important, the driving motivation for Army operations is to synchronize and remain in gear with the massive Army machine.

Manpower is a central preoccupation of the Army. As a mobilization engine, the service must be prepared for war during times of peace and must swell rapidly and capably to whatever degree a crisis requires. Generating sufficient manpower is the Army's first duty in national defense, so the service focuses more on people than on things. Drawing upon America's rich militia heritage, the individual soldier is the indispensable ingredient in making an Army. In turn, individuals aggregate into squads, regiments, and divisions, many of which boast long histories and distinctive traditions of dress and style. Joining the 1st Cavalry Division or the 101st Airborne Division means far more than just showing up to a new post—you are joining ranks with history itself. Commanding a division like these requires leaders with muddy boots; leading soldiers in the field is the most revered job in the Army.

As these brief descriptions suggest, the Army and the Marine Corps represent a study in contrasts. While both services pride themselves in being warriors, the Army and Marine Corps are in many ways cultural opposites. First, the Marines have been *wanted* but not necessarily *needed* throughout their organizational life, thus energizing the service with an organizationally focused survival instinct. The Army, however, grew up amidst a national aversion to standing armies; the Army has therefore been *needed* but largely unwanted, thus generating a nationally focused commitment to subservience. Regarding size, the Marine Corps is the smallest of the services with the most cohesive and unified culture, centered around the Marine infantryman. The Army, by contrast, is the largest service with the most diverse array of job specializations and, consequently, the least cohesive culture. As an illustration, the Marine Corps unifies its history and iconography at a single location: the National Museum of the Marine Corps near Quantico, Virginia. An aspiring student of Army history and culture, however, can visit any of 105 Army museums, spread across 42 states and three countries, and dedicated to specific branch and geographic subdivisions.[23]

The fundamental purpose of the two services differs as well. The Marine Corps exists as a middleweight expeditionary quick-reaction force, serving in effect as first responders to stabilize a critical situation. The Army is a massive heavyweight force, slower to deploy and even slower to return home, serving much like the full hospital staff that must care for the patient for the long term, until death or discharge. Finally, Marines cultivate an elite image—Marines are different, America at its polished best. The Army instead fosters an egalitarian image, a faithful reflection of the American people, serving as an armed microcosm of the nation itself.

The Air Force

In 1947, the US Air Force was born out of the Army, the offspring of a technology mated to an idea. Once aircraft broke into the third dimension, a rebel band of air-minded soldiers caught a vision for a new way of war. Why slug it out in the trenches when you can just fly over and take the fight to the heart of the enemy? Today's airmen, descendants of these rebels, hold fast to the belief that the aerospace domain comprises a distinct arena of warfare. Controlling the air requires separately focused organizational and intellectual commitments decoupled from the land and sea. Because the service argued for its autonomy on the basis of unique *ideas* about aerial employment, the Air Force's fight for independence birthed a persistent institutional insecurity. Its sense of security as an organization rises and falls with the broader acceptance of the Air Force's distinct ideas—and the commensurate success that can be achieved by following them. The Air Force therefore claims an exclusive expertise about employing aircraft, bristling at civilian intervention or limitations on its preferred use of aircraft and weapons.

Consequently, several beliefs in the Air Force's operational code orbit around the *right* way to use airpower. The service believes that when used appropriately, airpower has the potential to decide the outcome of a war. By targeting the enemy's war-making capacity and key means of national resistance, a fully committed and complete air campaign can bypass fielded forces and crush the heart of the enemy.

The Air Force believes that controlling the skies is the essential precondition for successful land and sea operations. Establishing air superiority is therefore the primary imperative for any US military mission. Similarly, the Air Force maintains a steady conviction that airpower must be centrally controlled by the senior airman in the region, who can flexibly direct air assets in accordance with the joint commander's objectives. Aircraft should not be preassigned and parceled out to independent field commanders, lest their inherent flexibility be compromised. The Air Force holds these truths to be self-evident, while the other services (the Army and Marine Corps, in particular) tend to believe otherwise.

Unsurprisingly, machines and technology play an important role in shaping the belief set of the Air Force. Created to exploit a disruptive new technology, the service has an abiding faith in the potential for new technologies to change the face of warfare. Lastly, the Air Force exhibits an informally collegial culture, unlike that in any of the other services. In the Air Force way of war, officers tend to fly and fight while enlisted airmen operate as skilled technicians, usually from relatively safe and secure air bases. Since most officer-enlisted relations therefore occur away from the battle zone, the resulting dynamic in the Air Force is generally respectful, but noticeably collegial and informal.

In sum, each service wields power according to an essential logic. Reducing each service to its core: Army power is fundamentally about *ultimate occupation*; wars are decided in the end by a "man on the scene with a gun."[24] The Navy is a force of *forward projection*; its carriers and escorts flexibly deliver five acres of sovereign US territory (and firepower) all across the world. The Marine Corps offers the power of *responsive intervention*; whenever called, whatever the task, the Marine Corps is ready to go, fight, and win. Lastly, the Air Force wields the power of *strategic interdiction*; it holds critical targets at risk anywhere in the world. Each service certainly does more, but at its core, each knows it must do no less.

Case Study Methodology

With these sketches of the services in mind, how do these differences translate into varying civil-military outcomes? To put the principled agent theory and cultural analyses to work, chapters 6 and 7 analyze the civil-military interactions in two important policy cases: (1) the creation story of the Rapid Deployment Joint Task Force, the organizational precursor to the military giant US Central Command, and (2) the prolonged political struggle to pass the Goldwater-Nichols Act in 1986. The two case studies weave theoretical analysis with historical narrative to reveal the insights from a culture-based principled agent framework. Within each case, I test the framework through a process-tracing methodology that looks for the observable implications of implicit causal mechanisms.[25] In other words, if the causal linkages I propose are really happening, what would we expect to see in the historical record? This approach generates numerous testable hypotheses within each case and imposes discipline on the analytic narrative.

The Rapid Deployment Joint Task Force

The first major case study captures the little-known story of the Rapid Deployment Joint Task Force (RDJTF). Since the massive campaign to liberate Kuwait in 1990–91, the US military has marched to the steady drumbeat of war in the Persian Gulf region. The American military machine arrived in Southwest Asia in 1990 and has never left. Throughout the past quarter-century of continual battle, the military organization directing the daily grind of war has been US Central Command (CENTCOM), headquartered at MacDill Air Force Base in Tampa, Florida. The preeminence of CENTCOM in recent military memory, however, tends to mask the highly uncertain political and military decisions that informed its initial creation.

When Iraqi tanks rumbled south into Kuwait in August 1990, CENTCOM was an unproven adolescent in the US military command structure. Just a decade earlier, no such entity existed. For much of the Cold War, in fact, the Middle East languished as the neglected hinterlands of European Command (EUCOM) and Pacific Command (PACOM), the two command titans focused on defending Western Europe, South Korea, and Japan. By 1977, new strategic realities finally prompted the Carter administration to create a US military organization focused on the Middle East. President Jimmy Carter signed a presidential directive in August 1977 ordering the formation of a deployment-ready force. After two and a half years, the Joint Chiefs of Staff cobbled together the RDJTF, combining (in theory) forces from all four services to deploy on short notice to the Persian Gulf region. Just three years later, after much controversy and debate, the hobbled RDJTF was deactivated and CENTCOM established in its place.

As an empirical demonstration of the principled agent model, chapter 6 presents a focused case study on the creation and development of the RDJTF. The chapter highlights the period from 1977 through 1983, from the Carter administration's specification of the Persian Gulf as a region of likely military conflict through President Ronald Reagan's decision to establish CENTCOM on January 1, 1983. If President Carter directed the creation of this force in 1977, why did it take nearly six years to establish CENTCOM? Is this a case of military foot-dragging, or were other dynamics in play? Why was the Army pushing for a new four-service organization, while the Marine Corps viewed the task as a routine part of Navy and Marine Corps operations? Were the military disagreements just another case of interservice rivalry, a mere competition for turf and prestige, or is there more to the story? The case study focuses attention specifically on the Army and the Marine Corps and their different approaches to the civil-military environment. While all four services were involved, the Army and Marine Corps received the bulk of the attention, both in the news of that day and in the later historical analyses that describe the interservice rivalry.

The Four-Year Fight to Pass Goldwater-Nichols

The second major case study of civil-military interaction examines the four-year period from 1982 to 1986 that led to passage of the Goldwater-Nichols Department of Defense Reorganization Act of 1986. During this period, major players in the defense establishment grappled with two fundamental political questions: who holds the power and how should it be exercised?

When it passed, the act fundamentally reshuffled the deck of power within the Department of Defense. The new law made the chairman of the Joint Chiefs of Staff (CJCS) the principal military advisor to the president, created the position of vice chairman of the Joint Chiefs of Staff, took steps to enhance the quality of officers assigned to the Joint Staff, specified that the Joint Staff works for the CJCS and not for the corporate Joint Chiefs, and strengthened the authority of the unified and specified commanders over their service components. While these provisions may appear merely administrative to an outsider, to factions within the military the stakes were incredibly high—even existential.

Chapter 7 focuses specifically on the actions of the Army and Navy and offers a compelling challenge to the conventional wisdom that the Pentagon was uniformly opposed to the law.[26] Instead, the case study presents clear evidence of substantive support from key factions within the Army; the principled agent model both predicts and explains why this would be the case. While the Navy opposed and fought the proposals at every step, the Army took a very different approach. As the debate raged in 1985, for example, the Army created a special review committee "to make an unbiased and open minded review of the validity of the major conclusions" of a controversial Senate staff study.[27] Furthermore, the group's charter included special instructions directing it to "look for positive directions in which Army can support constructive change," and clarified that the committee's review and conclusions "will not be constrained by preestablished Army/OSD [Office of the Secretary of Defense] positions."[28] In giving direction to the review committee, Brigadier General Howard Graves instructed it to "look at what the country needs. Let's get out of the green suit." Toward that end, Graves noted that "the Army might have to sacrifice some of its special interests for the greater good."[29] Clearly, the Army's institutional position can hardly be characterized as uniformly opposed.

The case of Goldwater-Nichols therefore shows meaningful variation in service responses, as the Army and Navy often held very different views and responded differently to the same policy proposals. This variation in responses is curious because the case did not involve issues where one traditionally expects to see variation and disagreement among the services. In this case, the Army and Navy were not fighting over limited defense dollars, or acquiring major weapon systems, or assigning roles and missions. Without these conventional bureaucratic issues in play, the diversity of service responses is all the more puzzling and in need of explanation.

As in the case of the RDJTF, all four services were very much involved in the Goldwater-Nichols debates. To allow for a deeper study of the civil-military dynamics, however, chapter 7 limits its scope to the Army and the Navy. These two services had the most variation between their overall patterns of conduct, and limiting the analytic focus to two services makes room for a more complete view of the principled agent framework in action.

Case Selection

These two cases were selected for several reasons.[30] The case of the RDJTF is largely understudied, empirically rich, and worthy of greater exposure and understanding. Additionally, the six-year span from 1977 to 1983 offers three distinct phases to evaluate both policy advising and interim execution. This case therefore illustrates one of the key pathways through figure I.1. To arrive at the top right square of traditional principal-agent theory, most policies must travel through either the left half or bottom half of the figure. The case of the RDJTF illustrates the hard slog across the bottom of the figure in which the policy debate remains largely incoherent, from advising through execution. At seemingly every step of the story, civilian and military leaders struggled to find a satisfying way ahead in a complex strategic environment. The ambiguity, inconsistency, and infeasibility of various policies rendered military compliance extremely difficult, if not impossible. Consequently, this case study usefully complicates a traditional understanding of military compliance and civilian control. Like the four services securing the building in four different ways in the opening anecdote, many of the military agents in the RDJTF story moved along culturally conditioned pathways of what they thought the job required.

The passage of Goldwater-Nichols was selected for complementary reasons. Most of the provisions in Goldwater-Nichols remain the law of the land, casting a long, 30-year shadow over modern military history. Its significant historical importance, wide array of sub-issues, and long period of debate and bargaining make it a compelling choice for deeper study. Furthermore, this case confronts the common bureaucratic assumption that the military services, like other large organizations, uniformly pursue greater autonomy; the varied responses of the Army and Navy suggest otherwise. The legislation also holds contemporary significance as defense experts trumpet the need to revisit Goldwater-Nichols for a subsequent reform of the defense establishment.[31] An understanding of the cultural barriers and possibilities that shaped the original legislation should prove useful for those attempting to undertake a similar effort today.

The four-year period leading to the passage of Goldwater-Nichols highlights the other primary pathway through figure I.1. Given its attention to the period leading up to passage of the law, the analysis in chapter 7 focuses on the left half of the figure. It traces the debate as it moved from low-coherence advising to higher-coherence advising. Once the issues became clear and well defined, the principal-agent dynamics became broadly *anticipatory*. The political debate focused not only on the substance of the policies but also on their implementation parameters and the amount of slack that would be available for future execution.

Plan of the Book

The book unfolds in several stages. First, chapter 1 establishes in greater detail the theoretical foundation of principled agent theory. It begins with the baseline agency model, and explains the three theoretically informed departures from the baseline. The chapter maps these extensions onto the 2 × 2 matrix shown in figure I.1, then describes in detail the observable implications one would expect to see in each of the four policy spaces.

Second, chapters 2 through 5 focus attention on the four services: first the Navy, then the Marine Corps, Army, and Air Force. Each chapter highlights the interaction of nature and nurture that conditions a particular worldview for the service. These chapters culminate in a slate of five or six key beliefs that each service holds about why it exists, what it exists to do, and with what resources. For readers with a keen interest in civil-military relations (both theory and practice), this four-service portrait establishes the basis for much of the service-level variation in the case studies. For readers solely interested in understanding the US military services—who want to know, for example, why airmen and Marines approach the world so differently—these four chapters may be a satisfying stand-alone primer. At the beginning of chapter 2, I explain in greater detail the research methodology that applies to all four of the service culture chapters.

Third, chapters 6 and 7 build deliberately on the theory in chapter 1 and the empirical cultural analyses in chapters 2 through 5. Chapter 6 details the creation narrative of the Rapid Deployment Joint Task Force, with a particular focus on the Army and Marine Corps. Chapter 7 charts the prolonged political struggle to pass the Goldwater-Nichols Act in 1986, focusing specifically on the varied responses of the Army and Navy.

The final chapter suggests some contemporary implications of the framework and then concludes the argument. It brings the analytic narrative into the present by identifying several defense issues currently faced by the four military services. Using the insights from chapters 2 through 5, it suggests likely pathways the services will take in their approach to these contemporary problems. In the challenging years ahead, the services will be told to secure many buildings. The concluding chapter offers a head start for figuring out how they might differ in their approaches. The final chapter ends by considering the civil-military implications for the United States.

In sum, the book offers new ways to think about the American military and its civil-military relationships. Traditional agency theory offered a strong and flexible approach for evaluating the relative strength of civilian control. The principled agent framework presented here takes the story further by expanding the scope of when, what, and who. The temporal expansion reveals the subtle interactions between the advising and executing phases of a policy. The contextual expansion shows the importance of considering the broader policy ecosystem when evaluating the quality of military compliance. And the service-level expansion demonstrates the powerful impact of service culture on American civil-military outcomes. The four services tend to act as principled agents, making sense of policy ambiguity with their own cultural logic. Ultimately, a responsible appraisal of American civil-military relations requires an authentic appreciation of the four military services and the complex political environments within which they live out the constitutional ethic of civilian control.

chapter 1

Principled Agent Theory

The point of civilian control is to make security subordinate to the
larger purposes of a nation, rather than the other way around. The
purpose of the military is to defend society, not to define it.
—Richard H. Kohn, "How Democracies Control the Military"

Civilian control of the military remains a sacred constitutional precept in
the United States. The American military takes pride in serving whomever the
people elect, Republican or Democrat, black or white, male or female. The
ethic of civilian control saturates military life, and American civil-military
relations have historically been strong—especially compared with the global
average. But a military service that submits to civilian control is still a service
with interests. And senior military leaders with 30–40 years of national service naturally harbor strong views about the best ways to defend the nation.
Military leaders with strong preferences, leading organizations with clear interests, exhibit varying degrees of cooperation with and resistance to their
civilian bosses. Civilian control is indeed unquestioned, but how far down
does this control extend?

I approach this question with a new framework for understanding and
appraising civil-military behavior. The theory described in this chapter offers
a reliable and reproducible way of generating informed hypotheses about
civil-military dynamics. The framework explains why the services act in specific ways and appraises the degree to which those actions contribute to a
strong or dysfunctional pattern of civil-military relations.

I begin by revisiting a fundamental question of civil-military politics: why
does the group with the guns take orders from unarmed politicians? After a
brief summary of major theoretical approaches to this question, I explain the
need to expand the scope of traditional agency theory in three dimensions. I
then discuss how the variables work together to generate new hypotheses about
civil-military outcomes.

Explaining Military Subordination

Who guards the guardians? Unless the ruling class also serves as the warriors, the governing elite must delegate the role of armed security to some other group. This act of delegation begets great potential risk. When political leaders provide their military with bombs and bullets, they seek to ensure that these weapons will be used on behalf of the state and not against it. This risky act of political delegation, however, routinely elicits a puzzling act of military subordination—particularly in the United States. Why does the military abide civilian control? Why do experts in the tradecraft of violence willingly submit to politicians unschooled in the grammar and logic of military affairs?

For decades, scholars and practitioners have relied on the answer provided by the titan of American civil-military relations. In 1957, Samuel Huntington penned his classic *The Soldier and the State*, anchoring the literature for over half a century. Writing in the early years of the Cold War, Huntington confronted a sea change in American civil-military relations, sparked by a new existential threat in the Soviet Union. For the first time in its history, the United States required a large military in perpetuity, not just for a short-run conflict. How, then, could the nation reconcile its new need for a standing military force with its long-standing liberal aversion to militarism? Huntington's famous prescription for "objective control" recommended a grand bargain between civilian and military leaders. To encourage military leaders to stay out of politics, Huntington argued, civilian leaders should cultivate a distinct military domain, a division of labor between the political and military spheres. A pattern of objective control carves out an autonomous sphere for the military, seeks to make the military politically neutral, and does so by granting it autonomy in the performance of its duties.[1]

How exactly does objective control encourage military subordination to civilian leaders? According to Huntington's logic, when civilians grant autonomy to the military, they fertilize the growth of a professional military ethic. The military professional, in his view, is defined by his "sense of social obligation to utilize his craft for the benefit of society."[2] As civilians grant the military autonomy, professionalism grows, fostering a subordinate conception of wielding military power, thus reinforcing civilian control. In essence, Huntington's theory of objective control rests on a reciprocal exchange between civilians and the military: civilians grant autonomy to the military in exchange for professional voluntary subordination.

Much of Huntington's 1957 work endures as the foundation of American civil-military thought. But as an explanation for the puzzle of American military subordination, Huntington's theory of objective control comes up short. Peter Feaver offers the most insightful critique, noting that Huntington's causal logic requires a uniquely self-serving definition of professionalism. Feaver argues that the mechanisms linking autonomy, professionalism, and willing subordination to civilian control are stipulations, not empirical observations.[3] The causal chain whereby autonomy leads to neutrality and professionalism, which lead to subordination, is a function of Huntington's particular definitions of those concepts. A different definition of professionalism, one that favored spirited advocacy for superior military policy, for example, would cause Huntington's causal chain to collapse.[4] In the end, Huntington's explanation for civilian control reduces to an unsatisfying platitude: the military obeys because it wants to.

Answering his own critique of Huntington, Feaver outlines an agency theory of civil-military relations. Instead of relying on apt definitions to explain military compliance, Feaver explores the rational materialist incentives that inform day-to-day calculations in the bureaucratic trenches. To explain a wide spectrum of civil-military behavior, Feaver draws on the robust principal-agent literature from economics.[5] Principal-agent relationships focus on the dynamics and incentives created by an act of delegation. How can a principal hire an agent to work on his behalf, securing the best possible outcome at the lowest cost of oversight? In a textbook principal-agent scenario, a principal hires an agent to perform a specified task, then shapes the relevant incentives to influence the agent's behavior.[6] The principal's core challenge is to grant latitude to the agent to perform unobserved work, while ensuring good-faith compliance with the principal's wishes. The ideal agent does exactly what the principal desires, with little or no oversight required. In a poor agency relationship, either the agent's work deviates far from the principal's intent or the degree of required supervision is prohibitively costly.

The challenges of a principal-agent relationship intensify when the agent is an expert in the relevant profession or craft. When the expert agent knows far more than the principal about the job at hand, the principal is poorly positioned to make smart agreements and monitor the work effectively. When hiring a mechanic to fix a car, for example, how can the untrained customer (i.e., the principal) verify what is truly wrong and needs to be done? Are those expensive brake pads being recommended for the benefit of the customer or the mechanic? How will the customer verify the quality of the work? A customer who barely understands the language or logic of the problem probably struggles to make reasoned judgments about prudent solutions. In such cases of expert delegation, informed agents have the advantage of asymmetric information, further complicating the principal's pursuit of optimal outcomes at low cost.

Car owners and civilian leaders share the same conundrum. A civilian official's decision to authorize a new artillery system or to send the military into battle operates by the same principal-agent logic as the car owner's decision to buy new brakes. In a civil-military context, elected civilian leaders serve as the principal, delegating the task of national security to an expert military agent.[7] In turn, these leaders attempt to structure the relationship to incentivize military agents to advise on and carry out a chosen policy as closely as possible to the civilians' intent. Aligning closely with the lexicon in principal-agent literature, Feaver uses the terms *working* and *shirking* to describe how closely military agents satisfy that intent.[8] A working agent does exactly what the principal wants done, while a shirking one carries out his own preference instead.

As Feaver's model suggests, civilian principals move three broad levers of influence to encourage military agents to work and not shirk: they shape (1) the monitoring regime, (2) the preference gap, and (3) the expectation of future rewards or punishments. First, civilians can choose how closely to monitor the military, with tighter scrutiny generally leading to better compliance, but at a higher cost. A lax monitoring regime reverses the tradeoff: civilian monitoring costs decrease, but the likelihood of military shirking increases. The second key lever is the gap between civilian and military policy preferences. When preferences converge, the gap closes and the motivation to shirk fades away. Conversely, divergent policy preferences yield large preference gaps that make shirking more likely. Finally, civilian leaders can shape the military's expectation of being meaningfully punished for shirking or rewarded for working. The anticipation of meaningful punishments or rewards affects the military's decision calculus to work or shirk.

Feaver's agency model makes a critical contribution to the study of civil-military relations. His elegant, flexible theory offers an insightful explanation of events in the domestic political sphere. Furthermore, the rational materialist assumptions move beyond normative prescriptions for civilian control, identifying the political conditions that vary to yield different civil-military outcomes. Overall, his theory does much to advance rigorous thinking about historical patterns of civil-military tension and cooperation.

Despite these obvious strengths, the theory serves as a flexible starting point rather than the final word on explaining American civil-military be-havior. For instance, the model focuses primarily on policy implementation and does not pay as close attention to the different dynamics that exist before and after a policy is set. The military mindset, however, experiences a qual-itative shift when its role changes from expert advisor to policy executor. How might the principal-agent model apply to the advisory stage as well? The model also simplifies civilian and military preferences as fixed, known, and isolated to single-issue cases. Yet in the early phases of a policy debate, a good deal of civil-military dialogue may be focused on understanding the problem at hand and defining preferences. And policies rarely are considered in isolation, but interact within a broader ecosystem of existing directives and debates. How do civil-military actors make sense of this complex political space on their way to the robust agency dynamics of Feaver's model? Finally, the model considers only two actors: a single civilian and single military actor. But what if the four military services tend to respond to policy debates differently, in ways that can be anticipated? How might a service-level view of agency dynamics offer more useful insight into American civil-military behavior?

Expanding the Scope of Agency Theory

To build profitably on the core insights of agency theory, a principled agent framework expands the scope of the model along three axes. First, it expands the temporal dimension to focus on the interaction between the advising and execution phases of a policy. Second, it expands the contextual dimen-sion to consider how the relative coherence of a policy affects a civil-military exchange: how do the clarity, consistency, and feasibility of a policy prescrip-tion affect the tenor of the civil-military dialogue? The third axis expands the number of key participants to see how an understanding of civil-military dynamics improves by paying attention to the four services as unique agents. The following discussion explains the need to expand the baseline theory along these three axes, then illustrates how they come together in a unified framework.

The X-Axis: Advising or Complying?

The first expansion of agency theory makes an analytic distinction between the military's role in advising on a proposal and in complying with a settled decision. The American military is both agent and expert advisor to its civil-ian principal; these related but distinct roles require different normative standards of behavior. In their role as expert advisors, senior military leaders have a statutory responsibility to provide their best military judgment to civilian policymakers. Contrarian views are not only encouraged but expected during policy debates. This noble contrarianism, though, must end when the debate concludes. Military society moves by obeying orders, and a crucial qualitative change in mindset occurs when a decision is made and an order is given. Consequently, the military's understanding of its proper role—whether advisor or agent—is considerably different on either side of a final decision. Before a policy is decided, the civil-military dialogue looks more like respectful bargaining—even brainstorming. Once a policy is set, the dynamics shift to monitoring and enforcement.[9]

A prudent civilian principal is likely to listen carefully to expert military counsel during the advising phase. The civilian's policy preference at the beginning of the debate may look quite different from the preference codified in the final decision. Whether the updated preference constitutes a compromise or simply a principled update in the light of received counsel, the civilian's preference can shift. This insight suggests that American civil-military relations are not a *pure* principal-agent problem as it is classically conceived. In a standard economics scenario, for example, the principal and the agent often have fundamentally opposed interests; the agent is assumed to want maximum pay for minimal work, while the principal prefers just the opposite. In a civil-military context, the civilian principal and military agent share a common goal in providing security for the state. They may differ, of course, in their preferred means for accomplishing that goal, but sharing a common end creates latitude for a healthy debate. This subtle departure from traditional agency dynamics punctuates the need to consider the advisory phase differently.

Finally, careful analysis of both the advising and the complying phases reveals the anticipatory interaction between the two periods. During a policy debate, as military agents offer expert counsel to civilian principals, the boundary conditions of the future are already taking shape. Both sides can see the future implications of the present debate, and those implications cast a long shadow back to the current dialogue.[10] When civil-military leaders discuss a proposed policy, they look ahead to the future political climate that the tentative policy language would create. Implicitly, both sides are asking questions such as: How much oversight and scrutiny are baked into the policy? If the memo is signed as currently written, could noncompliance even be detected?

Is there sufficient ambiguity to justify a favorable interpretation? In short, will the policy as written create any *implementation slack*, any maneuver room once the decision is made and the policy is set?

In this framework, implementation slack is a composite variable reflecting the endogenous monitoring conditions suggested by a given policy.[11] Four attributes combine to increase or decrease implementation slack: *specificity* of language, *imminence* of enactment, *durability* of the policy instrument, and implied *enforceability* of the policy issue. Implementation slack increases when: (1) the policy language is vague rather than specific; (2) a policy takes effect in the distant future, thereby leaving open the possibility of re-litigating the debate; (3) the policy instrument is ephemeral rather than enduring, like a policy memorandum rather than formal legislation; and (4) the policy is inherently difficult to enforce, perhaps due to a lack of empowered stakeholders who could serve as self-executing compliance monitors.[12] When the four attributes move in the opposite direction, implementation slack decreases, suggesting a more rigid compliance environment.

During the advisory stage, the anticipation of future implementation slack can yield surprising outcomes. Conventional wisdom suggests that one would see contentious debates when major disagreements exist. Similarly, one expects relatively peaceful dialogue when both sides agree on what needs to happen. But the temporal expansion of agency theory suggests an intriguing alternative. A contentious civil-military debate could occur when both sides *agree* on the policy substance, but the anticipated implementation slack is too high and one party fears that hard-fought gains could be easily overturned or ignored in the future. In that case, the military agent might push strongly for a policy with more specific language or with self-executing features, captured in a more enduring policy instrument, or one that takes effect sooner. For example, the services and the secretary of defense might agree on the need to reform the acquisition process by giving service chiefs more decision authority—the secretary might even codify this general agreement in a memorandum. The services, however, might continue to push the issue, keeping the debate alive until a much more specific agreement is captured in an official departmental instruction or even legislation. A heated debate could be all about the slack, not the substance.

The converse could also be the case. A benign civil-military debate might indicate a proposal that portends a great deal of implementation slack, not one in which the parties materially agree. If the looming maneuver room is wide enough, the letter of the law fades in importance. For these reasons, the principled agent framework focuses explicitly on both the advising and execution phases—and the surprising interactions that may ricochet between them.

The Y-Axis: How Clear Are the Policy Prescriptions?

One of agency theory's core contributions to civil-military relations theory is its rational materialist framework. Instead of relying on a particular norm or definition to secure civilian control, agency theory specifies clear variables and decisions made by key actors to maximize policy gains at the lowest bureaucratic costs. Cost-benefit calculations animate the theory, but these calculations require a coherent policy space. The issues and preferences must be clearly understood to give meaning to the work-or-shirk decision. But what happens when the issues are unclear, or when civilian and military leaders are just making sense of a chaotic or complex situation? What if the military agent's key decision is less *whether* to comply and more *how* to do so? Civil-military practitioners frequently testify that ambiguity, confusion, and complexity saturate the daily grind of civil-military policymaking. Issues at the highest level tend to be complicated, multilayered, ill-defined, and in tension with other policies. How should agency theory make room for the incoherence that dominates real-world civil-military dynamics?

To bring agency theory closer to the empirical reality in the Pentagon, the second expansion explicitly considers the relative coherence of the policy prescription at hand. Three attributes comprise this qualitative assessment of coherence: the clarity, consistency, and feasibility of what the military is being asked to do. The first component is the relative *clarity* of what is expected from the military agent. When all parties understand the issues at hand, what is expected, and what is at stake, traditional agency variables tend to apply quite well. But when a debate is just taking shape, or when a policy document contains ambiguous language subject to varying interpretation, agency variables have reduced explanatory leverage. A policy directive to restructure a headquarters or integrate homosexuals into the ranks may be difficult, but the expectations are relatively clear. On the other hand, a presidential request for policy options in Syria lives in a different category, where the "right answer" is far from obvious. The inherent complexity and ambiguity of such a task sets up a different style of civil-military exchange.

The second component of coherence is the degree of *consistency* in the policy prescription—both its internal consistency and its external consistency with the surrounding policy environment. Many policy decisions emerge from contentious compromise, with give and take embedded in the various provisions of the policy. But policy compromises can turn into compromised policies. Policies rife with internal inconsistencies make full-bodied compliance problematic at best. Similarly, policies rarely exist in bureaucratic isolation. Any civil-military policy enters a complex world of competing and even contradictory impulses. Working faithfully to carry out an arms control policy, for example, might entail shirking on a policy designed to strengthen the nation's deterrent posture in a particular region.

Third, the relative *feasibility* of the policy prescription shapes its composite coherence and likelihood for faithful compliance. Is the civilian's policy preference clearly achievable, or does it represent an aspirational goal? Policies sit on a spectrum of feasibility that shapes the military's ability to comply. Some policies can be straightforwardly accomplished, requiring only a decision and the commensurate will to carry it out ("increase the size of the force by 2%"). Other policy decisions, however, could be so aspirational or complex that even the hardest working agent fails to measure up ("fix the defense acquisition system"). If an agent is asked to do the impossible and comes up short, is shirking a fair verdict? Conversely, if a policy is quite clear, consistent, and achievable, the standard for faithful working should be correspondingly high. Forensic judgments of military behavior should consider the contextual elements that make working and shirking, even with the best of intentions, more or less likely.

Together, these three attributes shape the relative degree of coherence in a policy issue, which directly affects the military agent's approach to advising and complying with civilian direction. When coherence is low, uncertainty abounds and the services will tend to rely on their cultural beliefs to diagnose the stakes of the situation—perhaps moving in different directions as they do so. For a highly coherent policy, the relevant question is *whether* to comply; for a low-coherence policy, the question becomes *how*.

The Z-Axis: Civilian Control of Whom?

In American civil-military relations, who is the "military" with whom civilians relate? Most civil-military approaches treat the US military as a single, coherent actor. As a simplifying assumption, that level of analysis offers a reasonable first cut into American civil-military dynamics. But the first cut should not be the last word. In the United States, the term *military* overlooks a far more meaningful subcategory: the four major services. Peeling back the simple label of *military* to examine the four services represents the third key expansion of agency theory.

Fortunately for their civilian bosses, members of the US military wear their biases on their sleeves. A uniform is a starched résumé, displaying at a glance one's job specialty, rank, combat record, elite qualifications, special duties, and unit affiliations. Military members can rapidly size one another up at first glance, sniffing out tell-tale signs of accomplishment and prestige: a Ranger tab, a Navy SEAL trident, jump wings, an Air Force Weapons School patch, a Combat Infantryman Badge, or a Distinguished Flying Cross with valor—all of which convey history and confer credibility. The most telling attribute of the uniform, however, is its color. Uniforms are not uniform across the services, as each service sports its own colors, styles, and accoutrements. Despite the military's recent progress in fighting more jointly, each of the four services retains control over what its people wear, where they live, when they move, when they deploy, the equipment they operate, who gets promoted, and who has to leave. In short, the services control the dominant incentives of daily life.

Each military service profoundly shapes a way of life and pattern of thinking—a belief system closely guarded by the senior-most officers produced by the culture. The senior military officers most involved in civil-military dialogue are typically those most conditioned by the beliefs of their service culture; the winners selected by a value system rarely question the virtue of those values. So the American military's deployed operations may be increasingly "joint," but most of the *thinking* remains shaped by the distinct molds of the different services.

A study of American civil-military relations needs to take seriously these service-level differences. Just as people are products of their nature and nurture, military organizations are products of their distinct operating environment and unique political history. An Army soldier slogging it out in the mud, stewarding his service's Revolutionary era legacy, thinks very differently than an Air Force officer at 30,000 feet and 500 knots, whose service proudly pursues progress "unhindered by custom."[13] These different patterns of belief comprise the foundational elements in each service's culture, defined here as *a prevailing belief system about ends, ways, and means.* This belief system is an integrated set of ideas and assumptions that the service has found helpful in solving its past problems; those beliefs, in turn, are tacitly expected to be useful in the future as well.[14]

This approach recognizes that these beliefs do not inhere in the minds of every member of the service. Rather, the beliefs tend to take root at the aggregate service level, particularly in headquarters staff structures where the service takes on an anthropomorphic reality. Organizations, like organisms, seek to survive and prosper in changing environments.[15] Consequently, organizations such as the four services remain acutely aware of why they exist, what they exist to do, and what resources they require. These preoccupying categories of thought shape a prevailing belief structure that applies inconsistently to individuals but quite reliably to the organization writ large.

This use of service culture mirrors Alexander George's use of operational codes to study decision-makers. George found that political leaders facing ambiguous political environments relied on operational codes, or robust belief systems derived from both personality and personal history. Operational codes affected their "diagnostic and choice propensities"—the information the leaders paid attention to and the kinds of choices they made.[16] In the world of civil-military relations, cultural beliefs about ends, ways, and means similarly guide the four services through ambiguous policy spaces. Such beliefs affect what the services pay attention to and their preferences about particular policies.

Bringing the Three Axes Together

These three axes of expansion represent purposeful complications of Feaver's baseline agency model. Figure 1.1 illustrates conceptually the expansion of the framework relative to traditional agency theory. In a sense, these expansions of the theory refine and recalibrate its explanatory capacity. Theories are conceptual tools to explain empirical patterns. Different tools, calibrated for varying degrees of precision, accomplish similar tasks for different purposes. Chainsaws and scalpels are both made to cut—but tree removal calls for a different approach than brain surgery. So while Feaver's original model offers a helpful first cut in many cases, a deeper understanding of American civil-military relations requires conceptual tools calibrated for even finer precision.

The Principled Agent Framework

The expansions illustrated in figure 1.1 lay the conceptual foundation for the principled agent framework. The front face of the figure outlines a four-square typology defined by time on the *x*-axis and coherence on the *y*-axis. Traditional agency theory focused attention on the military's implementation of

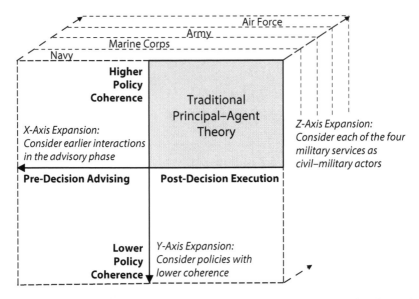

Figure 1.1. The principled agent framework is a conceptual expansion of traditional principal-agent theory along three axes: the policymaking timeline (*x*-axis), the degree of coherence in the policy (*y*-axis), and the relevant number of military agents (*z*-axis).

relatively clear policy decisions, depicted in the upper right square of the figure. Stretching back the *x*-axis of time to include the advising phase, then pulling down the *y*-axis of policy coherence to consider more ambiguous environments, opens up three new policy spaces to explain.

The four policy spaces rendered in figure 1.2 capture four different combinations of variables that affect American civil-military outcomes. They represent ideal-types, suggesting probable outcomes as real-world conditions approach the defining conditions. The dependent variable of this research—the specific event or outcome the theory seeks to explain—is the behavior of a military service while advising on a policy issue or while carrying out a settled decision. To explain variation in this outcome, the theory identifies the factors that most influence the services' civil-military interactions amid varying conditions. Given the importance of both time and coherence, as discussed above, the military services' decision calculus differs across the four variable combinations. The four spaces thus specify the different variables to look for in the empirical record. The discussion below, based on figure 1.2, outlines the optimal search pattern for each set of conditions, highlighting which variables matter when, and why. For emphasis, the discussion revisits

Principled Agent Framework

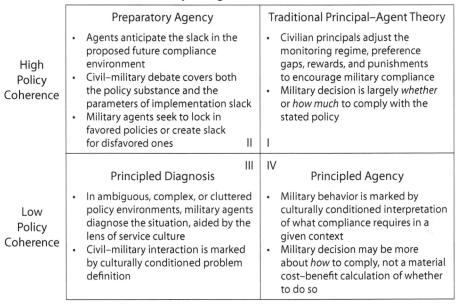

	Preparatory Agency	Traditional Principal–Agent Theory
High Policy Coherence	• Agents anticipate the slack in the proposed future compliance environment • Civil–military debate covers both the policy substance and the parameters of implementation slack • Military agents seek to lock in favored policies or create slack for disfavored ones **II**	**I** • Civilian principals adjust the monitoring regime, preference gaps, rewards, and punishments to encourage military compliance • Military decision is largely *whether* or *how much* to comply with the stated policy
Low Policy Coherence	**III** Principled Diagnosis • In ambiguous, complex, or cluttered policy environments, military agents diagnose the situation, aided by the lens of service culture • Civil–military interaction is marked by culturally conditioned problem definition	**IV** Principled Agency • Military behavior is marked by culturally conditioned interpretation of what compliance requires in a given context • Military decision may be more about *how* to comply, not a material cost–benefit calculation of whether to do so
	Advising	Executing

Figure 1.2. Summary of principled agent hypotheses as the timeline and coherence of the policy vary.

theoretical insights from earlier in the chapter to reinforce the causal logic in each square.

Square I: Traditional Principal-Agent Theory

The top right square in the typology depicts conditions of implementing higher-coherence policies. These conditions define the wheelhouse of traditional agency theory. This rational materialist approach models civil-military interaction as a strategic exchange in which each side makes cost-benefit calculations. Each rational actor pursues maximum policy benefit at minimum cost (whether bureaucratic, organizational, or personal). While Feaver's discussion of the model certainly recognizes the foundational role of normative ideals such as honor, pride, and service in shaping military behavior, the model holds fast to its rational baseline to see how much explanatory leverage it can generate.

In this top right space (square I), one expects military behavior to result primarily from the interaction of core agency variables: monitoring conditions, preference gaps, and expectations of meaningful rewards or punishments. First, civilian principals decide how closely or loosely to monitor the military agent's compliance efforts. Closer scrutiny encourages more compliant behavior, but is costly for the principal. A more lax monitoring regime is bureaucratically cheaper, but sets permissive conditions more likely to generate shirking by the agent. But shirking is only likely in the presence of the second key variable: a preference gap. When civilian and military leaders hold very different preferences about a given policy, a conceptual gap exists between the two positions. Large preference gaps tend to prompt shirking, while small preference gaps suggest close alignment of views and thus a higher likelihood of working.

This book's focus on the four services as distinct actors adds a new dimension of analysis to this traditional agency approach. It argues that service culture uniquely shapes the fact and form of a service's pre-strategic preferences. Agency theory, like other rationalist models, treats preferences as exogenous to the model—that is, preferences are an input to the model, not something explained by the model itself. Nevertheless, preferences are not exogenous to everything; they do not emerge *ex nihilo* without any explanation whatsoever.[17] A compelling explanation of actors' preferences improves the input to the rational model—and improves the output as well. Combining the strengths of both ideational and rational perspectives creates a unified view: an ideational approach predicts and explains the incoming preferences, while the rationalist framework explains the subsequent strategic interaction. By understanding what actors preferred before the interaction started, one can better appreciate the constraining effects of the decision-making environment.[18] Consequently, when examining the military services as separate agents, one can expect their unique cultural beliefs to shape different policy preferences and, in turn, preference gaps.

The third and final agency variable is the expectation of rewards or punishments. Civilian principals use both tacit and explicit methods to shape the military agent's expectations of being punished for shirking or rewarded for working. For example, a civilian boss with a recent reputation for firing military subordinates sets an expectation of meaningful punishment for perceived shirking. Such expectations in turn shape the military's work-or-shirk decision calculus.

These three variables interact qualitatively to make military compliance more or less likely. At one extreme, when civilians closely monitor the military, in the presence of a small preference gap and high expectations of meaningful punishment for noncompliance, the likelihood of compliance is quite high. At the other end of the spectrum, an unmonitored military agent with a contrarian policy position and no expectation of being caught or punished is far more likely to go its own way. Between the two extremes, one makes qualitative judgments about the relative strength of each variable to surmise the likely outcome.

Square II: Preparatory Agency

Moving from top right to top left, square II in the typology describes the dynamics of a military agent advising civilian leaders on relatively coherent issues before the policy decision is formally set. In this regime, both parties understand the coherent policy terrain and maneuver for preferred ground. But since the final decision has not yet been made, the core agency variables cannot be applied in the same way. In square II, agency variables apply anticipatively.

The central insight of this regime is that defining conditions of the future monitoring environment can be anticipated during a policy debate. Characteristics of the future monitoring regime become embedded in the policy itself, portending more or less implementation slack. When a policy uses very specific language, is self-executing, is codified in a robust form such as legislation, or will take effect soon, the stakes are higher and the advising phase is likely to be more contentious. Conversely, when a developing policy seems vague, largely unenforceable, easily changed, or temporally distant, the anticipated implementation slack is high and the debate may be more tepid.

The degree of expected slack interacts with the existing preference gaps to create intriguing outcomes. A large preference gap, for example, tends to create civil-military friction; when combined with a large degree of expected slack, however, the motivation to act on the gap fades away. Instead, the debate more likely focuses on keeping the slack wide—a negotiation to avoid the details. Conversely, small preference gaps indicate close agreement, suggesting the likelihood of only a mild debate. But combine the small gap with very little expected slack in the future and both sides will take a strong interest in negotiating the details—perhaps quite heatedly. Figure 1.3 summarizes the essence of these interaction effects.

Squares III and IV: Principled Diagnosis and Principled Agency

In the bottom half of the typology (squares III and IV), the policy space is dominated by ambiguity. Such ambiguity can arise from a variety of condi-

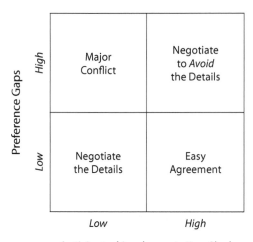

Figure 1.3. Hypothesized interactions between preference gaps and the anticipated implementation slack, which are most relevant during the advisory phase of more-coherent policies.

tions: perhaps the policy language is unclear, or the debate is at an immature stage, or the policy implications conflict with other demands—or perhaps it is just a bridge too far. These policy conditions are characterized as having low *coherence*, when the clarity, or consistency, or feasibility of the policy complicates a traditional agency framework. In principal-agent theory, decision-makers operate as utility maximizers; their decisions hinge on whether to comply, or how much to comply to earn acceptable gains at tolerable costs. However, when a policy environment is cluttered with more ambiguity than clarity, agency variables recede—and cultural factors fill the void.

In squares III and IV, military agents in environments of low policy coherence act less like utility maximizers and more like principled sense-makers. In these complex policy spaces, humans with bounded rationality make sense of their environment through the filters of worldview or operational code.[19] For a military service, its unique service culture tends to perform the function of both filter and script. The core beliefs of service culture condition what the services pay attention to, the ways they make sense of their environment, and their default pathways for action. In the bottom left space, square III, one therefore expects to see cultural interpretations predominate over agency calculations. As a policy issue takes shape, civilian and military actors work to clarify the issues at stake, bound the problem, and situate the policy relative to other demands in the policy ecosystem. This square is an arena of principled diagnosis, where cultural beliefs shape the ways in which the services approach their task of advising civilian principals. If the issues become more clear, consistent, and feasible before a decision is made, the scenario moves up to square II, animating the preparatory agency dynamics discussed above. But, if the issues remain incoherent even after the decision, the case shifts right to square IV.

In the bottom right arena of square IV, military agents must carry out policy decisions still clouded in uncertainty. The daily reality for many civil-military practitioners involves an overflowing inbox of insoluble demands, the tyranny of too little time to think, and the ambiguity of competing claims. In this world where cognitive demand overwhelms its supply, actors behave more reflexively than deliberately. They work from scripts and reflex, conforming to the patterns of institutional thought that surround them. They hew closely to long-standing beliefs that make each service distinctive. They may indeed be calculating options for organizational advantage, but the very idea of what constitutes advantage is likely to be rooted in service-oriented beliefs. When policy coherence is low and uncertainty is high, principled military agents are likely to move along culturally conditioned pathways. Their efforts to carry out ambiguous policy may simply be service-specific interpretations of what compliance is supposed to look like. These interpretations are likely to differ across the services and may well depart from the envisioned intent held by the civilian decision-maker.

These insights suggest that the work-shirk continuum for coding military behavior may be insufficient. Working and shirking, as described in traditional principal-agent theory, imply calculated decisions by an agent to satisfy the principal's intent or his own. However, in the arenas described above, good-faith efforts occasionally diverge, and shirking may be an unwarranted verdict. Military actions that deviate from the civilians' ideal point could be attributable to cultural interpretation, not malign calculation. In this bottom half of the matrix, therefore, a third condition of the dependent variable of military behavior may apply: culturally conditioned divergence.

Summary

The discussion in this chapter has orbited around a central political condition: every organized polity must decide who gets the guns. That decision inherently brings risk, as the weapons suited for conquering outsiders are equally well suited for suppressing insiders. For millennia, philosophers have wrestled with this puzzle of armed behavior: how should a society guard the guardians? The more recent puzzle, however, especially in the United States, is how our society has managed to solve that first puzzle so well. Why does a powerful million-person military submit to the control of unarmed civilians? In a world where "might makes right," the noble converse is a refreshing surprise: why does political right so often control military might?

The chapter has explored various theoretical approaches to these enduring political questions. The challenge of civil-military relations is as old as the Greek city-state and as current as today's *Washington Post*. Despite the long-standing nature of the problem, there is no settled solution. As political communities change over time, varying from place to place, civil-military dynamics change with them. The theories that explain and assess these dynamics continue to improve, offering more compelling explanations for civilian control and military action. Building on the normative bedrock of Samuel Huntington and modifying the rationalist architecture of Peter Feaver, the principled agent approach offers new understanding of ancient political dilemmas.

With the theoretical foundation in place, the next four chapters paint the four-service portrait that sits at the heart of the principled agent approach. These cultural portraits depict not just what the services think but why they tend to think that way. How have operational nature and political nurture conjoined in historically unique ways to create four services with distinctive worldviews?

chapter 2

Thinking Like a Sailor

The Service Culture of the United States Navy

To change anything in the Navy is like punching a feather bed. You punch it with your right and you punch it with your left until you are finally exhausted, and then you find the damn bed just as it was before you started punching!

—President Franklin Delano Roosevelt, quoted in
Roger Barnett's *Navy Strategic Culture*

The United States Navy dominates the world's oceans like no other navy in history. Boasting an extensive fleet of modern ships deployed across the globe, the US Navy is today's "global force for good."[1] The Navy's combat power is matched by the enduring power of its unique culture. The Navy celebrates a rich history of seafaring heroes and maintains a firm attachment to its traditions and values. How does this vivid organizational personality make its mark in American civil-military policymaking?

This chapter marks the beginning of a four-chapter, four-service portrait of the American military. The important contributions of each chapter are primarily methodological and analytic, not empirical. These chapters do not reveal new historical facts exhumed from declassified archives; instead, they arrange old ideas in new ways, allowing composite images to emerge. The research for each service canvased a wide array of primary and secondary sources, with a focus on answering two major questions: (1) What does the service tend to say and believe about its preferred ends, ways, and means? (2) How do the operational environment and specific organizational history lend strength to these beliefs? In looking at organizational history, the research focused on the founding context, major events, and notable exemplars that the service reveres. The discussion in each chapter arranges these historical insights thematically around the five or six most salient beliefs that emerge from each service's main narrative.

The historical surveys focus on each service's creation narrative up to the post-Vietnam era of the late 1970s. The analysis mentions more recent events where warranted, but the main effort focuses on a more settled historical period. Two primary issues inform this decision. First, the case studies (chapters 6 and 7) cover events from the early 1980s. Consequently, to see the impact of cultural beliefs in the case studies, the analysis required an empirical referent for service culture already in place at the time of the cases. Second, this approach to substantiating service culture focuses on long-endurance elements: inherent factors of operational environment and highly influential events of political history, especially early in the life of the service. Though the strategic context for the American military has changed significantly since the late 1970s, the core beliefs of each service have remained remarkably robust over time.

As discussed in the book's introduction, these portraits focus their cultural analysis at the *service* level. For a civil-military study, focusing on the services appears to be the optimal cost-benefit decision; I accept the tradeoffs of not focusing at a higher or lower level. At a higher level, some argue that the US military exhibits a national strategic culture; service variations, perhaps, are mere refractions of the national context.[2] The discussions in these four chapters note where similarities exist between the services—where beliefs reflect unique instantiations of national ideals—but the bulk of the analysis finds meaningful differences. At a lower level, focusing on the services willfully overlooks the subcultures and individuals within each service. These intra-service distinctions certainly affect life *within* the service, but at the civil-military level, the effect appears to be limited. When civilian principals craft policies for *all* of the services, service leaders typically transcend their internal divisions and operate from a consensus posture that spans the service. In his book on Navy culture, for example, Roger Barnett highlights the three main warfare communities in the Navy: surface warfare, aviation, and submarines. While each warfare community has subcultural idiosyncrasies, "when it comes to strategic culture, the three groups are in close, and even comfortable, agreement."[3] This first chapter on service culture, then, presents six enduring beliefs held by the US Navy, focusing on why it exists, how it operates, and the resources it requires.

An Armed Embassy of America: Anytime, Anywhere

What does the US Navy uniquely and indispensably do for the United States? The Navy is the dispersed muscle of American diplomacy, offering a unique instrument of national power. In a world dominated by water, the Navy offers sovereign US territory and combat power in almost any part of that world in very short order. Without needing to secure bases for aircraft or American boots, the Navy offers a full and flexible range of political-military options by its very presence. As a distributed fleet of warrior-diplomats, the Navy can show the flag while showing off the cannons. Consequently, naval power operates by a different logic than land-based military operations. It must be appreciated as a distinct instrument of national power, somewhere between military force and diplomatic presence. While this belief shapes America's Navy, it is not endemic to *every* navy in the world. How, then, did the US Navy arrive at its self-conception as the battleship ambassadors of America?

Operational Environment

The world's oceans cover nearly 70% of the globe, and 80% of the world's population lives on or near the coastline.[4] Consequently, ships at sea have the unique ability to transit the globe in the political sanctuary of international waters—while armed to the gills with military power. These geographic and demographic facts give a navy unique access to conduct discourse—armed or otherwise—with fellow states across the world. Furthermore, ships at sea carrying the flag of their home state represent sovereign territorial assets. When the Navy shows the flag and projects power abroad, it does so without needing anyone's permission. The mobility of ships at sea allows these sovereign assets to be moved where events warrant, without the political liability or logistical upheaval of establishing or vacating fixed bases. Such fluidity gives national leaders the flexibility to be anywhere—and *only* where—they want to be.

Finally, for the first 150 years of the nation's existence, ships offered the only means of intercontinental travel and power projection. Before the advent of aircraft in the early twentieth century, a deployed navy was the only way the United States could flexibly show its flag, boost its prestige, and conduct diplomacy in Europe, Africa, South America, and Asia. For a far-flung state like the United States to be involved in world affairs in the eighteenth and nineteenth centuries, it required a Navy to do so.

Founding Context

In general, organizational trajectories follow robust patterns, as "founding moments loom large" in establishing the fact and form of a given organization.[5] I focus here on the early events that shaped the US Navy, then consider how this seminal context was confirmed or reshaped by later events.

When does the life of the US Navy begin? The Navy celebrates its birthday each year on October 13, commemorating an appropriation by the Continental Congress on October 13, 1775, to convert two private vessels for official use.[6] But two vessels hardly comprise a navy. American naval forces during the Revolution also included state navies from 11 of the 13 colonies and small fleets raised and rented by Benedict Arnold and George Washington to support their troop movements. Together, this curious assemblage of ships did relatively little to win the war, prompting historian Ian Toll to regard the Continental Navy as "a wasteful and humiliating fiasco."[7] The Continental Navy, therefore, while nominally the ancestor of today's US Navy, was created only to help win a war. The more important organizational legacy emerged from the later decision to build a standing Navy for war *and peace*.

The constitutional debates, particularly as captured in the *Federalist Papers*, offered a compelling testimony for a national navy. As the colonies debated the terms of the drafted Constitution, a debate over the size, function, and cost of a navy raged alongside. The pro-navy arguments advanced by the Federalists ultimately shaped the culture of the US Navy, as they preached the inseparability of national prestige, diplomatic legitimacy, and a strong navy without which the first two would wither. Alexander Hamilton suggested in *Federalist* 11 that even a small US Navy could tip the European balance of power by its friendship or neutrality, but "a nation, despicable by its weakness, forfeits even the privilege of being neutral."[8] Given the strength of British and French naval forces, Edward Rutledge of South Carolina agreed: "We must hold our country by courtesy, unless we have a navy."[9] Ultimately, the arguments for a standing Navy prevailed, as the Constitution authorized Congress to "provide and maintain a Navy."[10] Unlike the impermanent army that could be "raised and supported" only for two-year periods, the navy was cast in a different constitutional mold. The United States created an enduring navy to serve as an adjunct to its diplomatic efforts abroad, providing legitimacy through strength and prestige through presence.

Events and Exemplars

The early constitutional debates offered the seminal context that later experiences reinforced in the naval mind. In many respects, the nation and its Navy sailed together through the nineteenth and twentieth centuries, as the Navy expanded its size and mandate to suit the emerging national character. The power and presence of the Navy buttressed American foreign policy throughout its history, underwriting presidential doctrines from James Monroe to Teddy Roosevelt to Ronald Reagan. As Barnett suggests, "The forward operations of the US Navy have always been, in large measure, for the purpose of lending operational muscle to these geostrategic policies."[11]

During the early and mid-nineteenth century, American foreign policy consisted largely of securing safe transit for American shipping, expanding commercial markets, and enlarging national borders. The Navy proved instrumental in the first two objectives, staying remarkably active as an emissary of American interests. Many of the nation's first treaties were negotiated not by State Department officials, but by enterprising captains of the US Navy.[12] In his 1820 report to Congress, Secretary of the Navy Smith Thompson reported on the activity of his deployed squadrons, which were keeping the Barbary powers in check in the Mediterranean, protecting trade and fisheries in the Pacific, securing trade routes to China in the East Indies, prosecuting the slave trade, and chasing pirates in the West Indies.[13] A decade later, in 1832–33, the USS *Peacock* cruised Asian waters, its ship captain negotiating trade agreements with the king of Siam and the sultan of Muscat—the first such agreements with Middle and Far Eastern states.[14] Perhaps the most famous diplomatic excursion of this period came from Commodore Matthew C. Perry, who received orders from President Millard Fillmore in March 1852 as "an envoy extraordinary and minister plenipotentiary" of the United States to Japan.[15] Perry, a distinguished naval officer commanding the only means of access to the island empire, was to carry out this high-profile diplomatic mission of the United States. Perry and his accompanying fleet arrived in Edo Bay (Tokyo) in July 1853, and returned the following spring to sign the historic Treaty of Kanagawa, on March 31, 1854.[16]

These early diplomatic missions by Navy ship captains established a trajectory of purpose that continued throughout the service's history. The Navy provided the big stick that allowed politicians to speak softly, as suggested by Secretary of the Navy Hilary Herbert in his 1893 annual report to Congress: "We must make and keep our Navy in such a condition of efficiency as to give weight and power to whatever policy it may be thought wise on the part of our Government to assume."[17] In 1907, in the midst of an escalating naval competition with Japan, the Navy launched its signature mission of big-stick diplomacy: the Great White Fleet, consisting of 16 new battleships and their auxiliaries, executing a 15-month, 46,000-mile cruise, and showing the flag—and the guns—to Japan and the rest of the world.[18]

In the border waters between diplomacy and war, the Navy maintained a similarly flexible posture during the starkly absolutist days of the Cold War.[19] As various international crises arose throughout the world, from the Suez Canal to Lebanon to the Taiwan Straits, the Navy offered the nation flexibility, nuance, and credible options across the diplomatic spectrum. While the Air Force competed during this era to be the new first line of defense, the airmen's vision for doing so became increasingly all-or-nothing, going from silent alert to nuclear war with limited calibration in between.[20] The Navy, by contrast, could provide a more measured response, as indicated by Admiral John S. McCain, Jr., in his testimony to the Senate Defense Appropriations Subcommittee in 1962: "Seaborne striking forces, because of their unique characteristics, are the ideal instrument for the execution of a policy of graduated deterrence or flexible response."[21]

The US Navy believes in its unique capacity to sail the ship of state between the Scylla and Charybdis of diplomacy and war. This distinction gives the Navy an esoteric conception of its role in American affairs. It believes that since no other group can fully appreciate or duplicate what the Navy provides, the Navy should have maximum latitude to do what only it can.

In summary, the first belief in Navy service culture is this: The US Navy provides a unique instrument of national power as a mobile archipelago of sovereign American presence and power anywhere in the world. The Navy offers a flexible and full continuum of diplomatic leverage, from showing the flag to full combat operations. American foreign policy is made credible by a large, powerful, and deployed fleet.

America and Its Navy Prosper Together

In addition to conducting armed diplomacy abroad, the US Navy uniquely enables American prosperity at home. When the new United States, stripped of its colonial protection from the Royal Navy, found its commercial shipping perilously at risk to Barbary pirates and raiding privateers, its need for a navy became acute. Born to protect the nation's shipping more than its coastlines, the US Navy inherited strands of mercantilist DNA, in which the prosperity of the Navy and the United States seemed woven together. The Navy's role in defending America included not only military protection of the homeland but vigorous protection of shipping and expansion of commercial markets. One of the early nineteenth-century textbooks at the US Naval Academy imparted to future Navy leaders this twin purpose: "To maintain the untarnished honor of the government and of the nation and, at the same time, *promote its commercial interests in peace*, is an obligation upon the Naval Officer equal with his obligation to defend his ship to the last moment in the hour of battle" (emphasis added).[22]

Operational Environment and Founding Context

The early constitutional debates revealed an acute awareness of the Navy's vital role in achieving national prosperity. The Federalists highlighted the essential role of navies in protecting trade and building economic infrastructure at home. In *Federalist* 11, Alexander Hamilton suggested that a federal navy could enable prosperity across the wide union of states. And such prosperity would not be limited to the northern states, argued Hamilton, as each region had something to contribute: sturdy wood from the south, iron from the middle states, and experienced seamen from the "Northern hive."[23]

Opponents of building a navy feared the cost, not the very existence, of a standing US fleet. The beneficial purpose of a navy was largely beyond dispute. In *Federalist* 41, in fact, James Madison commented on the rarity of such unanimous support for *any* provision in the Constitution: "The palpable necessity of the power to provide and maintain a navy has protected that part of the Constitution against a spirit of censure, which has spared few other parts."[24] The debate thus hinged on whether the benefits justified the financial burden. While fear of a standing army pervaded the early republic, no such fear accompanied the navy. Madison invoked this double advantage, arguing that "the [naval] batteries most capable of repelling foreign enterprises on our safety, are happily such as can never be turned by a perfidious government against our liberties."[25]

The Federalist arguments prevailed, but several years passed before Congress had reason to begin providing and maintaining a navy. US commercial shipping soon proved vulnerable to raiding Algerian pirates, and Congress passed "an Act to Provide a Naval Armament" on March 10, 1794.[26] The act authorized the construction of six frigates, four armed with 44 guns and two with 36 guns, to meet and destroy the Algerian corsairs. The first permanent ships of the US Navy—one of which, the USS *Constitution*, still sails today—therefore came into being explicitly to protect American commerce.

Born to protect American shipping, these first US Navy ships later survived the bureaucratic axe explicitly to protect American industry. A compromise provision in the original act stipulated that the six frigates were specifically to fight Algiers; construction of the frigates must stop should peace be made early. When diplomatic negotiations brought peace with Algiers in February 1796, the law required an end to construction of the frigates—at that point, all six were past due and over budget. Given the extensive infrastructure and financial commitments involved, however, President George Washington convinced Congress to keep the three frigates furthest along in construction. Washington argued that ceasing construction of all six would risk "derangement in the whole system."[27] These political decisions—to build six ships to protect shipping and to keep three ships to protect industry—strikingly reveal the early entanglement of naval and national interests. The Navy protected commerce at sea and provided jobs at home, both to good effect.

Events and Exemplars

These early experiences forged a strong belief within the naval service about the essential coupling of national and naval prosperity. In the periods that followed, this belief found its strongest reinforcement from one of the Navy's most celebrated thinkers: Alfred Thayer Mahan. In 1890, Mahan published a collection of his Naval War College lectures under the title *The Influence of Sea Power upon History, 1660–1783*, to instant acclaim. In fact, naval historian Kenneth Hagan argues, "Never has one book on naval history and strategy meant so much to so many."[28] Mahan captured the rising naval sentiments of his day, distilling lessons from history on the importance of sea power for national greatness and prosperity. As a central tenet of his argument, Mahan posited that "Naval strategy has for its end to found, support, and increase, as well in peace as in war, the sea power of a country."[29] Sea power, as Mahan conceived of it, comprised two entangled pursuits: first, commanding the seas with superior battle fleets; second, creating national prosperity through expansion of commercial markets and maritime commerce.[30] Mahan's concept of sea power wove together military strength and national economic growth, as superior warships enabled ever-expanding markets for commercial prosperity.

Mahan's popular, important, and influential work became a sacred text for "a theory of national prosperity and destiny founded upon a program of mercantilistic imperialism."[31] Mahan only tightened the knot already coupling the national and naval interest, capturing the prevailing sentiments of the times. Not a lone zealot at odds with his cohort, Mahan merely served as an articulate spokesman of the late nineteenth-century navy. "Far from being the atypical genius many have styled him," argues Peter Karsten, "Mahan was a quite conventional member of his generation of the naval aristocracy."[32]

Mahan offered the Navy its clearest and most forceful exposition for the natural entanglement of national and naval interests. This belief sank deep in the Navy mind, as Admiral Ernest King famously argued to the US Senate: "It follows that if the Navy's welfare is one of the prerequisites to the Nation's welfare—and I sincerely believe that to be the case—any step that is not good for the Navy is not good for the Nation."[33]

Contemporary evidence suggests that the Navy's organizational commitment to national prosperity continues. For the 200-year commemoration of the War of 1812, the US Navy promoted a campaign in 2012 that hailed the historical continuity of the Navy's purpose, using the slogan "America's Navy: Keeping the Sea Free for More Than 200 Years." As the Navy's online promotional material hailed, "90% of all our imports arrive by sea. Since 1812, the US Navy has ensured they get here."[34] The Navy and the nation continue to prosper together.

In summary, since its earliest days, the United States has wanted and needed a strong navy to establish its commercial interests abroad. The US Navy enabled a seafaring nation to expand its markets and continues to protect the freedom of the seas around the globe. Since a large navy poses no oppressive threat to its citizens, what is good for the Navy is good for America.

Survival through Enlisted Order and Commissioned Judgment

Sailors in the US Navy quickly learn that survival at sea requires every seaman to do his job, follow orders, and be prepared. The ocean is a dangerous place to live and work; threats from the sea, extreme weather, or an enemy fleet can surface at any time from any direction. To survive in this environment requires continual drilling for any possible contingency and a tight choreography of roles. Furthermore, life at sea requires a flexible standard for the ship's crew: enlisted sailors must obey quickly and fully, but commissioned officers need to abide by a different ethic. Given the unpredictability of the maritime environment, Naval officers perform best by relying on seasoned wisdom and sound judgment.

Operational Environment

Four key dimensions of life at sea contribute to this way of thinking. First, the sea is a vast and restless environment in which to work. Nearly every commentary on life at sea leads with an insight of this sort: "a seaman's first, visceral battle is with the environment. It is always trying to kill him."[35] Since "the first principle of a seaman's outlook is the safety of the ship," this primordial preoccupation conditions a specific manner of thinking and behavior among sailors.[36] To survive on a turbulent sea or in combat with an enemy across the horizon, everyone's safety hinges on a collective commitment to serving one's role and following orders smartly. The uncompromising ocean will make no bargains with a lax, undisciplined, or cavalier crew.

The emphasis on doing one's job is so profound in the Navy that sailors generally refer to their shipmates not by their names or rank but by their position. Identity and function are purposefully fused. For example, "Admin," "Ops," "XO," and "STAN" are job titles that sailors use as personal names to address the administrative officer, the operations officer, the executive officer, and the standardization officer, respectively. In fact, the Navy ritualizes this idea when announcing the arrival and departure of senior officers and ship captains aboard US Navy ships. When a commanding officer (CO) or senior leader arrives on board a ship, a member of the crew (the boatswain) announces not the name of the person but the name of the ship or organization that the officer commands.[37] When the CO of the USS *Nimitz* arrives on a ship, for example, the boatswain announces: "Nimitz arriving." If the secretary of the Navy departs a Navy ship, the announcement rings: "United States Navy, departing." In May 2003, this practice applied to the commander-in-chief himself—when President George W. Bush landed on the aircraft carrier USS *Abraham Lincoln*, the boatswain announced: "United States of America, arriving."

A second defining aspect of the Navy's environment is that sailors live in their weapon. Sailors at sea are never off-duty, since the transition from peace to war, from placid seas to threatening storms, and from calm to chaos can be immediate. In this uncertain environment, a ship captain "must always be ready to take his ship into action on a moment's notice. He must be able to use his ship as a single weapon in the way a swordsman uses his sword."[38] Being ready for anything—and responding as an integrated crew—requires vigilance, rehearsal, and incessant drill. Furthermore, even when the ship is not under active attack from an enemy or storm, the corrosive sea inflicts a steady assault against its integrity. Sailors must actively combat the persistent erosion with regular maintenance, servicing their home, their weapon, and their shelter with equal diligence.

A third dimension of the operational environment involves the paradoxical mixture of adventure and tedium that saturates life at sea. The allure of the open sea beckons sailors with a compelling romance that can only be experienced, not explained. This allure, however, quickly mingles with a pounding boredom, in which the flat expanse of the ocean offers a visual picture of the horizonless tedium of life afloat. "Most of the time on board a naval vessel," explains historian Peter Karsten, "was spent in eternal preparation for a situation—be it collision at sea, man overboard, a fire in the powder room, or war—that might never take place. Drills, routine upkeep, and watches filled the naval day."[39] For new midshipmen and sailors, the discipline of "the watch" brings order to the foreign and dizzying world at sea.

The routines of ship life also serve the purpose of maintaining good order and discipline in the midst of restless monotony. In the early days of the Navy, the rowdy sailors that comprised the ship's company formed a striking contrast to the aristocratic officer corps; two completely separate societies coexisted, and "the gulf between the two was unfathomable."[40] To guard against idle temptations, ship captains ensured that the crew remained purposefully occupied, doing what ship crews have always done: "Standing watches was about all there was to do. It was what seamen had done when at sea for three or four hundred years—a set of routines, arbitrary, clearly defined. They had a role to play. If you were at sea for as long as they were . . . it was necessary, having a ship's company that did not have too much to do, to have a set of rather arbitrary routines that held the whole society together."[41] This culture of purposeful arbitrariness persists even today; the commanding officer's official "watch bill" continues to be the central organizing directive that sets the circadian rhythms of a Navy unit, whether at sea or ashore.

Finally, since living and fighting at sea involves immersion in risk, the crew is expected to follow orders fully and quickly. But those in command of the ship must follow a different ethic. "At sea, context rules."[42] Ship captains cannot execute rote principles or rigidly follow rules when the shifting context calls for judgment and practical wisdom. As naval historian Clark Reynolds observes, "Practical common sense and the ability to improvise when short on doctrine or material are equally essential for survival at sea."[43] These observations have become part of the Navy's cultural belief system: if context rules, there is small value in specifying doctrine or a rulebook to cover every situation. The Navy thus holds a "long-standing aversion to written doctrine" and sustains a culture in which "definitions are often ignored when the chips are down and expediency—or, at the extreme, life and death—rules."[44] Since judgment comes mostly through experience, the Navy tends to reward its of-

ficers based on their proximity to sea spray. To be in the Navy is to be at sea—
everything else is secondary.

In summary, sailors afloat live in harm's way. The sea is a ruthless host, and
enemy ships may appear at any time from any direction. The crew must be
prepared at all times, and such readiness can come only through vigilance,
repetition, and obedience. Leadership in this environment requires experience at sea and sound naval judgment, not rote adherence to doctrine or
checklists.

The Glory of Independent Command at Sea

In his 2011 memorandum to prospective commanding officers, Chief of
Naval Operations (CNO) Admiral Gary Roughead opened with this declaration: "Command is the foundation upon which our Navy rests."[45] Later in the
memo, Roughead emphasized the historical legacy of this deep cultural tradition: "A Commanding Officer's authority must be commensurate with his
or her responsibility and accountability. This immutable truth has been the
very foundation of our Navy since 1775." As Admiral Roughead's memo suggests, the Navy takes seriously the role of the commanding officer, entrusting
COs with great responsibility and the latitude with which to carry out their
mission.[46] Armed with this institutional trust, COs in general—and ship captains more specifically—rule their domain with nearly impregnable authority. Consequently, naval officers covet the opportunity to command at sea—
very often the high-water mark of any career. A pattern of bold and daring
command fills the volumes of Navy history.

Operational Environment and Founding Context

Two elements of the Navy's environment contribute to its belief in the proper
role and authority of COs. First, ship captains at sea tend to operate at great
physical distance from higher echelons of command. Captains have the best
awareness of the current conditions of the floating organism that is their ship.
In the early days of the US Navy, the physical separation of a ship at sea also
meant a communicative separation, as messages could move from ship to
ship only at the rate of sail. Ship captains received initial guidance from superior military or political leaders and were trusted to exercise judgment in
carrying out those orders. While these geographic limitations on communication have certainly changed, operational justifications remain for trusting
captains at sea. According to Barnett, "The propensity to discount distant

authority when it differed from the commander's perception of the local situation [has] persisted in naval culture."[47] The Navy, in fact, is the only service that regularly uses the phrase "unless otherwise directed" and its associated acronym, UNODIR. Reflecting the Navy's unique principle of "command by negation," commanding officers are expected to inform their boss of plans and actions, not ask permission.[48] Silence from the superior officer implies consent, and COs proceed as planned unless otherwise directed.

Second, the demands of survival at sea require an intricate choreography of roles, underwritten by swift deference to authority—authority that culminates in the captain. The pervasive risk that saturates life at sea is the constant obsession of the ship captain, who bears a responsibility known by few others. Historian Eugene Ferguson writes that "the captain of a ship of war has—and in this respect conditions have changed almost none at all in two hundred years—a continuously sustained, minute-by-minute responsibility that can be understood only imperfectly by [a] landsman."[49] This shipboard reality confers a responsibility upon captains that, in turn, gives them nearly absolute authority to run the ship as they see fit.[50]

The early days of the US Navy reinforced these ideas. As highlighted earlier, the captains of the infant Navy enjoyed wide latitude in carrying out their varied diplomatic and military missions. Once their high-masted ships slipped over the horizon, captains ruled their maritime universe largely free of politicians' gravitational pull. Furthermore, to maintain good order and discipline at sea, captains received absolute deference from below as a fitting complement to the autonomy they enjoyed from above.

Bold Exemplars

The operational environment and founding context of the Navy clearly shaped the service's view of how to command at sea. The early generations of seafaring captains cemented the Navy way and left a legacy of bold, fearless, and daring command for subsequent Navy generations.

John Paul Jones, for example, occupies revered terrain in Navy hearts and on Navy grounds—entombed in an elaborate crypt beneath the Naval Academy chapel. Jones's example has become cherished Naval tradition.[51] During the fanfare attending Jones's interment in the Naval Academy crypt in 1906, President Teddy Roosevelt lionized Jones with high praise: "Every officer in our Navy should know by heart the deeds of John Paul Jones. Every officer in our Navy should feel in each fiber of his being an eager desire to emulate the energy, the professional capacity, the indomitable determination and dauntless scorn of death which marked John Paul Jones above all his fellows."[52] Jones's example during the Revolution included raiding the British coastline, wreaking havoc on British shipping, and winning a dramatic victory over HMS *Serapis* on September 23, 1779—the battle at which Jones uttered his most famous line. While his ship was burning and sinking, Jones received a demand for surrender from his British counterpart, to which Jones replied, "I have not yet begun to fight!"[53]

Jones's pugnacious example in the Revolution found ample reinforcement in fellow captains in the quasi-war with France (1798–1800) and the Barbary wars (1801–15). In February 1799, in the first major action of the quasi-war, Captain Thomas Truxtun commanded the USS *Constellation* on its way to finding, chasing, attacking, and capturing the French frigate *L'Insurgente*. When informed by the French captain that his actions were illegitimate given the official state of peace between their countries, Truxtun sent word to Secretary of the Navy Benjamin Stoddert: "The french Captain tells me, I have caused a War with France, if so I am glad of it, for I detest Things being done by Halves."[54] Truxtun became the hero of the quasi-war, and his example echoed through the ranks.

In the War of 1812, the Navy inaugurated another generation of intrepid ship captains whose legacy ripples through Navy history. The War of 1812 "must be the least remembered war in American history," writes historian Eric Larrabee, "the most disparaged as clumsy and inconclusive, yet it forged a national identity the Revolution had only begun to achieve—and the Navy remembers it."[55] The war bequeathed some of the Navy's most cherished mottos, such as Captain James Lawrence's "Don't give up the ship!"—a dying admonition to his crew of the USS *Chesapeake* in May 1813.[56] As a tribute to Lawrence, Captain Oliver Hazard Perry emblazoned those words on a flag, which he flew on his ship—fittingly, the USS *Lawrence*—in action on Lake Erie in September 1813. The original "Don't Give Up the Ship" flag features prominently in the Naval Academy museum, and a replica hangs just as prominently in the academy's ornate Memorial Hall.

Finally, the Civil War and the Spanish-American War provide two other cherished tales of fearless naval command. Commanding a column of ships to capture Mobile Bay in August 1864, Union Admiral David Farragut was unable to see the action in front of him. As Farragut climbed the mainmast of the USS *Hartford*, he asked a crewman to lash him in place—fixing his position on the ship and in naval legend. When the leading ship of his line hit a rebel mine, seeding confusion and doubt in his fleet, Farragut gave an order for the ages: "Damn the torpedoes! Full speed ahead."[57] Farragut's dauntless example clearly inspired one of his protégés, George Dewey, who had his own opportunity to lead warships into an enemy harbor. Thirty-five years later, as the United States was at war with Spain in 1898, Dewey sailed into Manila Bay in the Philippines, asking himself, "What would Farragut do?"[58] When Dewey's nephew, Lieutenant William Winder, eager for naval immortality, requested to lead the column of ships to detonate any potential mines ahead of the flagship, Dewey firmly replied, "Billy, I have waited sixty years for this opportunity. And much as I like you and know you are a fine officer—mines or no mines, I am leading the squadron in myself."[59]

In summary, ship captains have a unique responsibility to advance American interests, and they must be fully trusted to do so. On the ship, the captain is the sovereign, equipped with seasoned judgment, superior skill, and total authority. Command at sea is every officer's rightful aspiration and should be conducted with prudently bold independence.

A Professional and Permanent Navy

Since 1787, when the Constitution gave Congress the specified power "to provide and maintain a Navy," naval advocates have preached the importance of maintaining a standing navy. Unlike an army militia that can be temporarily mobilized in a local community, with citizen-farmers beating their plowshares into swords, navies require investment and time. All aspects of naval life—from shipbuilding to navigation to gunnery—require time, practice, infrastructure, and steady commitment. A credible naval fleet cannot be rallied to the village green by a town crier; it must be organized, drilled, and funded deliberately as a professional force.

Operational Environment

The Navy's operating environment, combined with its roles as America's warrior-diplomats and defenders of commerce, creates the ideological foundation for a professional full-time Navy. Life at sea is a world apart, bearing few resemblances to landlocked life. To survive and win at sea, crews must know their role, execute orders, and apply seasoned judgment that only time at sea can impart. Credible navies require expertise that only salty experience can provide. Any attempt to improvise a ship's crew, let alone a naval fleet, is a fool's errand. In his December 1945 testimony to the Senate, Fleet Admiral William Halsey emphasized this fact: "Let me remind you that a navy cannot be improvised overnight—it takes a long time to make a fighting ship. Naval leaders and naval air leaders achieved their skills by living on the sea, fighting over that sea, and beating the sea at its own game."[60]

Second, for the Navy to serve its roles as the deployed archipelago of American sovereignty and protector of American commerce, it must be *forward*. As the Armed Forces Officer guide explains, "The Navy culture is a *deployment* culture; deployments form the rhythm of Navy life for the Sailors and for their families."[61] The Navy cannot serve as warrior-diplomats or international trade police from home harbors or in dry dock. A militia serving as a last line of defense can be improvised from citizen-soldiers, but a navy serving as the *first* line of defense has no such luxury. It must live in a permanent state of readiness to protect American interests in peace, war, and everything in between.

Third, Navy warships require extensive infrastructure, technological currency, and industrial capacity. From the first six frigates authorized in 1794 to the nuclear-powered aircraft carriers of the twenty-first century, shipbuilding requires time, experience, funding, planning, and patience. To field a credible navy, a nation must maintain the industrial infrastructure to build, support, and sustain it. Navies are inherently expensive to build, are difficult to change, and require great investments of time and money. Such long time horizons and costly investments contribute to an abiding conservatism in the Navy, as decisions endure for decades.[62]

Founding Context and Reinforcing Events

Several events in the early life of the Navy reinforced this pattern of belief. First, the specific language of the Constitution clearly distinguished two different approaches to creating an army and navy. Congress held power to "raise and support" armies, limited to a two-year appropriation of funds; by contrast, it had power to "provide and maintain" a navy. The differentiation clearly mattered to the Constitution's drafters, as the pervasive fear of a standing army did not bleed over onto the navy.

Creation of the Navy Department in 1798 put the US Navy on the path to permanence. When Congress authorized the first six frigates of the US Navy in 1794, the War Department bore responsibility for both the army and navy. Soon, the burdens of shipbuilding and the mounting naval crisis with France became too much for the overwhelmed War Department staff. So Congress created a separate Navy Department, with a cabinet-level officer reporting directly to the president. This decision was one small step for Congress and one giant leap for the US Navy. While the appropriation to build the six frigates was an ad hoc response to the Barbary pirates, creation of the Navy Department comprised a major move in creating a standing Navy. By creating cabinet-level naval presence, Congress ensured that "control of naval operations [would be] directly under the nation's Commander-in-Chief rather than through the War Department—thus providing some insurance against the adverse effects suffered by other nations when naval operations had been subordinated to land warfare and sea power objectives were ignored."[63]

The nation's brief experiment with an alternative structure—a small, defensive, militia-style navy—provoked rampant criticism from Navy advocates. As president, Thomas Jefferson did not support a large standing navy, advocating instead for an affordable and defensively deployed gunboat navy. Reaping the brief peace dividend after the 1805 peace with Tripoli, Jefferson pursued a new fleet of small, defensively arrayed gunboats, while the larger frigates were put into inactive reserve status. Navalists of the period found such an arrangement "humiliating," while naval historians later decried the policy as "an unsound line of naval development" that clearly ignored the manifest lessons of the Revolution and the Barbary wars.[64]

The writings of Alfred T. Mahan cemented this conviction in the Naval mind. Mahan popularly argued for the use of powerful fleets-in-being to pursue offensive, not defensive, strategies. For generations of pro-Mahanian scholars and navalists, these convictions have applied universally and not contextually, offering the lens through which to read all history. The Civil War, for example, offered "clear and unmistakable" lessons to Mahanian scholars that naval fleets cannot be improvised, fleets-in-being are paramount, commerce raiding is inconsequential, and command of the seas makes all the difference.[65]

In summary, a credible naval fleet cannot be summoned in short order like a militia. Fighting ships and able crews require expensive investments, shipbuilding infrastructure, and continual drilling by full-time professionals. Navies are effective when their ships and sailors are active and deployed, not held in reserve.

The Bigger the Better

If the Navy should be organized as a standing force with a credible fleet-in-being, what should that fleet look like? The US Navy has consistently displayed a belief in the importance of organizing the fleet around major capital ships of the line, from its first six frigates to battleships to aircraft carriers. As the following discussion illustrates, a pervasive belief that "bigger is better" recurs throughout the Navy story, with various alternatives for smaller or more diverse fleets sparking significant resistance from the Naval core.

Operational Environment and Founding Context

In many aspects of life at sea, bigger is indeed better. In the early days of the Navy, engagements between warships required the massing of firepower in a concentrated space. The number of guns onboard became the defining characteristic of naval ships, and this all-important number became shorthand for the class of ship—commentators still refer to these ships as "36s," "44s," or "74s," for example. Size also allowed endurance, as larger ships could be self-sufficient for longer periods of time by carrying greater stores of provisions, thereby reducing the need for port visits.

Larger ships also provided the best classrooms for training new midshipmen and sailors. The biggest ships carried the largest crew, with the widest variety of roles and duties, and thus the greatest demand for order, discipline, and tight standards. The biggest ships were also the most seaworthy, so they sailed the farthest, explored the open oceans, and garnered a wider variety of experiences at sea and ashore. Finally, the biggest ships were commanded by the most senior and skilled officers, from whom junior officers and the crew could learn about all things Navy. In essence, the biggest ships were the Navy at its finest: the most orderly, most adventurous, and most skilled.

Big ships clearly appealed to the Navy, but the affection was hardly universal. As described earlier, the truce with Tripoli in 1805 concluded a major phase of the Barbary wars, prompting President Jefferson to attempt a citizen's militia of small gunboats for coastal and riverine defense. The Navy loathed the idea. Having established its credibility in the Mediterranean, the Navy did not want to yield oceanic control, retreating on gunboats into coastal-defense operations.[66] Gunboats, moreover, had none of the appeal of the grander frigates and battleships. "The anathematic vessel was the gunboat," writes historian Christopher McKee, "and the voices raised against it formed a nearly unanimous chorus."[67] Gunboats held none of the advantages of the frigates, with smaller crews, lax discipline, less experienced captains, and few opportunities to excel in seamanship on open waters. Beyond these functional arguments, gunboats lacked the aesthetic and glorious appeal of triple-masted frigates: "There was nothing at all heroic about [gunboats]: no soaring masts, no line of broadside guns, no showing of the flag overseas, no majesty."[68] Whether Jefferson's gunboat policy represented a prudent cost-benefit decision is an open question; the Navy's response to the policy is not.

Events and Exemplars

These early events in the life of the Navy set a pattern that echoed throughout the twentieth century. As discussed above, Mahan advocated fiercely for powerful fleets-in-being to command the seas and destroy the enemy's fleet. Imposing and powerful ships sailed at the heart of Mahanian theory. Even more importantly, Mahan argued that a powerful battle fleet was equally vital in peace. "The supreme essential condition to the assertion and maintenance of national power in external maritime regions," he wrote, "is the possession of a fleet superior to that of any probable opponent."[69] Mahan's ideas coincided with a period of rapid naval procurement. Beginning in 1883 with the authorization for four new steel ships, the Navy built its first three battleships in 1895 and had six by 1898.[70] With this new fleet, the Navy claimed dramatic sea victories in the Spanish-American War, first by George Dewey in Manila Bay (May 1898) using armored cruisers, then by William Sampson in Santiago de Cuba (July 1898) with battleships. The powerful combination of popular Mahanian doctrine with the glory of battleship victories formed an intoxicating brew for the Navy. This convergence "permanently wedded the US Navy to [Mahan's] preferred strategy of capital-ship warfare, the goal of which was command of the seas achieved through decisive engagements between battle fleets."[71]

From that point forward—until the morning of December 7, 1941—the Navy remained committed to the battleship as the core of its fleet, strategy, and tactics. After World War I, for example, the Naval War College focused great attention and wargaming on the only battleship contest of the war, the 1916 Battle of Jutland between the British and German navies.[72] Furthermore, as the development of submarines and aircraft carriers moved forward in the interwar years, these new assets were largely conceived as merely support for the battleship. Both submarines and carriers served initially as scouts for the battleships, with little independent role or strategic advantage to consider.[73] "The minds of the men in control were not attuned to the changes being wrought by advancing technology," submariner Captain Edward Beach observes. "Mahan's nearly mystical pronouncements had taken the place of reality for men who truly did not understand but were comfortable in not understanding."[74]

This resilient belief in the battleship lingered until the Japanese put most of the battleship fleet at the bottom of Pearl Harbor on December 7, 1941. For the remainder of World War II, the aircraft carrier served as the preeminent capital ship; its heroic success in the Pacific campaign became the stuff of legend. Since then, the aircraft carrier has assumed the sacred post once held by the battleship, with few mavericks willing or able to challenge the tenets of carrier-based orthodoxy. Despite mounting evidence that carriers are vulnerable to much smaller boats, submarines, and anti-ship missiles, such vulnerabilities have been rarely and reluctantly acknowledged.[75] While there are sound strategic reasons to downplay one's vulnerabilities, evidence suggests that even the Navy's internal narrative is largely resistant to dethroning the impregnable carrier.

In the early 1970s, an internal challenge to carrier orthodoxy revealed the strength and fervor of the belief. When Admiral Elmo Zumwalt became chief of naval operations in 1970, he perceived an imbalance in the Navy's fleet. The carrier-centric Navy was prepared to project power across the globe, but not to *control* the seas and waterways of the world with a sufficient number of ships—the Navy had quality but lacked quantity.[76] Compared with the growing Soviet navy, the US Navy had too few ships of the right mix, which Zumwalt sought to correct. High-end ships such as nuclear-powered carriers required complementary low-end ships such as Zumwalt's proposed sea control ship. These ships could be fielded with less capability but in higher numbers and in different types of water. Zumwalt knew his vision challenged the Navy's traditional insistence on "traveling first class," and his proposals were opposed vigorously by the aviation and submarine unions of the Navy.[77] Zumwalt's radical idea was "not acceptable to the naval leadership because it veered away from the very large, nuclear archetype that had become an *idee fixe* for US naval strategists."[78] Ultimately, the Navy's commitment to the carrier was written into law, as section 5062 of United States Code, Title X, stipulates: "The naval combat forces of the Navy shall include not less than 11 operational aircraft carriers."[79]

In summary, to project maximum power, the Navy should be organized around capital ships of the line—once battleships, now aircraft carriers. To destroy enemy fleets at their source, away from American shores, the Navy should assemble maximum firepower on superior ships.

Conclusion

This chapter has skimmed the surface of a deeply intriguing Navy history.[80] It provides only a first look at the personality of the Navy, differentiating it from its sister services in ways relevant to civil-military policymaking.

As explained at the beginning of the chapter, the contribution here is more methodological than empirical, both in the inductive approach to capturing the Navy's "operational code" and in the condensation of findings for subsequent deductive analysis. Figure 2.1 summarizes the beliefs of a complex Navy in a simple format. To the extent that these beliefs comprise an enduring cultural pattern for the Navy, its policy preferences are likely to follow logically from these beliefs.[81] Consequently, for the case study analyses (chapters 6 and 7), these six beliefs will be used first to predict and then to explain the fact and form of the Navy's policy preferences and political behavior. But with three other services still to consider, the next chapter shifts attention to the other service within the Department of the Navy: the United States Marine Corps.

		SUMMARY OF NAVY CULTURAL BELIEFS
Ends	**2.1** An Armed Embassy of America: Anytime, Anywhere	The US Navy provides a unique instrument of national power as a mobile archipelago of sovereign American presence and power anywhere in the world. The Navy offers a flexible and full continuum of diplomatic leverage, from showing the flag to full combat operations. American foreign policy is made credible by a large, powerful, and deployed fleet.
	2.2 America and Its Navy Prosper Together	Since its earliest days, the United States has wanted and needed a strong navy to establish its commercial interests abroad. The US Navy enabled a seafaring nation to expand its markets and continues to protect the freedom of the seas around the globe. Since a large navy poses no oppressive threat to its citizens, what is good for the Navy is good for America.
Ways	**2.3** Survival through Enlisted Order and Commissioned Judgment	Sailors afloat live in harm's way. The sea is a ruthless host, and enemy ships may appear at any time from any direction. The crew must be prepared at all times, and such readiness can come only through vigilance, repetition, and obedience. Leadership in this environment requires experience at sea and sound naval judgment, not rote adherence to doctrine or checklists.
	2.4 The Glory of Independent Command at Sea	Ship captains have a unique responsibility to advance American interests, and they must be fully trusted to do so. On the ship, the captain is the sovereign, equipped with seasoned judgment, superior skill, and total authority. Command at sea is every officer's rightful aspiration and should be conducted with prudently bold independence.
Means	**2.5** A Professional and Permanent Navy	A credible naval fleet cannot be summoned in short order like a militia. Fighting ships and able crews require expensive investments, shipbuilding infrastructure, and continual drilling by full-time professionals. Navies are effective when their ships and sailors are active and deployed, not held in reserve.
	2.6 The Bigger the Better	To project maximum power, the Navy should be organized around capital ships of the line—once battleships, now aircraft carriers. To destroy enemy fleets at their source, away from American shores, the Navy should assemble maximum firepower on superior ships.

Figure 2.1. A summary of the US Navy's cultural beliefs about its preferred ends, ways, and means.

chapter 3

The Few and the Proud

The Service Culture of the United States Marine Corps

We are not retreating. We are just attacking in a different direction.
—Major General Oliver P. Smith, Commanding Officer, 1st Marine
Division, quoted in Robert Heinl's, *Soldiers of the Sea*

Jarheads. Leathernecks. Devil Dogs. Marines. The United States Marine Corps is one of the most iconic fighting organizations in history. As rapid responders to violent crises, the Marines are "first to fight" anywhere in the world, for all types of hazardous missions. The Marine Corps boasts an elite fighting record, tackling the nation's fiercest conflicts with bravado and grit, while cultivating a sharply defined culture that Marines guard as vigilantly as any embassy. The other military services refer to their members as common-noun soldiers, sailors, and airmen—but there is nothing common about Marines, capitalized and elite. The other services provide jobs and opportunities; Marines create a new identity.

The Marine identity serves to unify the entire Corps. The other three services have internal status hierarchies and various subcultures. The Marine Corps, however, resists creating elite subdivisions within an already elite service. Other than aviator wings, dive qualification badges, and airborne badges, Marines do not wear job specialty insignia on their uniforms, nor do they display unit insignia for division, regimental, or battalion affiliations.[1] When Lieutenant General Chesty Puller was asked about changing this policy, he gruffly replied, "No unit insignia is required. Marine is enough."[2] Even the institutional divide between officers and enlisted Marines is minimized; all are Marines, baptized into the same rites and legends.[3] Functionally, the Marine Corps limits the variation of its jobs; it has no doctors, nurses, dentists, medical corpsmen, or chaplains—the Navy provides these services for Marines. This lack of internal strata, vertically in rank and laterally in specialty, strengthens Marine culture and makes it the most consistent and pervasive of the service cultures. Finally, the Marine Corps has the fewest number of four-star generals, with only three or four in active service at any time. The commandant of the Marine Corps therefore holds an unusual degree of authority *within* the service, allowing the Corps to line up squarely behind a single coherent message.[4]

The strength and consistency of Marine Corps culture is substantiated in the five beliefs that follow. The methodology behind this chapter mirrors that used for the Navy. Using both primary and secondary sources, the analysis pays close attention to the institutional history that the Marine Corps itself highlights as most central to its ethos. The portrait painted here relies on official histories appropriately salted with Marine-sanctioned legends and myths—with the distinctions noted as appropriate. As with chapter 2, the history presented here is neither comprehensive nor chronological, but organized topically around salient beliefs. Who, then, are these Marines?

Warriors from the Sea

As elite warriors organized within the Department of the Navy, Marines add the terrestrial punch to the Navy's power projection afloat. The Marine Corps is inherently a sea service, connected strategically and organizationally to the US Navy. Much of the Marine Corps narrative marches in step with the Navy story profiled in chapter 2, as the Corps has historically carved out new roles for itself alongside an ever-changing naval service. While the Navy serves as a mobile archipelago of American sovereignty around the world, the Marine Corps contributes the next step of political-military commitment. Marines offer the complementary staying power of American ground presence anywhere in the world to do anything the president asks.

Operational Environment and Founding Context

The Marine Corps–Navy connection has both historical and functional roots. The operational environment of eighteenth-century sailing ships required a cadre of armed soldiers to complement the sailing crew's core mission of "fighting the ship" against hostile seas and enemy fleets. Marines were "as much a part of a man-of-war's furniture as its spars, or sails, or guns," explains Marine Corps historian Edwin Simmons. "Marines preserved internal order and discipline. Marines gave national character to the ship. Marines were uniformed, sailors were not."[5] In this early operational environment, Marines formed an essential component of naval warfare, serving as boarding parties, sharpshooters, ship guards, landing forces, or whatever the ship captain might require.

The Continental Marines of the Revolutionary War served capably in this naval context. To prepare for an invasion of Halifax, Nova Scotia, the Continental Congress resolved on November 10, 1775, "that two Battalions of marines be raised," with careful consideration to include only "such as are good seamen, or so acquainted with maritime affairs as to be able to serve to advantage by sea when required."[6] Congress offered Samuel Nicholas the first commission as a Marine officer on November 28, 1775.[7] Nicholas then personally recruited the first American Marines, often staging his efforts from Tun Tavern in Philadelphia, which Marines still hallow as their organizational birthplace.[8]

After a successful recruiting effort, the first 288 Marines launched with the Continental Navy in February 1776, serving under the command of Commodore Esek Hopkins. The planned Nova Scotia mission had been cancelled, so the Marines and sailors went south to New Providence Island in the Bahamas to attack and secure British stores on the island—the Marines' first amphibious assault in what would become a long and storied pattern.[9] To the very end of the war, the Marines remained fundamentally linked to the Navy, as Marine officers and enlisted troops remained in service as long as Navy ships remained in commission.[10] When the end of war meant the end of the Continental Navy, the Marines likewise disappeared into the dividend of hard-won peace.

When the Barbary wars and quasi-war with France spurred Congress to authorize the first permanent ships of the US Navy, the Marines were likewise reborn. In fact, Congress organized an enduring *corps* of Marines, rather than raising them ad hoc to serve only on particular ships. On July 11, 1798, Congress passed "An Act for Establishing and Organizing a Marine Corps," specifying that "in addition to the present military establishment, there shall be raised and organized a corps of marines."[11] The Marines' hybrid character, serving capably by land and by sea, was firmly institutionalized in this act. The legislation subjected the Marines to the articles of war (like the Army) when serving on land and to Navy regulations (like the Navy) when serving at sea. Despite being organizationally wedged between the Army and Navy, the Marine Corps remained a sea service at its core. Situated within the Navy Department, the Corps defined itself in naval terms and in rhythm with naval developments.

Events and Exemplars

From these early days of the eighteenth century, the Marine Corps story continued to develop in parallel with the Navy. Wherever the Navy went, the Marines were with it; whatever glories the Navy compiled, the Marines helped make possible. As the Navy busily sailed around the world in the nineteenth century, showing the flag and negotiating treaties of commerce and protection, the Marines were there, planting the flag on foreign soil. Furthermore, the Marines were often dropped off on that soil, left ashore to handle protracted and thorny conflicts. Many pages of Marine Corps history hail its expertise in small wars, serving as colonial infantry and counterinsurgents in Nicaragua, Haiti, the Dominican Republic, and elsewhere across the globe.

The Marine Corps–Navy relationship experienced a major shock in the 1890s, when an epochal shift in the Navy prompted an equally foundational change for the Marine Corps. In the closing decade of the nineteenth century, the keel of the "new Navy" was laid, boasting a new fleet of steam-powered, steel-hulled ships. The logistical requirements of these new ships, coupled with the organizational dynamics of an evolving Navy, conspired to push the Marine Corps into a new era. Logistically, the new steam-powered ships required an extensive port infrastructure to keep them supplied with coal. The transition from sail to steam bore tradeoffs; ships exchanged their reliance on the wind for a dependence on coal. Extended cruises at sea now required coaling stations for resupply, which had to be secured at foreign ports from foreign rulers. This new dependence presented a challenge to the Navy and an opportunity for the Marine Corps. The visionary leader of the Marines during this crucial transition was John Lejeune, who intuitively understood the emerging connection. Overcoming significant opposition within the Corps, Lejeune recognized that the Navy's hunger for coal would need to be sustained by advanced bases, secured and defended by elite Marines.[12]

After World War I, interest in defending advanced bases evolved into planning for the seizure of bases through amphibious assaults. In 1921, with the Japanese naval threat on the rise, Lejeune supported the research of Major Earl Ellis, who actively devised a plan for fighting the Japanese in the Pacific.[13] Ellis's influential study, "Advanced Base Operations in Micronesia, 1921," became the blueprint for Navy and Marine Corps amphibious operations in the Pacific 20 years later. From that point forward, the Marine Corps began to organize, train, and equip its forces to perform amphibious assaults. In 1933, the Corps created the Fleet Marine Force to serve "in a state of readiness for operations with the Fleet," formalizing the structure required for amphibious operations.[14] Ten years later, when obscure Pacific islands such as Tarawa, Peleliu, and Iwo Jima became household names, the Marines' dedication to amphibious operations became their signature contribution to the Allied victory.

During the Cold War, the Marines' strategic attachment to the Navy remained largely in effect. Both sea services styled themselves as forces in readiness, with the Navy prepared to be anywhere at sea and the Marines prepared to do anything ashore. In an era of push-button nuclear absolutism, Marines remained decidedly conventional, expeditionary, and flexible. Marines deployed to hotspots like the Suez and Lebanon, performing various missions at the direction of the president. In sum, the Marines' vision in the decades after World War II was to serve, in the words of historian Allan Millett, as "minutemen . . . held in readiness to be moved instantly with the Fleet to any part of the world to strike hard and promptly to forestall at its beginning any attempt to disrupt the peace of the world."[15]

From the outset, Marines have been—and remain—a sea service of a distinctly hybrid character. In the conclusion to his insightful portrait of the Marine Corps, Lieutenant General Victor Krulak observes, "For the Marines, the maritime nature of the globe creates at once a grave responsibility and an elegant opportunity. It makes a powerful statement of a truth the Corps must never, never forget—that their future, as has their past, lies with the Navy."[16]

In summary, the Marine Corps is a maritime service, umbilically connected to the Navy through strategy and organization. The Corps serves as an embedded fighting force on the Naval archipelago, prepared to serve as needed on ships or on land. Marines are always prepared to fight their way onto any shore to conduct whatever mission the nation directs.

Survive to Serve

Marines sail the seas with the Navy, fight on land like the Army, and fly tactical and transport aircraft like the Air Force. Moreover, they do so on a much smaller scale than the other three services. Is this a wasteful duplication of effort, or does the Marine Corps offer a whole that exceeds the sum of its parts? The Corps is indeed a sea service, strategically linked to the Navy; in practice, however, the Marines' hybrid character puts them on contested ground. While the other three services have a clear domain of war that defines their existence, the Marines serve across all three domains of air, land, and sea. Like low-country inhabitants pushing back an encroaching sea, Marines have had to create their own institutional turf by reclaiming land and fighting for every square inch.

The Marines' fight for turf is a by-product of their charter. By creating an organization to serve on both land and sea, Congress birthed a military service that has lacked robust institutional protection for much of its life. At numerous points throughout its history, the Marine Corps has been considered unwanted surplus within the defense establishment; yet its unique attachment to the American public and Congress has kept it alive. Consequently, the Marines' precarious position confers an abiding institutional insecurity and a passion for public affairs. Marines are acutely aware that they serve at the pleasure of the American people; without their esteem, the Corps would likely have already perished. Absent a rational *need*, the Marines have to be *wanted*, and the Corps is thus passionate about being useful to the nation.

Operational Environment and Founding Context

The Marines have been wanted more than needed from the very beginning. The Continental Marines were originally proposed by the Nova Scotia committee of the Continental Congress to pursue an invasion of Halifax, Nova Scotia. On November 9, 1775, Congress considered the report of the Nova Scotia committee, which specified the necessary arms and organization for two battalions of Marines to conduct the invasion. The committee report also recognized that two battalions of Marines would prove useful even *without* the specific Halifax operation. The report offered this observation: "Should this Expedition by any Accident be found impra[c]ticable, these would be two Battalions of the Utmost service, being capable of serving either by sea or Land."[17] In other words, we are recommending two battalions of Marines to invade Nova Scotia, but should you decide to scrap the Nova Scotia mission, we still recommend those two battalions of Marines—we will be glad we have them. In the event, the Nova Scotia mission was indeed scrapped but the raising of two battalions of Marines was not.

The Army and Navy, however, did not share this esteem. The presence of Marines onboard Navy ships, while an essential complement in the eyes of the officers, served as an insult to the sailors.[18] The presence of Marines implied that the ship's crew needed constant oversight and would obey only at the point of a bayonet. Tension between Marines and sailors was woven into the very fabric of their joint work life, with little respect flowing in either direction.

Neither did the Army particularly care for the Marines, who constituted a partial duplication of the soldiers' terrestrial mission. According to the 1798 act that created the Marine Corps, Marines serving on land as sentries and guards were subject to Army regulations and processes, but the Army showed little interest in helping Marines with legal, administrative, or acquisition matters. Instead, one of the early commandants of the Marine Corps, Colonel Archibald Henderson, found himself institutionally unmoored. In a letter to the secretary of the Navy, Henderson complained that "[our] isolated Corps, with the Army on one side and the Navy on the other (neither friendly) has been struggling ever since its establishment for its very existence."[19] In fact, Marine Corps legend holds that after the Revolutionary War, all that was left was a corps of mules and the two battalions of Marines. The Army and Navy flipped a coin to decide who got the mules and who got the Marines; the Army won and chose the mules.[20]

Events and Exemplars

Born an orphan hybrid, the Marine Corps had to keep scrambling to stay alive. In fact, the Corps' existence has been threatened and attacked—but ultimately preserved by Congress—no less than 15 times in its history.[21] The Marines' strategy in response to all of these attacks has been to maintain a firm attachment to the American people and to prove their inestimable worth in whatever missions they have been given.

A major frontal assault on the Marine Corps came at the dawn of the twentieth century. The emergence of the new Navy in the late 1800s prompted a reconsideration of the Navy's organizational life. Led by Lieutenant William Fullam, a group of naval reformers reinvigorated an old cry to remove Marines from navy ships. Fullam suggested that the presence of Marines retarded the development of a professional navy, creating a "penal colony" atmosphere of suspicious supervision.[22] Instead, Fullam suggested, the Marine Corps should focus on expeditionary missions to secure advanced bases. While Fullam's idea proved prophetically invaluable to the life of the Corps, Marines were loath to give up *any* mission, even one with limited utility. A vocal debate raged for years among various factions in the Navy, with some calling for the removal of Marines from ships, others for the abolition of the Corps, and still others for maintaining the status quo.

The debate climaxed in 1908 when Navy reformers convinced President

Teddy Roosevelt to sign Executive Order 969 on November 12. Roosevelt believed the Marine Corps had grown too self-important and ordered Marines removed from Navy ships and relegated to garrison protection duties. Congress had other ideas. The chairman of the House Naval Affairs Committee was Thomas Butler, father of Marine Corps legend Smedley Butler, who would not let the Corps be dismissed so easily. Butler held hearings in January 1909, and the Marines ultimately won the day. Congress passed a rider to the appropriations bill on March 3, 1909, that put Marines back on Navy ships, preserving their original (though outdated) function. Historian Allan Millett notes how remarkable this bureaucratic feat truly was. The Marines repelled an assault from two presidents and key factions of the Navy and Army, and invoked nonfunctional arguments to do so. "When a military service can defend itself on grounds other than its present and future utility," Millett writes, "it has clearly reached a point of high institutional autonomy and stability. Such was the case of the Marine Corps in 1909."[23]

Another major attack began while bullets and bombs still streaked across Europe and the Pacific during World War II. While war raged, the American military services debated the merits of unifying the War and Navy departments into a single Department of Defense. The Army's proposed plan, which held sway with President Truman, involved unifying the services under a single department, with a single secretary of defense and a single military chief of staff.[24] Further, the proposed plan gave the secretary and the chief of staff power to determine the various roles and missions of the military services, a possibility that spelled disaster for the Marine Corps. The Marines vigorously pursued congressional protection, asking that their amphibious role and mission be coded into law, thus shielding the Corps from the eradicating whim of a future defense secretary.

The Marines' advocacy climaxed on May 6, 1946, with the testimony of the commandant of the Marine Corps, General Alexander Vandegrift. In his remarks, Vandegrift reminded Congress of its unique role in creating and preserving the Corps:

> In its capacity as a balance wheel this Congress has on five occasions since the year 1829 reflected the voice of the people in examining and casting aside a motion which would damage or destroy the United States Marine Corps ... The Marine Corps feels that the question of its continued existence is likewise a matter for determination by the Congress and not one to be resolved by departmental legerdemain or a quasi-legislative process enforced by the War De-

partment General Staff. The Marine Corps, then, believes that it has earned this right—to have its future decided by the legislative body which created it—nothing more.[25]

Ultimately, Congress sheltered the Marine Corps in the National Security Act of 1947, specifying its roles and missions so that no secretary or chief of staff could dismiss it with the stroke of a pen. Congress strengthened that protection five years later in the Douglas-Mansfield Act, passed on June 28, 1952, which stipulated the Marine Corps' minimum force structure as "not less than three combat divisions and three air wings."[26] Additionally, the act made the commandant of the Marine Corps a statutory member of the Joint Chiefs of Staff for all matters "which directly concern the United States Marine Corps." These pieces of legislation established the Corps on increasingly solid footing, reinforcing the legacy of congressional protection for a domestically besieged service.

The continual assaults on the Marine Corps' existence conditioned a willingness among Marines to perform any mission, big or small, as called upon by the nation. Recognizing their existence as contingent on the continuing esteem of the American people and Congress, Marines saw public excellence as an existential requirement. A trend of visible public service began with the very first commandant of the Marine Corps, William Burrows, who taxed each Marine officer $10 and used the funds to start the Marine Corps band. The band gave free concerts in Philadelphia and Washington, becoming much beloved by the American public.[27] The tradition continues to this day: the Marines still conduct public parades and concerts at the Marine Barracks in southeast Washington, DC, and at the Iwo Jima Memorial in Arlington, Virginia. In a very different public service role, Marines were once called to guard the US mail against robbers and thieves in the 1920s and did so with typical Marine pluck. Secretary of the Navy Edwin Denby gave shoot-to-kill orders and made it clear the mail *would* arrive or there would be a dead Marine at his post.[28]

Marine Corps hero Smedley Butler typified this public engagement while serving as base commander at Quantico, Virginia, in the 1920s. Butler, whose father chaired the House Naval Affairs Committee, understood the importance of endearing the Corps to the American people. He built a football stadium to host games between Marines and college teams; he staged Civil War reenactments at local battlefields; he even deployed Marines to Union Station in Washington, DC, to dig it out from a major snowstorm.[29] In 1947–48, as the existential debates raged about unifying the services into a single department, Marines started the "Toys for Tots" program, which continues to this day, to provide new toys to poor or disadvantaged children in local communities. Throughout its proud history, the Corps has understood the message plastered above the desk of Brigadier General Robert Denig, head of Marine Corps public affairs during World War II: "If the public becomes apathetic about the Marine Corps, the Marine Corps will cease to exist."[30]

Birthed by Congress into a liminal position between the Army and Navy, the Marine Corps has survived by doing any and every job, doing so with excellence, and maintaining an emotional connection with the American people. These trends help to resolve how Marines can be "paradoxically committed to *both* tradition and change."[31] In pursuit of organizational survival, the Corps has glorified its proud and unbroken tradition of service to the American people, while pursuing the technological and organizational changes necessary to maintain a viable mission.

In summary, the Marine Corps exists because the American people want it to exist. As the smallest of the four services, with tasks spanning the domains of warfare dominated by the other three, the Marine Corps risks being functionally eliminated or reduced to insignificance. Consequently, the Corps cares less about *how* it is used and more passionately that it be used and perpetuated.

Elite Warrior Identity

Being a Marine means forging a new identity—a new self-conception that supersedes all competing claims. The meta-identity of being a Marine involves stewarding the Marine Corps legacy and cultivating the elite warrior ethos that sets the Corps apart. Importantly, this emphasis on Marine identity reinforces the belief just discussed. When service in the Corps is not just something you do but *who you are*, all threats to the institution are taken seriously and eliminated swiftly. By making service in the Marine Corps a matter of existential reality, Marines heighten their vigilance against institutional extinction.

While members of the other three services often speak of being *in* the Army, Navy, or Air Force, members of the Marine Corps profess an identity: they *are* Marines. When recruiting new Marines, the Corps does not dangle incentives such as career benefits or job skills—it offers only the opportunity to be a Marine. Marine recruiting focuses almost entirely on the elite warrior image and the opportunity for battle. In 1907, the Army's recruiting posters hawked: "Join the Army and Learn a Trade"; the Navy offered the chance to "Join the Navy and See the World"; the Marine Corps declared simply, "First to Fight."[32]

This identity transformation begins immediately. Arriving for basic training, new recruits cross the causeway onto Parris Island, South Carolina, and see a sign declaring: "Where the Difference Begins." From their first moments, recruits are physically and emotionally stripped of identifying traits such as haircuts, personal space, or proper names. They are forbidden to use their own names or even personal pronouns; they must identify themselves as "this recruit."[33] Marine Lieutenant General (Ret.) Victor Krulak describes this process as an "egoectomy," the first step in replacing a self-centered persona with the new Marine identity.[34] Once recruits become Marines, they inherit the full heritage of the Corps and are expected to sustain the elite warrior spirit that defines it.

Operational Environment and Founding Context

Where did this collective warrior identity begin? The Marines' core attachment to the Navy created the first operational need for a disciplined, elite fighting force, distinct from the sailors nearby. To inculcate a higher disciplinary standard required of peacekeepers, mutiny-suppressors, and deserter-catchers, the infant Marine Corps maintained strict protocols for drill, dress, and appearance. The first official commandant of the Marine Corps, Lieutenant Colonel William Burrows, worked hard to burnish the reputation of the Corps in its earliest days. Fully aware of the Corps' cramped status in between the Army and Navy, Burrows turned the Corps' small size into an asset, cultivating eliteness as its comparative advantage.[35]

These institutional motivations for eliteness soon found support in the throes of combat. During the Barbary wars with Tripoli in the early nineteenth century, a tiny detachment of Marines famously fought on the "shores of Tripoli." While naval forces blockaded Tripoli in an effort to subjugate the Bashaw Yusuf Karamanli, Marine First Lieutenant Presley O'Bannon worked with American consul William Eaton to effect a different solution.[36] Eaton devised a plan to support Yusuf's exiled brother, Hamet, in a plot to take the throne by force. To support Eaton's mission, O'Bannon asked Navy Commodore Samuel Barron for 100 enlisted Marines to join him in the expedition; Barron granted only seven.[37] So Eaton, O'Bannon, and seven Marines gathered in Alexandria, Egypt, and cobbled together a force of several hundred

Greek and Arab mercenaries. This polyglot band of warriors marched 600 miles across North Africa, clashing with Yusuf's men at the battle of Derna on April 27, 1805. Despite suffering 50% casualties, with two Marines killed and two wounded, O'Bannon and his Marines prevailed and raised the American flag above the enemy fortification—the first of many times Marines would raise the stars and stripes on foreign soil.[38]

Despite this great military victory, Eaton's mission to put Hamet on the throne was superseded by a parallel American effort. On June 4, 1805, a separate diplomatic mission to Tripoli made peace with Yusuf, thereby undercutting the Marines' mission with Hamet. Nevertheless, the story of eight Marines fighting courageously on foreign soil sank deeply into the soul of the Corps. "To the Shores of Tripoli" served as the Marine Corps motto for a period and eventually became enshrined in the Marine Hymn. Marine Corps officers still carry the Mameluke sword, a curved blade reportedly given by Hamet to Presley O'Bannon in gratitude for the courageous work of his Marines.[39] The political insignificance of the battle does not matter to Marines. The approved lesson of Tripoli is that they went where they were sent, in the smallest of numbers, and fought valiantly to great effect.

Events and Exemplars

The elite action in Derna set the stage for two hundred more years of gallantry in combat. Marines have fought bravely and faithfully all over the world, serving as colonial infantry and counterinsurgents in Korea, Cuba, Samoa, the Dominican Republic, Honduras, Panama, Mexico, Nicaragua, Haiti, China, the Philippines, and beyond.[40] The War of 1812, the Indian wars in the American southeast (1836), the Mexican War (1846), the Spanish-American War (1898), the Boxer Rebellion (1900), and the military action in Veracruz, Mexico (1914)—all provide important instances of Marine Corps excellence in battle, but generally hold second-tier status in the Marine canon.

One of the first-tier battles to define the modern Marine Corps came on the outskirts of Paris during World War I, in the forests of Belleau Wood. There, the Marine Corps moved beyond its primitive role as colonial infantry and ship guards and met its first well-armed professional fighting force—"an acid test of the Marines' grit and dash."[41] In a monthlong campaign to defend the eastern approaches to Paris in June 1918, the Marines fought harder and suffered more than ever before. Between June 6 and June 12, the Marines lost 1,087 men, more than they had lost in their entire history to that point.[42]

The ferocious action at Belleau Wood added many cherished phrases to

Marine legend. When a retreating French officer counseled the newly arrived Marines to turn around, Marine Captain Lloyd Williams retorted, "Retreat, hell! We just got here!"[43] In other action, Sergeant Major Dan Daly urged the men of his platoon to join him in an assault by asking, "Come on, you sons-of-bitches. Do you want to live forever?"[44] Belleau Wood also birthed one of the enduring Marine Corps nicknames, as the German soldiers reportedly called the Marines *Teufelhunden,* or "Devil Dogs." Although German records include no historical evidence of the term, the beloved nickname and apocryphal story persist.[45] The legend of Belleau Wood is an enduring testimony to Marine grit and endurance, readiness for battle, and courage in the face of death.

The defining campaign in Marine Corps history is its amphibious dominance of the Pacific in World War II. From Guadalcanal (1942) to Tarawa (1943) to Peleliu (1944), Marines fought fierce battles against determined Japanese forces. The culmination of the Pacific campaign came in February 1945, on eight square miles of volcanic ash, against 22,000 entrenched Japanese fighting for their lives: the battle for Iwo Jima.[46] The month of savage fighting on Iwo Jima eclipsed anything the most grizzled of Marines had experienced. "I'm a veteran of three wars," recounted Major General Fred Haynes, the operations officer of the 28th Marine Regiment on Iwo Jima. "None of the other battles I've seen or even heard of compare to Iwo Jima. There's never been anything like it since . . . It was the definitive event of my life."[47] Four days into the battle, Associated Press photographer Joe Rosenthal captured its defining moment: the raising of the American flag on Iwo Jima's Mount Suribachi. Rosenthal's photo distilled the essence of the Marine Corps, with six faceless warriors striving corporately to raise an American flag in the midst of battle. Rosenthal's photo became the template for the Marine Corps Memorial in Arlington and the National Museum of the Marine Corps near Quantico. Iwo Jima remains the centerpiece of Marine warrior culture.

Lastly, a campaign cherished by Marines but unfamiliar to many Americans is their heroic action in the bitter cold of the Chosin Reservoir during the Korean War. After capturing Seoul in late 1950, American forces under General Douglas MacArthur raced north toward the Yalu River in four dispersed columns along detached mountain valleys. Sandwiched between two Army divisions, the 1st Marine Division advanced along a single narrow mountain road toward the Chosin Reservoir.[48] Fifteen thousand Marines, strung out along the narrow mountain pass, became perilously enveloped by more than 100,000 Chinese troops. In temperatures reaching 20 degrees below zero, the Chinese attacked the Marines on the night of November 27, 1950, at numerous points across the thin mountain line; when morning broke, the besieged Marines had somehow held their line.[49]

In desperately cold and brutal conditions, the operational commander of American forces in the region, Army Major General Edward Almond, ordered the Army and Marine Corps to retreat to the Korean coast. Almond ordered a rapid withdrawal, directing that any equipment, weapons, or supplies that slowed down progress should be jettisoned or destroyed. Marine Major General O. P. Smith, in command of the 1st Marine Division, replied that his Marines would fight their way out in an orderly and deliberate way, bringing out all of their men and equipment. The 1st Marine Division then conducted one of the epic fighting withdrawals in combat history—bringing out all its equipment and men in the process. No Marines were left behind; the wounded were carried out and the dead were properly buried. Along the way, in fact, the Marines accumulated *extra* trucks and equipment that the Army had left behind in its rush to the coast.[50]

Assessing the event, the Marines emphatically declared that this was no retreat. Colonel Chesty Puller, the most iconic Marine of them all, told reporters, "Remember, whatever you write, this was no retreat. All that happened was we found more Chinese behind us than in front of us. So we about-faced and attacked."[51] Whatever label one uses to describe it, Marines look to the Chosin campaign as a hallmark of enduring impossible conditions, persisting against great odds, and maintaining the military discipline to fight and care for one another no matter the cost—a point of pride heightened by the Marines' assessment of the Army's faltering performance under similar conditions.

The Hero of the Corps

Because collective identity is prized above personal ego in the Marine Corps, Marines tend to exalt the anonymous Marine rifleman above their great generals. The exceptions are few and only for the most deserving. And while the other services might name any of several heroes as their greatest, the Marine Corps clearly fixates on one: Lieutenant General Lewis "Chesty" Puller. "There is absolutely no doubt that Puller is *the* mythological hero of the Corps—the very icon of the entire institution," writes Marine historian Jon Hoffman. "His larger-than-life image is etched indelibly in every Marine almost from the first day at boot camp or officer candidate school."[52] During basic training, recruits in their bunks intone together, "Goodnight Chesty, wherever you are!"[53] Marines doing pull-ups prod one another by exhorting, "One more for Chesty!" The Marine Corps mascot, an English bulldog that resides at the Marine Barracks at 8th and I Streets in southeast Washington, is named "Chesty." Puller's funeral in 1971 was attended by the commandant of the Marine Corps, 43 general officers, and 1,500 former and active duty Marines.[54] Each year, a detachment of Marines continues to travel from Quantico to Puller's grave in Saluda, Virginia, to lay a wreath on the anniversary of his death.[55]

Puller's legendary status derives from his embodiment of the Marine warrior image: a gruff, aggressive combativeness coupled with a religious commitment to leading from the front and taking care of his Marines.[56] The most decorated Marine in history, Puller was awarded five Navy Crosses for valor in combat—a decoration second only to the Medal of Honor. Puller famously led his troops from the front, subjecting himself to all of the same dangers they faced. On Guadalcanal in 1942, one of his fellow officers saw in Puller "the greatest exhibition of utter disregard for personal safety I ever saw."[57] Consequently, Puller could lead his men into the worst fights, suffering the highest casualty rates, while still earning their fierce loyalty and veneration. Puller embodied the Marine ethos: he marched straight into the toughest fights, pulled no punches, never surrendered, served across the globe, and doggedly cared for his Marines at every step.

To be a Marine is to join an elite warrior fraternity. Marines know and celebrate their organizational history, as the ghosts of Derna, Belleau Wood, Iwo Jima, and the Chosin Reservoir all chant the same chorus: Marines fight fiercely and together.

In summary, being a Marine is fundamentally an identity, not a profession. All other identities are subsumed and secondary, as Marines today steward the legacy of Marines past. The Corps then and now is an elite warrior fraternity that runs toward the sound of the guns, wins battles, never retreats, and takes care of its own.

Faithful Stewards of the National Trust

Marines proudly recount their many battle successes, while proudly noting that they win those battles using only six cents of every defense dollar. Historically, the Marine Corps has received a smaller proportional share of the defense budget than the other three services. So it has learned to be creative and resourceful with what it *does* have. Marines see themselves as faithful stewards of the national trust; as their motto *Semper Fidelis* suggests, a Marine is always faithful. If the American people will trust the Marine Corps enough to keep it around, the Corps will honor that trust by husbanding its tax dollars effectively and creatively. The Corps' belief in frugality, faithfulness, and creativity receives the shortest treatment in this chapter, but this does not indicate a lack of importance. Frugal resourcefulness is a core element of Marine culture.

As the neglected stepchild in the Navy Department, the early Marine Corps developed a creative and scrappy approach to securing its equipment. Funded through the Navy Department, but requiring weapons and gear like the Army, the early Marine Corps had to fight for every resource. Without a separate budget or cabinet-level representation, the Corps relied on the secretary of the Navy to represent its interests sufficiently. In practice, this often meant that Marines received second-hand goods or manufacturing defects. Consequently, Marines cared religiously for the resources they *did* receive. Commandant of the Marine Corps Archibald Henderson, who led the Corps for 39 years, ensured that no Marine resource was wasted and "set the tune in establishing institutional frugality as a Marine Corps principle."[58] Future commandants extended that legacy, as John Lejeune made it a point as commandant always to return a portion of the Marine Corps' appropriation to the Treasury each year.

As Krulak describes in a lively narration of Marine Corps creativity over the years, Marines have never discarded equipment just because it is old; equipment is cared for and used until broken beyond repair. Further, Marines have a proud though illicit history of institutional "borrowing"—or, opportunistic theft—from other military services or fellow units too careless to guard their gear. According to Krulak, a resourceful sergeant once constructed an entire building at the Marine Corps Recruit Depot, San Diego, using only "borrowed" supplies. According to the official base register, the building did not even exist.[59]

The Marine Corps' ability to maximize its combat power on the cheap is a point of institutional pride. In his memorable testimony to the US Senate on May 6, 1946, General Alexander Vandegrift painted a striking contrast between the Army's and Marine Corps' stewardship of the American taxpayer's investment: "In the days of peace preceding the recent war, the United States was possessed of the world's top ranking Marine Corps. In 1938, that investment in security cost the Nation about $1,500 per marine. At the same time the United States possessed the world's eighteenth place army—at an annual cost of over $2,000 per soldier."[60] Marines are committed to doing more with less, having grown accustomed over their history to maximizing every investment made in the Corps.

In summary, the Marine Corps is a faithful steward of the national trust and the American taxpayer's investment. With a creative spirit, Marines make do with what they are given and care for it religiously. Marines are the best "victory per dollar" investment in military history.

Every Marine a Rifleman

General John Pershing of the US Army once declared, "The deadliest weapon in the world is a Marine with his rifle."[61] The Marine Corps believes, preaches, and lives the dictum that *every Marine is a rifleman*, and every Marine officer is a rifle platoon commander. So the most important resource on the Marine equipment ledger is the potent and inseparable coupling of the Marine and his rifle. This belief derives from the first principles of using military force, memorably conveyed by historian T. R. Fehrenbach: "You may fly over a land forever; you may bomb it, atomize it, pulverize it and wipe it clean of life—but if you desire to defend it, protect it, and keep it for civilization, you must do this on the ground, the way the Roman legions did, by putting your young men into the mud."[62] The Marine infantryman, equipped with his rifle, is the venerated icon of the Marine Corps and the critical resource for the Corps' success.

Marines and Their Rifles

No other American military service has a creed about its weapons. The Army, Navy, and Air Force all profess creeds about the high calling and the excellence demanded of being a soldier, sailor, or airman. These creeds nobly canonize a virtuous ethos for how to perform the service's mission. But since World War II, Marines have memorized, recited, and abided by a creed about their *guns*—the Rifleman's Creed, written by Major General William Rupertus. The creed venerates the Marine-rifle coupling:

> This is my rifle. There are many like it, but this one is mine. My rifle is my best friend. It is my life. I must master it as I must master my life. My rifle, without me, is useless. Without my rifle, I am useless . . . My rifle is human, even as I, because it is my life. Thus, I will learn it as a brother . . . We will become part of each other . . . Before God, I swear this creed. My rifle and myself are the

defenders of my country. We are the masters of our enemy. We are the saviors of my life.[63]

The Rifleman's Creed codifies the mystical union of Marines and their rifles, prompting historian James Warren to suggest, "The rifle is at the core of the Marine Corps' tumultuous history, its organizational mind-set, and its ethos."[64] The rifle is not a disembodied weapon or glorified technology for the Marine Corps; it is always conjoined to its Marine sibling. Across the lifespan of the Marine Corps' institutional saga, its most ardent and protracted fights were about *Marines themselves*, not their stuff or their task. "For the Marine Corps," writes historian Allan Millett, "the first priority in defining the Corps has always been its people, not its functions or its technology."[65]

The Culminating Belief

The Marine-rifle union comprises *the* essential resource with which the Marine Corps performs its service to the nation. Marines do many things through many different career specialties, but all Marines are first trained as riflemen and understand that any other specialty explicitly supports the rifleman on the front lines. Marine Corps aviators, for example, seek no independent role in their employment; instead, they specialize in close air support to the Marine infantry, focusing their tactics and doctrine accordingly. Major Alfred Cunningham summarized the Marines' long-standing view on aviation in a 1920 article in the *Marine Corps Gazette*: "It is fully realized that the only excuse for aviation in any service is its usefulness in assisting the troops on the ground to successfully carry out their operations."[66] Cunningham's seminal belief persists within the Corps—but certainly not outside it, particularly among Air Force airmen.

In a sense, the primacy of the Marine-rifle union can be seen as the culmination of the other four beliefs outlined in this chapter. The first belief highlights the Marine Corps' role as an expeditionary force-in-readiness, the ground-based punch to the Navy's sea-based projection. The legacy of the first Marines, serving on Navy ships with only their muskets, persists in spirit and in fact. As light infantry forces in an expeditionary role, Marines must travel light and be prepared at all times. Rifles comprise the ultimate expeditionary weapon, kept in readiness by their conjoined Marine twins, prepared for anything.

The second belief identifies the Marine Corps' precarious institutional state and the corollary search for an ongoing viable mission. By focusing on the Marines and their rifles, the Corps defends an irreducible mission that is never outdated or irrelevant. "Trained men who will stand and fight are never obsolete," writes Marine Corps historian Robert Heinl. "Men—the man, the individual who is the Marine Corps symbol and stock in trade—constitute the one element which never changes."[67] By focusing on the Marine and her rifle, the Marine Corps ensures its institutional relevance; no technology or technique can fully replace Marines in the mud.

The third belief expresses the supremacy of the Marine identity and elite warrior fraternity. The warrior image finds no greater fulfillment than a "man on the scene with a gun."[68] Rifle-toting Marine warriors resist antiseptic attempts to outsource combat to kinder or gentler means. "The Marines are an assemblage of warriors, nothing more," writes Krulak. "Paper massaging and computer competitions do not kill the enemy, which is what Marines are supposed to do."[69] Lastly, the fourth belief highlights Marine frugality and faithfulness, which a rifle exemplifies. A rifle costs relatively little, has a long service life, and is maintained religiously by its creed-coupled Marine. Thus, the Marine Corps' veneration of the Marine and his rifle is a core institutional belief and a picture of the other four beliefs in action.

In summary, the last word belongs to the "man on the scene with a gun," and the crux of battle is the Marine infantryman closing with the enemy. All efforts in the Marine Corps must focus on supporting the rifle-shooting Marine engaged on the front lines.

Conclusion

The US Marine Corps inherits its swagger honestly, forged in combat for the nation. Moreover, its battle record abroad only barely eclipses its combat prowess in defense politics. Often fighting for its life in bureaucratic battles, the Marine Corps has deftly managed to stay alive while staying true to its maritime roots; it remains under the Department of the Navy, yet an institution all its own.

All the while, the Marine Corps has crafted an elite warrior fraternity that accomplishes the seemingly impossible: it succeeds in performing wholesale "egoectomies" on thousands of 18-year-olds every year. What other institution anywhere in the world so consistently overcomes the gravitational pull of teenage self-centeredness? A personal identification with the Corps over the isolated individual remains an enduring legacy of the Marine Corps way.

The five cultural beliefs outlined in this chapter, summarized in figure 3.1,

SUMMARY OF MARINE CORPS CULTURAL BELIEFS		
Ends	**3.1** Warriors from the Sea	The Marine Corps is a maritime service, umbilically connected to the Navy through strategy and organization. The Corps serves as an embedded fighting force on the Naval archipelago, prepared to serve as needed on ships or on land. Marines are always prepared to fight their way onto any shore to conduct whatever mission the nation directs.
	3.2 Survive to Serve	The Marine Corps exists because the American people want it to exist. As the smallest of the four services, with tasks spanning the domains of warfare dominated by the other three, the Marine Corps risks being eliminated or reduced to insignificance. Consequently, the Corps cares less about *how* it is used and more passionately *that* it be used and perpetuated.
Ways	**3.3** Elite Warrior Identity	Being a Marine is fundamentally an identity, not a profession. All other identities are subsumed and secondary, as Marines today steward the legacy of Marines past. The Corps then and now is an elite warrior fraternity that runs toward the sound of the guns, wins battles, never retreats, and takes care of its own.
	3.4 Faithful Stewards of the National Trust	The Marine Corps is a faithful steward of the national trust and the American taxpayer's investment. With a creative spirit, Marines make do with what they are given and care for it religiously. Marines are the best "victory per dollar" investment in military history.
Means	**3.5** Every Marine a Rifleman	The last word belongs to the "man on the scene with a gun," and the crux of battle is the Marine infantryman closing with the enemy. All efforts in the Marine Corps must focus on supporting the rifle-shooting Marine engaged on the front lines.

Figure 3.1. A summary of the US Marine Corps' cultural beliefs about its preferred ends, ways, and means.

capture the core ideas that distinguish the Marine Corps from its sister services. As described in chapter 2 for the Navy, the Marine Corps' core ideas overlap and reinforce one another, highlighting what the Corps tends to believe about why it exists, how it does its job, and the resources it requires. The history presented here is inductive and broad in its collection, but deductively selective in its presentation. These beliefs emerge as consistent thematic elements of an ideationally neutral reading of Marine Corps history and legend. As the forthcoming analysis will demonstrate, these distinctive beliefs of the Marine Corps condition a unique set of preferences and behaviors in the trenches of civil-military policymaking. Before exploring those trenches, however, the next chapter leaves behind the maritime services and turns to the terrestrial giant of the US Army.

chapter 4

Washington's Own

The Service Culture of the United States Army

I'll be damned if I permit the United States Army, its institutions, its
doctrine, and its traditions, to be destroyed just to win this lousy war.
—Senior Army officer in Vietnam, quoted in Brian Jenkins's
The Unchangeable War

The story of the United States Army is the story of the United States itself. The
Army's battle record comprises the "shorter catechism" of American history:
Lexington and Concord, Valley Forge, Gettysburg, Appomattox, Meuse-
Argonne, Normandy, and Saigon. The Army is the oldest of the services, tracing its roots to 1775 and the Continental Army led by George Washington.
During the Revolutionary War, the Army was the very icon of the fledgling
republic, an island of federalism in the colonial sea. Washington understood
that the failure of his straggling army would mean the ruin of America's re-
bellious cause. When the Continental Army ultimately prevailed, nationhood
moved from dream to reality. The US Army proudly claims its Revolutionary
War heritage and essential role in birthing, developing, sustaining, and protecting the nation. From its humble beginning as a rabble of militiamen on
Lexington Green, the Army has swelled into a vast, complex, and highly dif-
ferentiated military service.

I present here a thematic survey of the Army's historical record and internal commentary. As with previous chapters, the background research focused
on the Army's organizational history from its inception through the Vietnam
era, paying close attention to the Army's self-conception of its enduring ends,
ways, and means. Given the vast history of the service, few attempts are made
to recount the specifics of famous battles; instead, the focus is on the lessons
the Army drew from these key events. The chapter outlines six elements in the
Army's pervasive belief structure about why it exists, how it should do its job,
and the resources it requires.

Apolitical Servants of the Nation

The United States Army's commitment to civilian control of the military is branded into the soul of the institution. Born among a colonial people deeply averse to standing armies, the US Army has long understood its tenuous place in American political life. From its earliest days, the Army has looked to the example of George Washington in the Revolutionary War as the paragon of military deference to civilian authority.[1] Steeped in this historical awareness, the Army remains deeply committed to healthy civil-military relations, orienting itself as a robustly apolitical entity—a faithful extension of the American people. The service's founding context and early exemplars did much to sear this apolitical mindset into Army culture.

Founding Context

Colonial America brought together disparate peoples, practices, and beliefs, with relatively few universal precepts. One of the near-universals, however, was a shared hatred of standing armies. The American colonists viewed the British army as an arbitrary instrument of repression and coercion. Fueled by excesses such as the Boston Massacre and the forced quartering of British soldiers, the antipathy to standing armies became a central plank in the Revolutionary platform. At the conclusion of the Revolutionary War, the founding fathers debated the proper structure of military defense for a newly independent United States. During the debates, the deep-rooted aversion to standing armies evolved into a fear of what unchecked political power *might do* with such an army. Consequently, as Samuel Huntington observed, "the Framers' concept of civilian control was to control the uses to which civilians might put military force rather than to control the military themselves."[2]

The specific language of the Constitution puts this idea in sharp relief. The Constitution divides power over the military between the executive and legislative branches, as well as between the federal and state governments. The president serves as commander-in-chief, but Congress has the power to declare war and to create and structure the armed forces. Toward that end, the Constitution gives Congress power "to provide and maintain a Navy," implying a perpetual arrangement for a standing Navy. The power to create the Army looks ephemeral by comparison; Congress has authority "to raise and support armies, but no appropriation of money for that use shall be for a longer term than two years." This language lacks the permanence of the naval arrangement, implying the purposeful expansion and retraction of a short-term army, called to arms for a specific purpose and duration. From its earliest days, the Army has felt needed but unwanted by the people it has pledged to serve.

Events and Exemplars

Embedded in a nation wary of its existence, the Army found its shining exemplar in George Washington. The Revolutionary War shaped the ethos of the US Army in many ways, but a clear legacy of the war is the deference to civilian authority that guided Washington's steady conduct. In a short historical piece authored for the Army's Center of Military History, historian David Hogan avers that "having won independence, the Continental Army now made perhaps its most important contribution to the nation—deference to civilian authority."[3] Washington exercised only the specified powers granted him by the Congress and respected civil authority at seemingly every turn.

Washington's civil-military finesse involved wise advocacy in two directions: toward both the Army *and* the Congress. To his men in the Continental Army, he modeled the importance of abiding by civilian control, adjusting his strategy and even tactics accordingly. And Washington's example to his civilian superiors proved equally instructive. Through his words and actions, he dampened congressional (and public) suspicion of the army. In a letter to Congress in September 1776, Washington acknowledged the widespread aversion to standing armies, but he approached the issue with balanced wisdom: "The Jealousies of a standing Army, and the Evils to be apprehended from one, are remote; and in my judgment, situated and circumstanced as we are, not at all to be dreaded; but the consequence of wanting one, according to my Ideas, formed from the present view of things, is certain, and inevitable Ruin."[4] As an exemplar of military subordination to civilian leadership, Washington put the Army in its rightful supporting position, while coaching Congress to appreciate the sacrificial and essential role the Army served.

Echoes in the Army

How, then, did Washington's early example affect the mindset of the Army? Of the four American military services, the Army appears most concerned with its civil-military relationship. In fact, much of the contemporary civil-military scholarship generated by military scholars comes from Army officers, many of whom have been on the faculty at West Point or the Army War College. Jack Marsh, former secretary of the Army and member of Congress, reinforces the Army's unique interest: "Deeply ingrained in the Army's ethos is its *subservience to civilian control*; much more so than you find in the Navy, or Marine Corps or more recently the Air Force. The selfless service legacy of George Washington, in our revolutionary Army, and his sensitivity to civilian concerns that went beyond the Army institution's self-interests were ingrained in the Army."[5] The discussion here considers three corollary ways in which Washington's legacy continues to reverberate in the Army's ranks.

Apolitical, for Better or Worse Paradoxically, the Army's noble commitment to civilian control inspires both helpful and harmful patterns of conduct. The Army professes a staunchly apolitical nature, fully obedient to its political masters, and thus works hard to keep its distance from all things political. This admirable desire to remain above the political fray, however, can have the pernicious effect of keeping the Army sidelined in its legitimate political sphere. Army officer Stephen Scroggs details the Army's discomfort in liaising with Congress, fearing that this may be misperceived as improper lobbying. "Senior Army leaders," writes Scroggs, "have difficulty adopting a perspective that views proactively engaging Congress on behalf of their service's interests as a legitimate and appropriate component of their professional responsibility."[6] The Army's noble high-mindedness results in a lack of congressional exposure to legitimate Army needs. "There is a belief in the Army," observes Norman Augustine, former undersecretary of the Army, "that the merit of the Army cause speaks for itself. You shouldn't have to involve yourself in politics in selling the greatness and relevancy of the Army. The Army cause by itself tells the story. No lobbying is necessary. Unfortunately, Washington doesn't work that way."[7] The Army's admirable resistance to improper political conduct has a side effect: the Army also remains leery of proper political conduct.

Nationally and Professionally Committed As reflected in its congressional relations, the Army does not want to be its own cheerleader. While the other three services gladly trumpet their services' interests, the Army often deflects its loyalty toward the higher ideals of the nation and the enduring profession of arms. Army officer and historian William Ganoe captured the supra-organizational identification of the American soldier: "It is his invariable rule when confronted with any task, to think first of his duty to his nation. His superiors often change, but his employer—his country—always stays."[8] Similarly, in describing the tenets of the Army's professional ethic, Colonel Matthew Moten puts "[an embrace of] national service" and "loyalty to the Constitution" at the top two spots in the list.[9] The Army tends to subordinate its organizational identity to a higher loyalty to the nation.

The Army also sees itself as the national steward of the profession of arms, a historical and noble tradition with ancient roots. In 1986, for example, the Army's Center of Military History published a new edition of Sir John Winthrop Hackett's classic collection of lectures, *The Profession of Arms*. In his introduction to the Army's edition, Chief of Staff of the Army General John Wickham reminded his readers that in "an age that sets high store on technological expertise, it is well for military officers to remind ourselves that we are members of an ancient and honorable profession."[10] Similarly, the Army's extensive project entitled "The Future of the Army Profession" listed four dimensions of the Army officer's identity: warrior, member of profession, servant of country, and leader of character.[11] Conspicuously, none of these identities focus on the Army organizationally; instead, they point to higher callings of national service and professional legacy.

An Extension of the National Will   Since the Army looks beyond its borders and identifies with the nation as a whole, it nurtures an explicit commitment to and connection with the American people. The Army sees itself as an extension of the citizenry, on whom it relies for manpower, funding, and most importantly, willpower. Committing the American Army to a conflict demonstrates national intent and a serious commitment of resources—both blood and treasure. Consequently, the Army does not want to be sent abroad on cavalier missions at odds with the national will. Much of the Army's internal historiography about the Vietnam War, for example, emphasizes this concern. "Vietnam was a reaffirmation of the peculiar relationship between the American Army and the American people," wrote General Fred Weyand, then chief of staff of the Army. "The American Army really is a people's Army in the sense that it belongs to the American people who take a jealous and proprietary interest in its involvement . . . In the final analysis, the American Army is not so much an arm of the Executive Branch as it is an arm of the American people."[12]

In summary, the Army exists to serve the nation as an obedient and apolitical junior partner to its civilian leaders. The Army is a faithful extension of the American people, on whom it depends for manpower, resources, and national will. Loyalty to the Army as a service is less important than serving the nation as a member of the honorable profession of arms.

A Land Force of Last Resort

The US Army exists to defend territory and fight land battles. But as a national land army, it serves as a force of last resort and must be prepared for whatever is demanded of it. Throughout its history, the nation has asked the Army to perform some of its most unsavory domestic missions. The Army thus offers not only a last line of defense but an organized labor force of last resort. When no other group has been willing or able to do a job, the Army has answered the nation's call—to build railroads, cut canals, deliver the mail, explore the frontier, or forcibly resettle Native American tribes. In many respects, the Army paralleled the Navy during the nation's first century, doing domestically what the Navy did abroad: exploring new land, showing the flag, negotiating treaties, and establishing a prosperous infrastructure for a new nation. Along the way, the Army grew accustomed to being stuck with the nation's messiest jobs. A resigned "suck it up" mentality endures as part of Army life.

Operational Environment

A distinguished Navy admiral understood well the indispensable nature of a land army. In his 1962 testimony to Congress, Admiral John S. McCain, Jr., commented, "All wars are brought to a successful conclusion by a man with a gun on his shoulder going in, sitting down, and saying 'This belongs to me.'"[13] Admiral McCain's insight is the glory and bane of the Army soldier—he must finish the job, whatever it might be, for there is no one else to whom he can hand the mess. Among the four services, the Army typically runs the anchor leg and must carry the national baton across the finish line. The Marines, generally speaking, serve as a middleweight quick-reaction force to prepare for heavier follow-on forces. Airmen and sailors shape the battlefield in critical ways but do not have the capacity to *occupy* it. The Army is the nation's long-term heavyweight force, tasked to occupy territory and *finish* the task. And since wars are typically much easier to start than finish, the Army inherits complex political tasks that defy easy completion. "If the nation loses a war, the Army gets blamed," lamented one Army senior officer. "*No one will blame the other services for losing our nation's wars. If the Air Force screws it up, it just means the Army has to finish it.*"[14] The Army keenly understands its role as the custodial guardian of the nation's hardest conflicts.

Founding Context

How has the Army's history reinforced this idea? For the first hundred years of the republic, the Army did most of the heavy lifting in building the country's infrastructure. The government had difficult jobs to be done, and the Army could not say no. As observed by Army scholars Leonard Wong and Douglas Johnson, "As a young nation, the United States had only the Army to turn to for numerous functions. Fighting the nation's wars was the fundamental purpose of its existence, but frontier protection and infrastructure-building dominated the early years of the Army's existence."[15] Army officers served as civil engineers for the nation, as West Point was founded in 1802 almost exclusively as an engineering school—only later did it begin educating in military art and science.[16] Until 1835, in fact, West Point was the only school in the nation producing qualified engineers; this gave the Army responsibility for surveying roads, canals, railroads, bridges, aqueducts, the Capitol dome, the Washington Monument, and the Smithsonian museum.[17] Army Captain Meriwether Lewis and his partner, William Clark, himself an Army veteran, led the most memorable Army expedition to explore the Louisiana Purchase and the western tract of the United States. But Lewis and Clark merely headlined a much broader trend, as many Army soldiers performed similar tasks of internal exploration across the continent.

The Army led some of the grandest engineering projects in national history. The Army Corps of Engineers, for example, proudly celebrates the legacy of Major George Goethals, the engineer who overcame profound challenges to complete the Panama Canal. President Theodore Roosevelt had struggled to find a capable leader for such an epic undertaking; when two civilian engineers resigned after short periods, Roosevelt announced that "the next chief would be an Army officer, who, if he walked off the job, would find himself facing a court martial."[18] Goethals completed the job, ahead of schedule and under budget—emblematic of the Army's skill and fortitude. In other venues, Army officers led the construction of the Union Pacific railroad, guarded the national parks until creation of the National Park Service in 1918, and managed the Civilian Conservation Corps during the New Deal by providing camps, food, fuel, leadership, and supervision. Army historian David Hogan rightly comments that the Army's "ready availability as a source of disciplined and skilled personnel has made it an attractive option for American leaders confronted with a wide array of nonmilitary demands and crises."[19]

In addition to these massive public works projects, the US government gave the Army some of its most troublesome domestic and foreign assignments. Samuel Huntington recounts the types of missions given to the Army and, more importantly, their effects on Army culture. The Army inherited such complexities as:

Southern reconstruction, Indian fighting, labor disorders, the Spanish War, Cuban occupation, Philippine pacification, construction and operation of the

Panama canal, [and] the Mexican punitive expedition. Accordingly, the Army developed an image of itself as the government's obedient handyman performing without question or hesitation the jobs assigned to it . . . It had no particular field of responsibility; instead, it was a vast, organic, human machine, blindly following orders from on high . . . By following all orders literally the Army attempted to divest itself of political responsibility and political controversy despite the political nature of the tasks it was frequently called upon to perform.[20]

The Army's indispensability gives its officers a sense of grave responsibility and professional inevitability. The Army understands that it serves as the last line of defense, the force for the long haul, and the organized force of last resort to do the messiest of jobs. A sometimes grumbling acceptance of this inevitability endures across the service. This resigned acceptance only reinforces the Army's apolitical posture discussed earlier in the chapter, reducing any motivation the Army might have to protect its turf. One former chief of staff of the Army commented, "There has always been an Army . . . We don't have to justify the need or relevancy of an Army. America requires an Army. The other services have to justify themselves in terms of their platforms or weapon systems . . . There will always be an Army."[21]

In summary, land forces in sufficient mass are an essential precondition for victory in war, and the Army must be that indispensable last line of defense. Furthermore, the Army as an organized and skilled group of national servants must accept glorious and menial tasks alike, serving as a labor force of last resort to do the nation's messiest jobs, prepared to take more blame than credit.

The Army Way of Battle

Over time, the US Army has cultivated a preferred approach to combat. This tacit preference seeks out complete victories, earned through the enemy's unconditional surrender, and fought with superior firepower and technology. While the Army has fought a wide array of conflicts in its history with a variety of tactics, it tends to favor this one particular approach. Like most organizations, the Army remembers best what it prefers the most. This pattern of selective memory is at the heart of any organization's culture. "What we choose to remember and the way we choose to remember it may unduly flatter or unfairly condemn our military forebears, may indeed be more legend than history," writes historian Robert Utley. "Legends thus form a conspicuous part of our military tradition and are often far more influential in shaping our attitudes and beliefs than the complex, contradictory, and ambiguous truth."[22] The Army tends to prefer a way of war that decouples military action from political calculation, while pitting superior firepower and technology against a conventional foe. In short, *the Army is most comfortable when the categories are clear.* The service strongly pursues clear military objectives, mechanized by clear processes, enabled by clear working relationships, to remove a clearly defined enemy from the battlefield.

Operational Environment

Elements of belief derive from selective memory but also from the visceral demands of a military service's operational context. Understanding the Army's preferred way of battle thus requires an appreciation for the context of ground combat. An epic description of battle, quoted at length for its vivid insight, comes from one of the Army's celebrated citizen-soldiers of the Civil War. Colonel Joshua Chamberlain, a professor of rhetoric at Bowdoin College, joined the Union Army and led the 20th Maine regiment throughout the war. He is best remembered for defending the southern flank of the Union line at Gettysburg's Little Round Top, which he described in a 1913 piece in *Hearst's Magazine*:

> It was a stirring, not to say, appalling sight; here a whole battery of shot and shell cutting a ragged chasm through a serried mass, flinging men and horses like drift aside; there, a rifle volley at close range, with reeling shock, hands tossed in the air, muskets dropped with death's quick reflex, or clutched with last, convulsive energy, men falling like grass before the scythe . . . here, a defiant regiment of ours, broken, slaughtered, captured; or survivors of both sides crouching among the rocks for shelter from the terrible crossfire where there is no rear! But all advancing—all the frenzied force, victors and vanquished, each scarcely knowing which—surging and foaming towards us; death around, behind, before, and madness everywhere![23]

As Chamberlain vividly captured, the wail of ground combat defies the imagination of the unbaptized. War reduces to a zero-sum business of *kill or be killed*, complicated by the inevitable fog and friction of battle. The stark distinctions of life and death preoccupy a soldier, conditioning similarly stark habits of mind. Those involved in the complex and lethal business of combat inevitably gravitate toward measures of simplification. Soldiers prefer clear categories to simplify the chaos: good or bad, us or them, all or nothing, victory or defeat, kill or be killed. They understand Clausewitz's fundamental insight that war is an extension of politics by other means, merely a different grammar of the same logic. But the grammar of war is life and death, while politics requires compromise and ambiguity. The complexities of politics feel intolerable to a vulnerable soldier facing the uncompromising choice between life and death. So war and politics may be logically adjacent, but the experience of them is worlds apart.

Events and Exemplars

The Army's unique battle record reinforces this discontinuity. Russell Weigley's sweeping analysis of America at war depicts the US Army cultivating a novel practice of *unlimited war*, fought for unlimited political ends. Whereas the pattern of war in seventeenth- and eighteenth-century Europe had been one of limited war, the American experience quickly departed from that trend. "When the English colonists in America fought the Indians," Weigley writes, "they often fought in what both sides recognized as a contest for survival . . . The logic of a contest for survival was always implicit in the Indian wars, as it never was in the eighteenth-century wars wherein European powers competed for possession of fortresses and counties, but always shared an awareness of their common participation in one civilization."[24]

The Army's signature experiences at war reinforced this abnormal trend of unlimited war. The Revolutionary War, though fought defensively by George Washington, was an existential total war, fought to the finish to give birth to a new nation. After the Revolution, the Army began policing the frontier, commencing its hundred-year history of fighting the so-called Indian Wars. Two key trends emerged from the Indian Wars: first, an institutional aversion to guerrilla warfare, and second, yet another experience of an existential war of survival. On the frontier, the Army refused to believe its constabulary mission of fighting the Indians deserved explicit preparation in strategy, tactics, or materiel. Instead, "military leaders looked upon Indian warfare as a fleeting bother."[25] Consequently, the Army was preoccupied with conventional, orthodox war, even while fully engaged in unconventional guerrilla war on the frontier. Weigley identified this preoccupation as part of a larger phenomenon: "A historical pattern was beginning to work itself out: occasionally the American Army has had to wage a guerrilla war, but guerrilla warfare is so incongruous to the natural methods and habits of a stable and well-to-do society that the American Army has tended to regard it as abnormal and to forget about it whenever possible."[26]

The Army's defining event of the nineteenth century—the Civil War—compounded this trend. Again, the Army found itself in an existential fight to the finish, as the Confederate Army fought for the unlimited aim of complete secession. "'Complete conquest' had to be the Union aim," suggests Weigley, "because the southern people believed that their very way of life was at stake, and they would submit to nothing less . . . Henceforth the Civil War afforded the American Army its conception of a major war." Naturally, the Civil War came to dominate the curriculum at West Point after the war, and wars of "'power unrestrained' unleashed for 'complete conquest'" became the template for American Army warfighting.[27]

The US Army's experience in World War II provided a culminating exemplar of the Army's ideal ends, ways, and means. The Army fought yet another total war, pursuing unconditional surrender with massive firepower and abundant materiel produced by a fully committed homeland. It was the Army's finest hour, which it would not soon forget. "Something happened to the Army in its passage through World War II that it liked," observes defense analyst Carl Builder. "And it has not been able to free itself from the sweet memories of the Army that liberated France and swept victoriously into Germany."[28]

In Korea, however, the Army could not replicate its glorious drive through Europe. Instead, it had to adjust to the chafing fetters of political restraint. In Korea, "Americans adopted a course not new to the world, but [new] to them," writes historian T. R. Fehrenbach. "They accepted limitations on warfare, and accepted controlled violence as the means to an end."[29] They accepted such limitations only begrudgingly, however, and not without challenge. In perhaps the most notorious civil-military conflict in national history, General Douglas MacArthur tried to take the war aggressively into North Korea, accepting war with China as a result. MacArthur famously insisted "we must win. There is no substitute for victory."[30] In his confrontation with President Harry Truman, MacArthur ultimately fell victim to his larger-than-life status and argued a preferred way of battle too far.

Finally, while all the services left Vietnam vowing "never again," the Army's experience in Vietnam appears most devastating to the heart and soul of the service. The complex political, military, and geographic terrain in Vietnam offered none of the clarity the Army craves. Murky objectives, a shadowy enemy, stifling rules of engagement, and harsh terrain all conspired against the Army's preferred approach. Nevertheless, the service held fast to what Andrew Krepinevich called the "Army Concept." According to Krepinevich, a retired Army officer, the two key characteristics of the Army Concept include "a focus on mid-intensity, or conventional, war and a reliance on high volumes of firepower to minimize casualties—in effect, the substitution of material costs at every available opportunity to avoid payment in blood."[31] As a consequence, the Army was ill-prepared for the type of fight it faced in Vietnam, defaulting to the only strategy it knew: firepower. Brian Jenkins of RAND wrote in 1970 that "the Army simply performed its repertoire even though it was frequently irrelevant to the situation."[32]

After the war, the Army moved quickly to cleanse Vietnam from its collective memory, focusing again on conventional war in Europe and studying mid-intensity conflicts like the 1973 Arab-Israeli War. The 1976 edition of the Army's operational field manual, for example, did not even mention counterinsurgency, and in 1979 the Army's Command and General Staff College scaled back training on low-intensity conflict from 40 hours to just 9 hours.[33] The Army clearly showed it was ready to move on from Vietnam—an experience better forgotten than remembered.

In summary, the US Army tends to believe that it should be used to win complete victories with overwhelming firepower. When civilians send the Army to fight, they should send it to win with maximum resources and minimum restraints. Given the nature of war, there are things the Army should not be asked to do, and civilian leaders are wise to heed these limitations.

Synchronizing the Fragments

As a massive organization tasked to perform a wide array of missions, the US Army must be varied and subspecialized in its structure. The core of the Army lives in its three main combat arms branches—the infantry, field artillery, and armor—but more than 30 other branches complement the big three.[34] Furthermore, the Army spreads its force structure across both state and federal control, with various degrees of readiness, from active duty through guard and reserve forces. The Army is therefore the largest and most fragmented of the services. Ultimately, the Army's high degree of fragmentation creates a strong imperative to coordinate and synchronize its forces, making teamwork and coordination a core tenet of Army operations. As journalist Arthur Hadley observed, "The new-fledged Army lieutenant soon learns that he can make no movement without coordination. He cannot go right, left, backward, or forward without informing units on his right and left, artillery, tanks, supply trains, his superiors—all in detail."[35] The scope of the

Army's mission requires a diversity of specialization, and the scale of the mission demands tight synchronization among those specialties.

Operational Environment

Several factors in the Army's operational environment generate the firm belief in the need to centralize, coordinate, and synchronize. First, the inherent complexities of fighting, moving, feeding, paying, equipping, and sustaining a massive land force create an organizational need for many branches and specialties. Even at the end of the Revolutionary War, when the Continental Army was quite small, George Washington's combat elements received support from an adjutant general, inspector general, judge advocate general, quartermaster, commissary general, medical corps, and corps of engineers.[36] These essential combat and support functions persist, along with dozens of new branches that have developed since. Ever-increasing specialization and subdivision have created recurring challenges for an Army pursuing unified action. In 1938, for example, the War Department occupied no less than 20 buildings throughout Washington, DC, frustrating sincere attempts to coordinate Army policy. Workers broke ground on the massively consolidated Pentagon three years later.[37]

The inherent vulnerability of exposed ground forces reinforces this drive to centralize and synchronize. Whereas Navy and Air Force combat operations tend to be episodic, Army operations are more continuous—a sustained posture against an enemy force. Furthermore, the Army organizes, plans, and thinks along clear geographic boundaries; coordinating the geographic seams between units is essential. The Army's terrestrial exposure creates a core need to secure its perimeter and lash together adjacent units to coordinate fire support.

Because contact with the enemy is a constant threat and preoccupying concern, the Army naturally wants to control as many of its supporting elements as possible. So-called organic support is pursued and prized by Army commanders. Organic, dedicated support can be tasked and held accountable, while support from other services may get diverted to someone else's higher priority. Nevertheless, the Army understands it cannot control all of its support and thus depends extensively on the other services. Admiral J. C. Wylie notes well the soldier's state: "The soldier cannot function alone. His flanks are bare, his rear is vulnerable, and he looks aloft with a cautious eye. He needs the airman and the sailor for his own security in doing his own job."[38] This dependency, however, eventually reaches an operational limit.

While support from the other services is critical, it often feels *absent when needed*. So the service may recoil into an Army-only posture, using whatever organic support can be found, since outside support can be too hard to coordinate and too fickle to plan on. Thus, while the Army relies on the other services, its vulnerability can motivate a self-fulfilling prophecy: since we do not know for sure that external support will be there, we should act conservatively and make an Army-only plan. When the Army pushes forward with that plan, uncoordinated with the other services, it often finds the inevitable: supporting elements are unprepared and do not provide any support.

A final element of the Army's operational environment generates yet another paradox of employment. Given the chaos and fog of battle, tactical doctrine drives the need to trust sub-echelon commanders to operate with creativity, flexibility, and initiative. Consequently, the Army emphasizes these ideals in theory, but the ideal succumbs to a different reality. In his survey-based study of Army organizational culture, James Pierce finds that soldiers broadly recognize that Army culture *should* be one that "emphasizes flexibility, discretion, participation, human resource development, innovation, creativity, [and] risk-taking." Instead of this ideal, however, the underlying assumptions that actually inform the Army emphasize "organizational stability and control."[39] Life in the Army is strongly shaped by adhering to established processes, working linearly through problems in a standardized way, and defaulting to doctrine. The Army's devoted attachment to its doctrine shapes much of its approach to organizing, training, and equipping its force.

Here, the Army gets pulled in different directions by its twin nature as both profession and bureaucracy.[40] The dictates of the profession call for flexibility and creativity, while the ponderous inertia of the bureaucracy muffles any attempts to be flexible or creative. A 2001 study on officer training and development in the Army, authored by a 37-member panel, reached this conclusion: "Army officers suffer from stifling micromanagement—a fact long known and broadly acknowledged."[41] Leonard Wong, a professor at the Army War College, also studied Army leadership development and found this same contradiction at work: "A serious disconnect remains between current leader development practices and the type of leaders required by the future force. Put bluntly, the Army is relying on a leader development system that encourages reactive instead of proactive thought, compliance instead of creativity, and adherence instead of audacity."[42] An Army leader's incentive structure encourages this micromanagement, as leaders are ultimately accountable for everything that takes place under their command; their interest in every sub-echelon is thus very high. At the same time, there are no tangible rewards associated with developing the next generation of Army leaders by entrusting them with responsibility. Consequently, both incentives shove in the same direction: toward micromanagement and control. The vast Army machine needs reliable cogs, not freelancing artists.

Echoes in the Army

How does this belief reverberate throughout the Army? First, the fragmentary nature of the Army often leads to a strong identification with one's branch specialty, rather than with the Army as a whole. Members of various branches are readily identifiable in their uniforms, with different branch insignia and differently colored accoutrements.[43] The first professional journals in the Army were branch-specific technical journals, emphasizing the unique crafts of the infantry, cavalry, engineers, or artillery. These dynamics dilute the coherence of an *Army* culture, as many members constitute their professional identity at multiple levels: proudly with their branch, weakly with the Army writ large, and strongly with the nation as a whole (as discussed earlier in the chapter). Whereas Marines identify themselves first and last with the Marine Corps, Army soldiers have their professional identities scattered more broadly.

A second echo within the Army is related to the first. Carl Builder describes the Army as a fraternity of professional "guilds," each plying its trade in concert with the others.[44] These guilds—dominated by the infantry, artillery, and armor—all have strong internal Army support and are led by very senior officers. With so many senior-ranking officers in the Army, each overseeing a disparate clan of soldiers, a climate of egalitarianism and fairness pervades.[45] The job of the chief of staff of the Army becomes one of extensive coordination among the branches and various Army agencies. Generating a coherent and consistent Army viewpoint is a herculean task of persistent staff work.

This drive for internal agreement yields a distinctly *inward* orientation for the Army.[46] In its relations with Congress, for example, the Army struggles to translate its internal dialogue into externally meaningful terms. According to Stephen Scroggs, congressional staffers typically find the Army's communication efforts to be "murky, complicated, odd, and suited for internal rather than external audiences. Unlike the Marine Corps approach, the Army message tends to glaze rather than water the eyes of a sympathetic congressional audience."[47] Similarly, once an internal consensus has finally been reached, the chief of staff of the Army may be hard-pressed to compromise the Army's position with an external actor. The chief of staff may find his position more tenable within the Army if policy changes get imposed by civilian leaders rather than through proactive political compromises.

In summary, the diversity of the Army mission creates a fragmented array of branches, specialties, and units. But controlling and directing military forces requires intricate coordination and complete synchronization. While leaders in the Army should exhibit creativity and initiative, the need for coordination and standardization is the much stronger imperative.

Fielding an Army: Regulars and the Militia

How can a nation with a pervasive distrust of standing armies adequately prepare for an uncertain defense? In Weigley's history of the US Army, the dominant subplot is not about war and peace—it is a story of *manpower*. From the colonial militia to the large standing army of the Cold War, the nation has searched for a right-sized army suited to its character and needs. Fearing the repressive potential and burdensome cost of a large army, the nation's default choice has been a small force. Yet the nation needs an army of suitable size, strength, and readiness when war comes. This tension has shaped an enduring debate over the size and structure of the Army: How much of it should be regular (i.e., active duty)? How much should the Army rely on a reserve citizen-militia? And how should the service expand to face crises? Weigley concludes that both the regular and the reserve components have forged the character of the American Army: "The duality of the American military tradition has given the United States Army both many of its historic perplexities and its best qualities too. At once an expert army and a people's army, it has served as the nation's sword without endangering the nation's democracy."[48] The discussion here explores these ideas further, confirming Army historian Edgar Raines's assessment that, at its core, the Army is essentially "a mobilization organization."[49]

Operational Environment and National Experience

Choosing the size and structure of a national army requires reconciliation of an army's cost with a state's anticipated needs. A state must have enough ready strength to handle an initial attack, combined with a suitable method for expanding rapidly to finish the task. The approach each nation adopts is ultimately a political question, informed by the character of its national institutions. How has the United States brokered this dilemma? The Army's own history textbook, developed for use in its Reserve Officers' Training Corps (ROTC), explains it this way:

> The Army is essentially an institutional form adapted by American society to meet military requirements. The American military system has been developed so as to place a minimum burden upon the people and give the nation a reasonable defense without sacrificing its fundamental values. From the beginning, the United States has sought to reconcile individual liberty with national security without becoming a nation in arms.[50]

Historically, the American colonists embraced the militia tradition of the citizen-soldier, a tradition deeply rooted in the British colonial experience. This militia character fueled the early violence of the Revolution, as citizen-soldiers in Lexington, Concord, and Bunker Hill stared down and traded blows with British regulars. These seminal battles "went far to create the American tradition that the citizen soldier when aroused is more than a match for the trained professional," an impression often disputed by the trained professionals of the regular Army.[51]

George Washington's own experience with the militia was mixed. Struggling to keep the Army intact, Washington kept losing militiamen as their enlistments expired. In September 1776, he lamented to Congress, "We are now as it were, upon the eve of another dissolution of our Army . . . To place any dependence upon Militia, is, assuredly, resting upon a broken staff."[52] But Washington's dissatisfaction was neither a total condemnation of the militia nor an endorsement of full reliance on regular forces. Instead, as expressed in his *Sentiments on a Peace Establishment* after the war, Washington suggested the need for a strong core of regular forces, augmented by a *well-organized* militia, trained and standardized across the states.[53]

Congress, however, had other plans. In June 1784, Congress directed Henry Knox, then the senior officer in the Continental Army, to discharge all but 80 men for the entire Army.[54] With such a remarkably small regular force, the nation relied upon state militias to guard the frontier. After several years of inglorious defeats of these militia forces by Native American tribes, Congress created the Legion of the United States, in December 1792, under Major General Anthony Wayne. Soon, Wayne had crafted a credible fighting force: "With good reason he could be called the Father of the Regular Army."[55] Not long after, the War of 1812 brought together regulars and militia forces once again. After the scarring battle of Bladensburg, when militia forces abandoned the White House and Capitol to British fires, the regular Army concluded that "the lesson of the recent war [of 1812] was simple. The militia was utterly worthless."[56]

While the regular Army held fast to its belief in the inadequacy of militia forces, Brigadier General John Palmer eventually offered a different view. His 1941 study of army force structure revealed rare insight into the *political* aspect of fielding an army. Palmer recognized that earlier analysis by Major General Emory Upton had unduly glorified the Prussian model, a militaristic approach out of step with American democratic values. Instead, Palmer argued that the size and character of a national army must remain congruent with the political character of the state: "the form of military institutions must be determined on political grounds, with due regard to national genius and tradition."[57] In Palmer's view, a small regular force, complemented by an expansible militia, prudently sacrificed a degree of capability so as to preserve American values. Ultimately, through various legislative attempts and national experiments with local and global war, the United States arrived at a three-part system of regular (active) forces, reserve forces, and national guard forces—first established as such in the National Defense Act of 1916. Since then, the essential logic and structure have persisted, though the specific forms have continued to evolve.

Echoes in the Army

This overriding question of manpower creates several echoes within the Army. First, a volunteer Army must work hard to recruit able-bodied members into its force. And given the scope and diversity of the Army's requirements, its approach to recruiting is markedly different from that of the Marines, for example. While Marine Corps recruiting focuses on being "first to fight" and never hawks any side benefits, the Army—with its higher quota for recruits—takes a more egalitarian and populist approach. In the 1920s, for example, the Army promised recruits the chance to learn any hobby they wanted, from playing the flute to wood-carving.[58] In the early 1970s, the Army's populism informed its recruiting slogan, "Today's Army Wants to Join You!"[59] The service replaced this slogan with "Be All You Can Be!" in the 1980s, but the message still focused on the individual, not on service, on the Army, or on the nation. The Army does what it must to fill its ranks.

A second echo created by the manpower obsession is the vital requirement for readiness, training, and standardization. The active duty Army must always be ready, trained, and equipped for immediate action. General Creighton Abrams, former chief of staff of the Army, considered "the basic task of the Army to be readiness."[60] Most Army histories emphasize, however, the perpetual trend of unpreparedness that has marked American adventures in war. The tragic poster-boys for the Army's lack of readiness were the members of Task Force Smith, the woefully undersized force that met the North Korean Army in July 1950. "That forlorn hope spearhead—Task Force Smith, a name to be added to Army annals—shattered itself against the Red blow by July 5, 1950."[61] The name "Task Force Smith" endures in the Army as a shorthand cautionary tale—a warning against being caught flat-footed, ill-prepared, and forced to send too few to do too much.

The requirement to be always ready extends to guard and reserve forces as well. These crucial augmentation forces must fulfill George Washington's design as a *well-organized* force, with standardized and routine training aligned with that in the active force. The core of regulars must seamlessly expand through the addition of reserve and guard forces, all cut from the same cloth. The Army therefore emphasizes standardization and breaks down nearly any endeavor into a uniform checklist, acronym, or procedure. The service leads with its doctrine, relying on a codified consensus to bring predictability to its vast and varied enterprise. Everyone must do each task in the same way, forging interchangeable parts to equip the massive Army machine.

In summary, the Army must be prepared for war in times of peace and must be in a position to expand rapidly and capably to whatever degree a crisis requires. The Army's cultivation of suitably trained manpower is the first and most critical aspect of providing for the national defense.

Soldiers, Units, and Leaders

The Army is ultimately an enterprise of *people*, consisting of individuals, units, and leaders. A million-person Army is built one soldier at a time, so the Army emphasizes the individual soldier as the backbone of the service. These individual soldiers, however, must be organized into cohesive fighting units, so the Army pays great attention to the organization and structure of its various units. In fact, the service venerates its regiments and divisions as anthropomorphic patriarchs of the service, whose personalities persist despite rotations of assigned personnel. Lastly, the Army recognizes that units must be led, so it celebrates the great battle captains who lead soldiers in the field. The service tends to hold a "muddy boots bias," valuing and promoting leaders with the strongest pedigrees of leading troops in the field.[62] Reflecting the Army's focus on heroic leaders, the central parade ground at West Point is flanked by statues of the Army's iconic generals, not by empty hulks of its great tanks. Ultimately, the Army sees itself as a profession of soldiers, recruited individually, organized collectively, and led courageously. This brief final discussion highlights these hierarchical emphases across the service.

The soldier is the essential building block of the Army, so the service rightly focuses on the need to recruit, train, and equip the individual soldier to fight when called upon to do so. General Creighton Abrams insisted that "people are not *in* the Army. People *are* the Army."[63] Efforts at reform, change, or rehabilitation typically begin, therefore, with the individual soldier.

But soldiers do not fight as isolated individuals. For obvious reasons, soldiers must be organized efficiently into fighting units. The Army is a massive hierarchy of units and subunits: squads, platoons, companies, battalions, brigades, divisions, corps, and field armies, all commanded by ever-higher-ranking officers. The first task of an assembled mass of soldiers is to organize. During the massive mobilization for World War II, for example, a young lieutenant recalled the phone call that notified him of his first assignment: "Ryder, come right on over, you've been selected and our first job is to write a TO&E [Table of Organization and Equipment] for the platoon."[64] Similarly, General John Pershing recalled his early days in the Army, when "every army officer carried an army organization bill in his vest pocket."[65] When the Army activates its guard and reserve forces for deployment, it places great emphasis on moving the unit, activating the flag, and keeping organizational identities intact.[66] While the Air Force and Navy often activate and deploy *individual* reservists, the Army insists on activating entire *units*.

This emphasis on organization creates the distinctively anthropomorphic veneration of the Army's major divisions. These heralded units each create their own subculture, traditions, uniform accoutrements, and slogans. Joining the 1st Cavalry Division or the 101st Airborne Division means far more than just showing up to a new post—you are joining ranks with history itself. Unit patches and insignia are essential iconography, instantly recognizable to soldiers across the service. Division and regimental flags adorn the Army corridors of the Pentagon, with battle streamers indicating the unit's proud contributions to major campaigns.

The Army's emphasis on people culminates in the great generals who lead the Army in battle. The Army's renowned heroes are its senior combat-proven generals: Washington, Scott, Grant, Sherman, Pershing, Marshall, Eisenhower, MacArthur, Patton, Bradley, and Ridgway, among others. The service prizes and cultivates combat leaders, starting from a young lieutenant's first leadership assignment as a platoon leader. This belief leads to what numerous observers call a "muddy boots bias" within the Army. The Army's culture, career pathways, and promotion criteria all appear "rigged to favor those who have served the most time with troops."[67]

Historian Brian Linn calls this phenomenon "muddy-boots fundamentalism, the anti-intellectual reductionism manifested in slogans such as 'War means fighting and fighting means killing,' or 'The Army's job is to kill people and break things.'"[68] The life-and-death nature of combat compels soldiers to reduce complex equations into simpler terms. So this anti-intellectual reductionism is not difficult to understand, particularly for enlisted soldiers at the front. But to the extent that it permeates all levels of the Army, it can impoverish the capacity of senior leaders to appreciate the political and strategic nuances required of them. If senior Army leaders are promoted on the basis of their muddy-boot field credentials, they may be tempted to apply the same muddy habits of thought to political-military jobs required at the higher ranks. "Winning the nation's wars is most important for the Army," stated one Army general. "That produces the division commander mentality that is so prevalent in the Army and is so out of place in Washington."[69] Army generals with muddy boots may excel in the field, but a different skill set may be needed to tackle the unique bureaucratic challenges of the Pentagon and Congress.

In summary, the individual soldier is the building block and indispensable ingredient in making an Army. But individuals must be subsumed by units. Fighting units organize and inspire their members as part of an ancient and honorable hierarchy. Leading these troops in the field is the highest calling and most sacred job in the Army.

Conclusion

The US Army is a vast and complex institution, a colossus that cannot be tied down in a single chapter, and the Army's history and scope surpass any one person's experience of it. The discussion presented here is by no means an exhaustive description of the Army's belief structure—readers with their own experience in the Army may find other ideas to be more salient. Nevertheless, the chapter specifies trend lines that emerge from a disinterested immersion in Army history and organization. Focusing on enduring ends, ways, and means, the analysis finds that these six cultural beliefs are likely to inform the Army's policy preferences and civil-military interactions, as shown in figure 4.1. The next chapter completes the analysis of the four military services, introducing the group of ambitious airmen who seceded from the Army—the United States Air Force.

SUMMARY OF ARMY CULTURAL BELIEFS		
Ends	**4.1** Apolitical Servants of the Nation	The Army exists to serve the nation as an obedient and apolitical junior partner to its civilian leaders. The Army is a faithful extension of the American people, on whom it depends for manpower, resources, and national will. Loyalty to the Army as a service is less important than serving the nation as a member of the honorable profession of arms.
	4.2 A Land Force of Last Resort	Land forces in sufficient mass are an essential precondition for victory in war, and the Army must be that indispensable last line of defense. Furthermore, the Army as an organized and skilled group of national servants must accept glorious and menial tasks alike, serving as a labor force of last resort to do the nation's messiest jobs, prepared to take more blame than credit.
Ways	**4.3** The Army Way of Battle	The Army should be used to win complete victories with overwhelming firepower. When civilians send the Army to fight, they should send it to win with maximum resources and minimum restraints. Given the nature of war, there are things the Army should not be asked to do, and civilian leaders are wise to heed these limitations.
	4.4 Synchronizing the Fragments	The diversity of the Army mission creates a fragmented array of branches, specialties, and units. But controlling and directing militaries requires intricate coordination and complete synchronization. Leaders in the Army should exhibit creativity and initiative, but the need for coordination and standardization is the much stronger imperative.
Means	**4.5** Fielding an Army: Regulars and the Militia	The Army must be prepared for war in times of peace and must be in a position to expand rapidly and capably to whatever degree a crisis requires. The Army's cultivation of suitably trained manpower is the first and most critical aspect of providing for the national defense.
	4.6 Soldiers, Units, and Leaders	The individual soldier is the building block and indispensable ingredient in making an Army. But individuals must be subsumed by units. Fighting units organize and inspire their members as part of an ancient and honorable hierarchy. Leading these troops in the field is the highest calling and most sacred job in the Army.

Figure 4.1. A summary of the US Army's cultural beliefs about its preferred ends, ways, and means.

chapter 5

Fighting for Air

The Service Culture of the United States Air Force

Nothing man can do on the surface of the earth can interfere with a
plane in flight, moving freely in the third dimension.

—Giulio Douhet, *The Command of the Air*

The United States Air Force is the upstart new arrival in the American military, more than 150 years younger than its three older siblings. Today's Air Force clawed its way into formal existence in 1947 through persistent advocacy, born as the offspring of an invention mated to an idea: the technology of the airplane coupled with the belief that strategic bombing could win wars. The primary justification for creating a separate air force rested on the conviction that airpower in the hands of the other three services would be suffocated, used only to support gravity-bound ways of war. So an air-minded band of secessionists broke away from the Army, arguing for and ultimately inheriting a new military service to think differently about how to command the air and win the nation's wars.

The Air Force's quest for organizational autonomy continues to reverberate in the service, as a preoccupation with proving itself still lingers. The Air Force feels most secure when it can clearly demonstrate its *independent* contribution to a war effort. Because its autonomy is predicated on unique doctrines of employment, the Air Force must prove itself by using airpower in ways the other three services would not think to pursue. As a result, the Air Force harbors strong and clear beliefs about the *right ways* to use airpower—beliefs that the other three services often dispute.

The formal creation of the Air Force sparked inherent tensions with the other three services, whose professional jurisdictions had to be renegotiated when the service was born.[1] Before the airplane, the division of labor between the War Department and Navy Department was clearly delineated: the Army fought on land, the Navy at sea. But breaking into the third dimension forced a redrawing of the borders between the services' professional jurisdictions. For the services, such delineations of "roles and missions" were like tenuous peace treaties with existential implications—secure organizations require enduring missions. Given its role as the great disruptor and its strong beliefs in the right way to use airpower, the Air Force's relationship with its sister services has often been contested.

Using the same methodology as in the previous three chapters, I present here some of the core beliefs that shape Air Force service culture. The analysis emerges from an inductive survey of Air Force history, with a focus on discovering enduring ideas that the service maintains about its preferred ends, ways, and means. The chapter focuses on six beliefs, with analysis detailing the contribution of the operational environment, founding context, and key events in forming and sustaining these beliefs. Together, these six beliefs shape the Air Force's policy preferences, its political behaviors, and the tenor of its civil-military interactions.

Air Controlled by Airmen

Did the airplane merely improve existing tactics, or did it fundamentally transform the art of war? In the early decades of the twentieth century, no one was quite sure. The Army, Navy, and Marine Corps clearly saw great potential for manned aircraft to support their core missions by observing enemy troop locations, spotting artillery, supporting ground battles, and harassing enemy fleets. A rising chorus of airpower advocates, however, had grander ambitions. They believed the airplane changed nearly everything, rendering old ways of war obsolete. The nation must organize accordingly, they argued, to cultivate a new breed of warriors to control and exploit the third dimension. As one of these early zealots quipped, "to entrust the development of aviation to either the Army or the Navy is just as sensible as entrusting the development of the electric light to a candle factory."[2] Through a mixture of prophecy, logic, and trial, these early airmen eventually carved out the separate Air Force in 1947. The first enduring belief of the Air Force is the need to focus an organization exclusively around the task of employing independent airpower.

The Air Force also believes its creation story is emblematic of the service's larger commitment to finding creative solutions to status quo problems. The service continues to assert its unique capacity to think creatively and nonlinearly, going "over not through" tactical and strategic problems alike.[3]

Founding Context and Key Events

Creation of the separate Air Force emerged through the interaction of political choice and early experimentation. On August 1, 1907, less than four years after the Wright brothers' first flight, the Army made its first organizational commitment to aviation by creating the Aeronautical division within its Signal Corps. With two enlisted men assigned to his support, the chief signal officer was "to take charge of all matters pertaining to military ballooning, air machines and all kindred subjects."[4] This small organizational act, uncertain as it was, created the first lineal ancestor of today's modern Air Force.

In July 1914, Congress upgraded the small Aeronautical division and established the Aviation Section within the Signal Corps, equipping it with 60 officers and 260 enlisted personnel. During World War I, the Aviation Section became the Air Service, which by the end of the war had swelled to more than 19,000 officers and 178,000 enlisted airmen.[5] While the Air Service carried out independent actions during the war, it focused primarily on supporting the ground army through observation. At war's end, Army General John Pershing concluded that military aircraft were best suited to "drive off hostile airplanes and procure for the infantry and artillery information concerning the enemy's movements."[6]

After the war, airmen made a slow but steady advance toward independence. In 1920, Congress reaffirmed the Air Service as a separate combatant branch within the Army, upgrading it to the Army Air Corps in 1926. Nine years later, on March 1, 1935, the Army activated the General Headquarters (GHQ) Air Force, which gave airmen tactical control over aviation assets in the United States, rather than having these assets parceled out among Army units in the field—a major development on the path to independence.[7] In June 1941, the Army Air Corps was renamed the Army Air Forces (AAF), under the command of General Henry "Hap" Arnold. Throughout World War II, the AAF enjoyed significant autonomy, due in large part to the personal rapport between General Arnold and Chief of Staff of the Army General George Marshall. Marshall appreciated the strategic potential of air forces, and though Arnold was his subordinate, their conduct during the war was largely that of colleagues.[8]

The path toward an independent air force took a major leap in 1943 following operations in North Africa, when, on July 21, the War Department published Field Manual 100-20. Entitled *Command and Employment of Air Power*, this seminal manual captured the airmen's perspective with stark clarity. The very first point in section 1 of the manual made this essential claim: "Land power and air power are co-equal and interdependent forces; neither is an auxiliary of the other."[9] Arnold himself dubbed FM 100-20 the "emancipation proclamation" for airpower, finally liberating the Army Air Forces from any notion of doctrinal subservience to ground forces.[10]

At war's end, a separate Air Force was nearly a foregone conclusion, though the actual legislation did not come easily. The autonomy of the Air Force became part of the contentious debates over unification of the armed services, finally resulting in the National Security Act of 1947. With passage of this act on September 18, the Air Force was born as a separate military service to provide "prompt and sustained offensive and defensive air operations."[11]

The Outspoken Exemplar

As the Army's air component grew and pressed for independence, impassioned airmen propelled the movement forward. Among the many outspoken advocates for a separate air force, Brigadier General William "Billy" Mitchell outspoke them all. A brash officer with a penchant for publicity, Mitchell helped forge the independent Air Force as both its prophet and its martyr. Although he was not one of the Army's initial cadre of airmen, Mitchell sensed that the airplane would revolutionize warfare and paid for his own flight lessons in 1916.[12] During World War I, he became the Air Service First Brigade commander working for General John Pershing, ultimately commanding more than 1,500 allied aircraft in the Saint-Mihiel offensive in 1918. Mitchell emerged from the war with two convictions: first, airpower was now the decisive element of warfare; and second, airpower must be controlled by an independent service.[13]

During the interwar years, Mitchell led an incendiary campaign against the Navy, proclaiming both the obsolescence and the impotence of the battleship-focused fleet. Two key events headlined Mitchell's tireless crusade: the sinking of captured Germans ships in 1921 and his own court-martial in 1925. First, after a series of claims and counter-claims about the vulnerability of Navy ships, Mitchell and the Navy agreed to a clinical trial in which airmen would attack two captured German warships. On July 18, 1921, Mitchell's airmen took aim at the cruiser *Frankfort*; playing by the established rules, they inflicted moderate damage on the ship.[14] Three days later, with movie cameras rolling, the Martin MB-2 bombers relentlessly attacked the 24,000-ton battleship *Ostfriesland*, without the agreed-upon pauses, and in full defiance of the Navy's calls to wave off the attacks.[15] The *Ostfriesland* sank in 21 minutes, after which Mitchell informed his boss that "the problem of the destruction of sea craft by Air Forces had been solved and is finished."[16] The sunken hull of the *Ostfriesland* became an icon of Mitchell's campaign for a preeminent air force.

Mitchell's fervency proved unquenchable, despite attempts by War Department leaders to temper his rhetoric. Banished from Washington, DC, to a post in Texas, Mitchell brought his disruptive advocacy to a climax in September 1925 after the crash of a Navy dirigible. He publicly blamed the fatal crash on "the incompetency, criminal negligence, and almost treasonable administration of the National Defense by the Navy and War Departments."[17] Unable to tolerate this final stroke of insubordination, President Calvin Coolidge levied charges against Mitchell and summoned him to Washington for a court-martial. His court-martial became a much-publicized affair, a pseudo-referendum on the role of aviation in civil and military affairs. Ultimately found guilty of insubordination, Mitchell was reduced in grade to colonel and subsequently retired from the service.

In the end, the Air Force's ongoing attitude toward Billy Mitchell involves conflicted appreciation. Mitchell's vision, voice, and advocacy clearly helped to establish the independent Air Force. Furthermore, his understanding of airpower provided the nascent force with its seminal doctrines. "More than any other individual," writes former Air Force officer and historian Mark Clodfelter, "[Mitchell] was responsible for molding the airpower convictions that would serve as the doctrinal cornerstones of the United States Air Force."[18] Similarly, Mitchell's outspoken candor is admired by a service that prides itself on finding new possibilities by challenging convention. Major General Charles Dunlap notes strains of "assertive individualism" in Air Force culture and suggests that Mitchell's example of questioning authority in defiance of the status quo "set[s] a tone for the Airman's attitude that still resounds today."[19]

Nevertheless, given Mitchell's brash zealotry and insubordination, the Air Force struggles to embrace him as a pure hero. The service seems conflicted about whether Mitchell's incendiary tactics were a necessary part of his message or unprofessional excess. The Air Force appears to have enduring pride in Mitchell for his outspoken candor, complicated by the fact that its hero was court-martialed. Mitchell's example is not one that senior Air Force leaders typically encourage their junior airmen to follow wholeheartedly.

In summary, the aerospace domain is a distinct arena of warfare. Controlling the air requires separately focused organizations and mindsets, decoupled from land and sea. As a service, the Air Force maintains an ongoing commitment to finding creative ways to bypass conventional conflict and conventional thinking.

Decisive Strategic Potential

As aircraft entered the military inventory in the early twentieth century, soldiers and sailors envisioned service-specific applications. The Army focused on supporting ground maneuvers and the Navy on supporting the fleet, but airmen insisted that airpower could make an independent war-winning contribution. Employed independently, bombers could bypass static trench lines, striking directly at the heart of the enemy homeland to cripple its war-making capacity and enervate its national will to resist. Convinced of airpower's great potential, combined with a belief in the need for a separate air force, airpower advocates viewed the doctrine of strategic bombing as the logical pathway to independence.

The doctrine of strategic bombing and the pursuit of organizational autonomy were tangled strands—logically distinct, but in practice inseparable. Since the viability of strategic bombing had existential implications, airmen were hardly in a position to admit any defects in their doctrine. But as Major General Perry Smith argued, "this is not to imply that the Air Force planners were cynics who were searching for ways to justify their existence. These men believed that airpower was the most effective way to maintain national security, but they came to this belief not by a scholarly weighing of a number of alternatives."[20] Since achieving independence in 1947, the Air Force's experiences in war have revealed practical limitations to this once-absolute theory of strategic bombing. Despite these limitations, the Air Force continues to hold a core belief in the decisive strategic potential of airpower to bypass conventional fielded forces, strike the enemy's center of gravity, and achieve decisive impact in war.

Operational Environment

In what ways does the aerial environment influence the Air Force's belief in the decisive potential of strategic bombing? As aircraft entered World War I, their remarkable mobility and speed offered a striking contrast to the static blood-letting in the trenches below. While opposing armies conjured new ways to trade large swaths of men for small tracts of ground, aircraft could overfly the tragedy below and strike deep in the enemy heartland. New targets came within reach, unlocking new pathways to influence the enemy's decision calculus and will to resist. Aircraft democratized warfighting, exposing civilian populations and political leaders to lethal risks that had once been reserved for professional armies. These opportunities to strike the enemy's heart and soul carried revolutionary potential, which visionary airmen quickly intuited. While reality proved more problematic than theory, the strategic potential of the air could not be ignored.

Founding Context

Informed by the British and American experience in World War I, the Army Air Corps developed a theory of strategic bombing during the interwar years. With the goal of organizational autonomy always in view, sincere airpower advocates believed that strategic bombing would prove effective both in winning wars and in gaining organizational independence. At the Air Corps Tactical School (ACTS) at Maxwell Field, Alabama, airmen began developing a theory of industrial-web targeting. The theory conceptualized the enemy as a sensitive network of factories, supply centers, distribution hubs, and raw materials. By striking key nodes in this industrial web, airpower could cripple the enemy's war-making capacity, ultimately choking it into capitulation. While the airmen at ACTS recognized the flexibility of airpower to perform diverse missions, they clearly emphasized its *strategic* potential. Teaching materials at ACTS in 1938 affirmed that "air warfare may be waged against hostile land forces, sea forces, and air forces, or it may be waged directly against the enemy nation. The possibility for the application of military force against the vital structure of a nation directly and immediately upon the outbreak of hostilities is the most important and far reaching development of modern times."[21]

After the United States entered World War II, the renamed Army Air Forces began employing their preferred doctrine of high-altitude daylight precision bombing. Launching from airfields across Great Britain, American and British bombers targeted German cities and industry, providing the only means of Allied attack against Hitler's forces in Europe until June 1944. The American component of this effort, the Eighth Air Force, pursued its strategy at great cost. Ultimately, 77% of AAF crewmen who flew against Germany before D-Day became casualties. By war's end, the Eighth Air Force alone had suffered more fatalities (~26,000) than the US Marine Corps (~20,000).[22]

The heroic efforts of the Eighth Air Force comprised only a fraction of the total campaign wrought by the AAF. Across the globe, airmen advanced the Allied war effort through close air support, troop transport, air defense, cargo and materiel transport, reconnaissance, and convoy support. Despite the diversity of the AAF's contribution, its leaders concentrated primary attention on the unique dimension of strategic bombing. Even before the war ended, AAF leaders commissioned the United States Strategic Bombing Survey (USSBS) to assess and validate the overall impact of strategic bombing, much like the British had done after World War I.[23] Historian John Huston summarized the hopes of the USBSS effort: "At long last, Arnold and other Army aviators hoped the realities to be found among the ruins of German industries and cities by this group would validate the theories and unfulfilled promises of air advocates over the past two decades."[24] The conclusions of the USBSS helped confirm for airmen the value of the AAF's extensive bombing campaign in defeating Germany and Japan.

When the atomic bombs of August 1945 hastened the surrender of Japan, airmen had their ultimate proof of the decisive potential of strategic airpower. The prewar theory developed at ACTS, combined with the experiences of the AAF during the war, forged a seemingly unassailable belief in the value of strategic bombing to win wars quickly and decisively. This belief, however, was more fragile than its advocates admitted, and future air campaigns struggled to match the expectations created by the AAF over Germany and Japan.

Vietnam: Exception or Rule?

The Air Force's belief in the value of strategic bombing, shaped by the unlimited context of World War II, yielded great frustration in the limited wars of Korea and Vietnam. The early air campaign against North Vietnam proved particularly antithetical to airmen's belief in the right way to employ airpower. During the Rolling Thunder campaign, from March 1965 through October 1968, the United States fought to convince North Vietnam to stop supporting the Viet Cong in the south.[25] Toward that end, US political leaders did not want a full-scale air campaign to flatten North Vietnam—they merely wanted to apply increasing pressure on the regime. The resulting air campaign proved woefully ineffective, hamstrung in part by restrictive rules of engagement, targets hand-picked by political leaders in Washington, and disunity of command—to the profound frustration of the Air Force.[26]

The air war in Vietnam ended, however, with a more effective effort by American airmen. In response to the North Vietnamese Easter Offensive in 1972, President Richard Nixon ordered robust bombing of North Vietnamese industrial and military targets.[27] With more precise technology thrown against a conventional army, and restricted by fewer political constraints, the Air Force achieved more effective results in the Linebacker campaigns than it did during Rolling Thunder. Linebacker conformed more closely to the Air Force's preferred vision for strategic bombing and ultimately succeeded in bringing the North Vietnamese to the negotiating table.

The most balanced historical analyses argue that Linebacker succeeded where Rolling Thunder failed because conventional bombing was able to threaten and destroy valuable targets in 1972 that did not exist in 1965–68.[28] Linebacker successfully threatened North Vietnam's vital concerns and targeted its heavy conventional forces. Moreover, the political and military objectives changed between 1968 and 1972, as President Nixon sought to extract the United States from Vietnam and therefore pursued more limited ends. The Rolling Thunder campaign, however, had misaligned the chosen strategy with the type of war being waged by the enemy. Bombing North Vietnam had little effect on the Viet Cong's nonindustrial guerrilla campaign in the south and could do little to achieve the ambitious political objectives set by President Lyndon Johnson.[29]

The conclusions reached by the mainstream Air Force, however, look quite different from this balanced analysis. The relative success of Linebacker I and Linebacker II at the end of the war "allowed airmen to believe they might have won the war had they been allowed to run it."[30] General Curtis LeMay, the face of Air Force strategic bombing, suggested in 1986 that the Air Force could have won the Vietnam War in "any two week period you want to mention."[31] Airmen remained convinced that had they been allowed to bomb freely and massively much earlier in the campaign—as they could during Linebacker in 1972—the whole tragic mess could have been avoided. In his history of the Air Force, Colonel Walter Boyne captures the service's conventional wisdom about Vietnam in a particularly ambitious counterfactual:

> The result of Linebacker II was exactly what had been predicted for the total application of air power in North Vietnam: quick military victory. Had it been applied in the first years of the war, the lives of millions of people would have been spared, hundreds of billions of dollars would have been saved, South Vietnam would not have been ravaged, Cambodia would have not had to endure the Khmer Rouge, and the United States would have not had the ugly experience of the disaffected 1960s and 1970s with the continuing cynicism of the media and the general disaffection of the populace with its government.[32]

In summary, the service tends to believe that when used appropriately, airpower has the potential to decide the outcome of a war. By targeting the enemy's war-making capacity and key means of national resistance, a fully committed and complete air campaign can bypass fielded forces and crush the heart of the enemy.

Command the Air

The Air Force tends to believe that the battle for the air decides the battle on the ground. For airmen, commanding the air domain—operating in the skies without prohibitive interference from ground or air attack—is the first critical step toward ultimate victory. Air superiority thus comprises the essential precondition for victory on land or sea. In the first of his 10 propositions of airpower, Colonel Phillip Meilinger asserts that "whoever controls the air generally controls the surface."[33] This belief gives airmen a sense of their essential importance—*and* a sense of being taken for granted by the other services, which profit from the Air Force's nontrivial efforts. While this belief may seem like an esoteric doctrine with limited applicability to civil-military relations, it is a core element in the Air Force's concept of the *right* way to employ airpower. It is one of the reverberating truths the Air Force holds to be self-evident, though it is contested by the other services. The following discussion illustrates why.

Operational Environment

The relationship among the air, sea, and land environments gives inherent advantages to the air. By commanding the high ground with great reach and velocity, aircraft can exert a disproportionate effect on the land and sea domains. The air environment thus becomes an essential contested space, as whoever controls it stands a much higher chance of controlling what is below. Consequently, air forces prioritize gaining and maintaining air superiority by defeating enemy air forces and air defense systems that could disrupt friendly air and surface activity.

As early airpower theorists considered how best to fight in the third dimension, "command of the air" became a central tenet. Billy Mitchell, for example, prioritized air superiority in his writings, arguing that complete control of the air directly translates into mastery of the earth.[34] His confidence in this translation was so strong, in fact, that he suggested that the loss of air superiority is itself sufficient cause for a warring nation to capitulate. Once the air war is decided, Mitchell argued, the ultimate outcome is foreordained—the surface action merely fulfills what airpower has determined. Mitchell was not alone in this opinion. Marshal of the Royal Air Force (RAF) Sir Arthur Tedder opined similarly, asserting that "when [the air battle] is won, the war is all but won," and confidently concluded that "air superiority is the prerequisite to all war-winning operations."[35]

The beliefs of these airpower theorists informed the War Department's Field Manual 100-20. After the preamble declaring air and ground forces to be coequals, the next section detailed the proper employment of air forces. The first doctrinal statement reads:

> The gaining of air superiority is the first requirement for the success of any major land operation. Air forces may be properly and profitably employed against enemy sea power, land power, and air power. However, land forces operating without air superiority must take such extensive security measures against hostile air attack that their mobility and ability to defeat the enemy land forces are greatly reduced. Therefore, air forces must be employed primarily against the enemy's air forces until air superiority is obtained.[36]

These doctrinal commitments carry far-reaching implications, particularly as they relate to interservice relations. According to this published doctrine, the battle for air superiority is the first task for any campaign and the essential enabler for land and sea action. By implication, enemy air forces must be the first targeting priority for the joint force. Consider the tensions inherent in this belief. Gaining and maintaining air superiority is ultimately a means to an end, not an end in itself; air superiority is a condition provided by the air force so that land and sea (or strategic bombing) operations can occur without interference by enemy air forces. Yet by establishing air superiority as the first and highest targeting priority, airmen can be perceived as fighting a self-justifying air war while downgrading or delaying support requests from surface forces. Mutual misunderstanding can easily occur. The surface forces disparage the Air Force for fighting its own air war, away from the "important" action on the surface. The Air Force feels justified in its approach; it provides the most essential service possible, all the while feeling unappreciated by those below.

A reciprocal misunderstanding can exist as well. Since airmen tend to believe that the air war determines the outcome of land or sea battles, they may feel impatient with surface forces that enjoy complete protection from the air but still struggle to win. *Nobody's bombing you guys, we've hit every target there is to hit—what's taking you guys so long?* With an institutional commitment to commanding the air, the Air Force inherits frequent interservice tensions.

Founding Context and Key Events

During the interwar years and throughout World War II, the relationship between command of the air and success on the surface was largely beyond dispute. Initially, airmen pointed to Mitchell's famous sinking of the battleship *Ostfriesland* in 1921 as stark evidence of the ability of air forces to disrupt and dominate surface activity. Alexander de Seversky, one of Mitchell's fervent disciples, echoed his patron in 1942, writing matter-of-factly: "True, our two-ocean navy is almost completed; by general acclaim it adds up to the finest and strongest naval force the world has ever seen. Yet it can now do nothing, literally nothing, against the locust swarms of giant airplanes."[37]

The Allied preparations for D-Day in June 1944 reinforced this close connection between air battles and surface outcomes. In March 1944, General Dwight Eisenhower and his British deputy, Air Chief Marshal Arthur Tedder, met with the Allied air chiefs to discuss aerial preparations for Operation Overlord. They decided on the "transportation plan" of interdicting railways, marshaling yards, and other sources of German army mobility.[38] Simultaneously, however, the RAF and AAF maintained steady pressure on the Luftwaffe itself, destroying the enemy air force wherever it could be found. The effects of the sustained battle for air superiority were apparent; the Luftwaffe launched a meager 200 sorties on D-Day, compared with 13,000 from the Allies, whose invasion proceeded without meaningful interference. Eisenhower clearly appreciated the connection. In testimony to the Senate on November 16, 1945, he stated, "Unless we had that faith in the air power to intervene and to make safe that landing, it would have been more than fantastic, it would have been criminal."[39]

After World War II, the Air Force fought its last meaningful battle for air superiority in Korea, from 1950 to 1953. In fact, airmen fondly recite the historical fact that the last American ground soldier killed by air attack was in 1953.[40] Since then, American ground forces have enjoyed a complete aerial sanctuary, free from any attacks by enemy air forces. Having gained and maintained air superiority with relative ease for the past 60 years, however, the Air Force feels like the victim of its own success. Outsiders are prone to regard such a feat as easy or trivial, exacerbating the mutual lack of appreciation identified earlier.[41] But airmen firmly believe that air superiority comes not as an automatic birthright, but from the deliberate cultivation of skilled pilots, quality training, and leading-edge technology.

In summary, controlling the skies is the essential precondition for successful land and sea operations. Air superiority determines battlefield success: you cannot win a war without it, and once you have it, you should not lose. Establishing air superiority is therefore the first—and most important—imperative for any US military mission.

Centrally Controlled Flexibility

The first belief described in this chapter focused on the conviction that airpower should be controlled by a separate organization of dedicated airmen. Another belief amplifies this: not only should airpower be controlled by airmen, but it should be *centrally* controlled as a unified fighting element. One of the most common refrains in the Air Force is that "flexibility is the key to air power."[42] The speed, range, and mobility of aircraft provide the flexibility to mass one's force for concentrated effect, both geographically and temporally. Furthermore, aircraft represent an inherently *limited* resource. Limited resources drive the need to be efficient in order to be effective. Consequently, the Air Force believes that air assets should be centrally controlled by the senior airman in the theater of operations, who can decide where best to concentrate forces in pursuit of larger objectives. Parceling out dedicated air assets to dispersed ground units is anathema to airmen; such a policy nullifies the inherent flexibility of an air force and potentially squanders limited resources. Airmen naturally apply this line of thinking to the management of other assets too—not just aircraft. The service tends to favor centrally managing resources of all kinds (e.g., money, personnel, equipment), flexibly distributing them to the point of need as the situation warrants.

Operational Environment

The inherent speed, range, and mobility of aircraft confer both possibilities and limitations on the air forces that employ them. One of the advantages of the air domain is that strategists are not committed to any single line of action. Airpower can be directed and redirected as situations develop, which "enables the commander to correct many errors in foresight."[43] By controlling aircraft with central direction and common vision, one can achieve a decisive application of force with greater speed and surprise than ground forces could otherwise accomplish.

A second inherent attribute of aircraft is their limited numbers. Most aircraft are expensive, requiring extensive infrastructure to design, build, and operate—and commanders seemingly never have as many as they would like. Furthermore, airpower operations comprise a long value-chain of parts, equipment, training, logistics, planning, and coordination. To be effective with this long chain of limited resources, one must be efficient. To be efficient with airpower, airmen strongly believe in the need to consolidate assets, manage them centrally, and direct them conditionally to areas of greatest temporal need. Consequently, the eighth of Meilinger's 10 propositions on airpower is this: "Air Power's unique characteristics necessitate that it be centrally controlled by airmen."[44]

Key Events

This belief in centralized control emerged through experiments with its alternative. During the early phases of World War I, tactical ground commanders controlled their own dedicated aircraft in support of conventional ground maneuvers. By the later stages of the war, senior air leaders such as Billy Mitchell, Benjamin Foulois, and Lewis Brereton already believed that centralized control of airpower was fundamental to its sound employment. Mitchell, as the Air Service First Brigade commander, clashed with various ground commanders over airpower control in the Chateau-Thierry campaign in July 1918. During the Saint-Mihiel and Meuse-Argonne offensives in September 1918, he managed to secure greater control, centrally directing more than 1,500 aircraft in a coordinated campaign.[45]

In the interwar years, airpower advocates carried this conviction forward, consistently preaching the value of centralizing control of air assets. Their insights, however, were poorly applied during the initial North Africa campaign of World War II. As Operation Torch began in November 1942, the RAF and AAF maintained separate command and employment structures, with their respective commanders housed in separate headquarters. The two air forces retained separate control of their assets, then assigned specific aircraft to particular ground commanders. With the air forces already suffering from aircraft shortages, this so-called penny packeting of airpower further weakened their effect, as existing aircraft were not concentrated for maximum effect on key targets. By February 1943, the system proved thoroughly ineffectual, and the British and American leaders instituted reforms that central-ized control over the tactical aviation assets.[46] The new system succeeded, and once again vindicated the early doctrine preached by Mitchell and others after World War I.

Two months after the end of the North Africa campaign, the War Depart-ment published the now-familiar Field Manual 100-20. The lessons of North Africa clearly informed this seminal doctrinal statement:

> The inherent flexibility of air power is its greatest asset. This flexibility makes it possible to employ the whole weight of the available air power against se-lected areas in turn; such concentrated use of the air striking force is a battle winning factor of the first importance. Control of available air power must be centralized and command must be exercised through the air force commander if this inherent flexibility and ability to deliver a decisive blow are to be fully exploited.[47]

This doctrine remained intact throughout World War II and played a cen-tral role in one of the Air Force's first official codifications of doctrine, Air Force Manual 1-2, published on April 1, 1955. That publication declared:

> The medium in which air forces operate—space—is an indivisible field of activ-ity. This medium, in combination with the characteristics of air vehicles, invests air forces with the great flexibility that is the basis of their strength. For this flexibility to be exploited fully, the air forces must be responsive at all levels of operation to employment as a single, aggregate instrument. All command ar-rangements must be in accord with the precept that neither air forces nor their field of activity can be segmented and partitioned among different interests.[48]

This belief once again creates tension with other services that approach the role of airpower in different ways. For example, the Air Force's insistent belief in centrally controlling air assets pits it squarely against the Marine Corps, which reserves all of its air assets for the sole passion of the Corps: supporting the infantry. Some of the fiercest interservice tensions since World War II have orbited around this issue. The Air Force has reliably argued that efficient operations require the pooling of limited resources for flexible application at the point of greatest need. As the Air Force has extended its logic to the joint force, it has asked all the services to make available their aviation assets for centralized control. The Marine Corps, with its religious commitment to sup-porting Marine infantry first and always, has resisted relinquishing control of Marine air to an Air Force commander. Marine air is for Marines on the ground. Similar disagreements have plagued Air Force relations with the other services, as airmen argued for "single management" of all air assets.[49] These substantive disagreements are more than mere interservice rivalry: they represent clashing first principles of deeply held beliefs.

Another interservice misunderstanding flows from this belief. Since the Air Force focuses on centrally controlled assets, it tends to think like a portfolio manager about its broad *capabilities*—things it can do, or effects it can create. The other services—particularly the Army—tend to think and communicate in terms of physical things. As described in chapter 4, the Army assigns physical assets to specific commanders, who then have formal responsibility for maintaining and employing those assets. Consequently, when the Army requests support from the Air Force to move equipment or drop a bomb, it tends to ask for a thing: "I need a C-130," or, "Send me four A-10s!" The Air Force, thinking like a portfolio manager of centrally controlled assets, counters: "Just tell me what needs to happen and I'll create the effect you're looking for. Tell me you need two pallets of ammunition moved to a forward operating base—don't ask for a C-130. Tell me you need battlefield interdiction for troops in contact at specific coordinates—don't ask for A-10s!" So one service thinks and talks in terms of physical assets; the other thinks and talks in terms of net capabilities and effects—yet another clash of cultural first principles.

In summary, the Air Force tends to believe that the unique flexibility of airpower requires that limited resources be centrally controlled by the senior airman in theater, who can direct those resources to the highest-priority location or task. For maximum efficiency and effectiveness, all US military aviation assets should be centrally controlled, not held in reserve for service-specific agendas. In general, centralized control of assets, distributed as needs dictate, is the preferred method for managing resources.

Technology and Identity

Technology features prominently in Air Force identity and culture. The Air Force's very existence is a deliberate response to a disruptive new technology. Like the Navy, which cannot exist without ships, the Air Force is no force at all without aircraft. The service prospers in concert with the sophistication of its technology, which makes the Air Force keenly interested in the quantity and quality of its aerial fleet—particularly its *quality*. Defense analyst Carl Builder suggests that "to be outnumbered may be tolerable, but to be outflown is not. The way to get the American flier's attention is to confront him with a superior machine."[50] The Air Force thus focuses on both the general and the specific: the service prizes new technology in general, while valuing the aircraft as a specific embodiment of that technological progress.[51]

An observer's first impression of the Air Force, rendered through its visible artifacts, reveals this organizational passion for the airplane. Nearly every Air Force base showcases airplane monuments, often right at the entrance to the base. As a point of comparison, the parade ground at the US Military Academy at West Point is flanked by monuments to the Army's great generals: Washington, Patton, MacArthur, and Thayer. The Terrazzo at the US Air Force Academy is cornered by sleek airplanes: the F-15, F-16, F-4, and F-105. Walking through the halls of the Pentagon yields similar impressions, as dramatic paintings and photographs of aircraft dominate the Air Force's corporate territory.

Operational Environment

The Air Force's unique operating environment contributes strongly to its fascination with new technology. In fact, the only reason the Air Force *has* an operational environment is that technology pushed back against gravity, allowing aircraft to "slip the surly bonds of earth."[52] More than sailors or soldiers, airmen rely profoundly on a sustained technological achievement to do their job. An airman in flight inhabits a precarious space, vulnerable to threats seen and unseen, natural and manmade, and his occupation thereof is inherently temporary. These dynamics give airmen both an appreciation for and a profound dependence on their machines. They develop a mindset for emergency preparedness, shaped by the vulnerability of speeding 500 miles per hour, five miles above the earth, precariously perched in front of 10,000 gallons of jet fuel steadily exploding in the engine bays behind them. The technological dependence of airmen thus confers an institutional commitment to detailed planning, fallback options, contingency plans, and scripted emergency procedures when red lights start flashing.

A second aspect of the Air Force technological environment also affects its culture. Given the engineering complexity of aerospace systems, the service faces very long timelines for research, development, and fielding of major weapon systems. Like the Navy and its ships, the Air Force must go to war with assets already designed and built. Similarly, the service must prepare today to build the Air Force that will be airborne decades from now. This reality orients the Air Force far into the future and creates the paradox of fielding "next generation" technological marvels that may be nearly obsolete by the time they reach the operational force.

Echoes and Implications

The Air Force's commitment to new technology and aircraft may seem relatively straightforward, but it spawns a series of more subtle echoes and implications within the service. First, since technological machines feature prominently in the service, the loyalties and identities of airmen naturally migrate toward these machines. Given the unique experiences and vulnerabilities afforded by the human-machine union, airmen commonly identify themselves with their primary aircraft or weapons system—"I'm an F-15 pilot," or, "I'm a C-17 maintainer." This dynamic tends to dilute common bonds across the service, giving rise instead to a "fractionated confederation of subcultures rather than a cohesive military service."[53] The Air Force struggles to find a unifying narrative among such a diverse group of clans and tribes, with each subgroup defined largely by the machine it operates.

A second echo affects motivation and loyalty in the Air Force, as many airmen find their particular technological experience to be the sustaining factor in their service—more so than a commitment to the Air Force as an institution or to national service in general. In his study of Air Force cultural cohesion, James Smith noted the high level of occupational versus institutional loyalties in the officer corps, particularly among pilots.[54] Carl Builder identified a similar theme, noting that across the Air Force's history, "People found themselves in an institution because that was the place to do what they wanted to do—to fly airplanes, to work on rockets, to develop missiles, to learn an interesting or promising trade, etc."[55]

This level of identity construction stands in contrast to that in the Army or Marine Corps. Marines identify most strongly with their service and are all about the Marine Corps. Army soldiers tend to identify *above* the service level, as servants of the nation and as members of the historical profession of arms. Air Force airmen, however, tend to identify *below* the service level, with loyalties that gravitate toward their machine-centric experiences and sub-communities.

In summary, the Air Force was created to exploit a disruptive new technology and has an abiding faith in the potential for new technologies to change the face of warfare. These technologies naturally attract the loyalty and identity of the airmen who operate them. Due to the length and complexity of research and development processes, the nation must invest today to have a world-class Air Force tomorrow.

Informal Collegiality

Finally, the Air Force has a unique social dimension to its culture. Of the four military services, the Air Force is the least formal in its relations between officers and enlisted troops and among officers of varying ranks. A collegial social atmosphere permeates most Air Force units, conditioned by several unique facets of the service's mission environment. Unlike in the other three services, officers do most of the combat fighting in the Air Force, while enlisted troops anchor the essential support and maintenance infrastructure. Furthermore, this disparity between officer and enlisted experiences reflects a larger phenomenon in the Air Force: across the service, relatively few airmen serve in harm's way. And those flyers who sortie forth into combat do so in short bursts, on discrete missions, and then return to base.[56] Lastly, leadership in the tactical flying environment is based not on individual rank but on mission qualification and specific roles designated for specific missions. These social dynamics create a collegial environment that makes the Air Force successful and unique, while mystifying its sister services, which sometimes find the environment odd at best and unmilitary at worst.

Operational Environment

Soldiers, sailors, and Marines typically experience combat in a communal way, aboard their ships or as part of a combined-arms team in a battle zone. Airmen encounter war differently, segregating the experience of combat in several ways. First, only a minority of airmen participate in flying jobs, of which only a portion actually fly forward into a combat zone. Across the Air Force, then, there are large asymmetries of exposure to the bombs and bullets associated with combat. The second dimension along which airmen segregate combat duties is between rank structures. Due to the training and education required to operate advanced equipment, the vast majority of flyers are officers. This means that officers do most of the fighting in the Air Force, while the enlisted force comprises an essential support structure of maintenance, supply, and logistics.

Another segregating element is the distance from which most airmen experience war. Even in combat, much of Air Force life takes place on secure bases, typically—though certainly not always—at a safe distance from enemy threats. Airmen whose jobs are confined to the base discover their war duties to be eerily similar to their peacetime routines back home. Consequently, the Air Force's experience of war can become an exercise in process management, staged at a psychological and geographic remove from the sound and fury of battle. Airmen can find themselves living and working in a dissonant no-man's-land between war and peace, where day-to-day routines feel neither like home nor like one's expectations of combat.

A further unique element of the Air Force operational environment is the flyer's short-duration exposure to the extremes of the human condition. A combat flyer's experience of trading bombs and bullets is inherently limited in time, typically sandwiched between periods of relative safety and comfort on a base. Historian Donald Miller captures this experience well in his description of the bomber crews in World War II: "Bomber warfare was intermittent warfare. Bouts of inactivity and boredom were followed by short bursts of fury and fear; and men returned from sky fights to clean sheets, hot food, and adoring English girls."[57] These psychological extremes tend to confer a unique outlook on those subjected to them.[58]

Echoes and Effects

Since most combat exposure in the Air Force is limited to highly trained officers, its flying culture takes a different approach to combat leadership than the other services. In the Army, Navy, and Marine Corps, the senior-most officer on the scene typically has ongoing tactical and operational command over assigned forces. In the Air Force, however, combat leadership gets conferred episodically, not perpetually. For a given Air Force mission, a qualified aircrew member is anointed the "mission commander," tasked to plan and execute a particular mission along with dozens of other aircraft assigned for that event. The mission commander could well be a captain, with authority to command higher-ranking majors, lieutenant colonels, and colonels across the span of the scheduled mission. This rank-blind meritocracy creates a more informal approach to hierarchy and rank structures, particularly in flying squadrons where airmen refer to one another more frequently by clan-given nicknames than as "sir" or "ma'am."

A second echo extends these implications to officer-enlisted relations. Most enlisted airmen perform technical jobs away from the combat zone, so expectations of these troops differ from those of the other services. This has long been the case. In 1926, Major William Sherman commented on the unique enlisted environment of the Air Service:

[The enlisted airman] is not called upon, as the infantryman may be, to follow his officer forward in the charge, through the heated atmosphere of danger and death. The duties of the air service enlisted man are complex, but are performed under conditions of comparative security . . . Among the enlisted personnel of the air force, the discipline needed is that of the shop rather than of the battlefield.[59]

Furthermore, officers rely on their enlisted troops in a very dependent way, entrusting them with their lives as these enlisted airmen service their aircraft and pack their parachutes. The accepted tenor of officer-enlisted relations in the Air Force is thus quite collegial, informal, and egalitarian.[60] While standard customs and courtesies are generally observed, fraternal practices such as using aviator call-signs or first names are common.

In summary, in the Air Force way of war, relatively few airmen experience the perils of combat; most who do are circumscribed by their machines. Consequently, operational culture is meritocratic and rank-agnostic, not hierarchical. Since most face-to-face interactions occur away from the battle zone, social dynamics in the Air Force should be respectful but collegial and informal.

Conclusion

This short, selective history of the US Air Force yields several summary observations. The Air Force appears particularly susceptible to being misunderstood by outsiders, in part because esoteric claims are an essential part of the service's creation narrative. The service's founding ethos was rooted in its gnostic proclamations about airpower: the other three military services, left to their own devices, would have mishandled and underutilized the air weapon. Consequently, the very existence of the Air Force is an organizational rebuke of the other services' inadequate appreciation of airpower's full potential. Many of the Air Force's cultural beliefs are thus deliberately novel and contrarian. Moreover, many of these beliefs have been not only contrarian but triumphalist. In one of its first doctrinal publications, the service proclaimed that its dominance knew no limits: "Of the various types of military forces, those which conduct air operations are most capable of decisive results . . . They provide the dominant military means of exercising the initiative and gaining decisions in all forms of international relations, including full peace, cold war, limited wars of all types, and total war."[61] Unsurprisingly, then, many elements of the Air Force's history and culture put the service at odds with the Army, Navy, and Marine Corps. The advent of human flight disturbed existing service arrangements and forced a fundamental renegotiation of all of the services' tasks and jurisdictions.[62] The Air Force, born amid competition and strife, inherits some misunderstanding and rivalry as part of its birthright. To its credit, and to the good of the nation, it has added excellence, professionalism, and faithful service to that pedigree as well. The salient beliefs of Air Force service culture are summarized in figure 5.1.

This concludes the cultural portraits of the four American military services. As stated at the outset, the primary contribution of these four chapters is their methodological consistency and the creative synthesis of existing histories. They are portraits sketched in pencil, not exhaustive biographies—but the pencil lines give more than enough detail to distinguish one from another. By conducting a structured, focused comparison oriented around the concepts of ends, ways, and means, these chapters specify a novel slate of beliefs for each service. These beliefs provide enough specificity to differentiate each service as a unique political actor, but they retain sufficient flexibility and generality to apply to a wide variety of issues and cases. These composite arrays of belief are used in the case studies in the following chapters, and they may also be used in future research, across disparate issues and historical periods, to predict or explain the policy preferences and civil-military behavior of each military service.

The next two chapters enter the trenches of civil-military policymaking to assess how unique cultural beliefs condition different patterns of civil-military behavior. When asked to prepare forces for possible deployment to the Middle East, how did the Army and Marine Corps respond? The creation of the Rapid Deployment Joint Task Force in the late 1970s serves as the first demonstration of the principled agent framework in action.

SUMMARY OF AIR FORCE CULTURAL BELIEFS		
Ends	**5.1** Air Controlled by Airmen	The aerospace domain is a distinct arena of warfare. Controlling the air requires separately focused organizations and mindsets, decoupled from land and sea. As a service, the Air Force maintains an ongoing commitment to finding creative ways to bypass conventional conflict and conventional thinking.
Ways	**5.2** Decisive Strategic Potential	When used appropriately, airpower has the potential to decide the outcome of a war. By targeting the enemy's war-making capacity and key means of national resistance, a fully committed and complete air campaign can bypass fielded forces and crush the heart of the enemy.
	5.3 Command the Air	Controlling the skies is the essential precondition for successful land and sea operations. Air superiority determines battlefield success: you cannot win a war without it, and once you have it, you should not lose. Establishing air superiority is therefore the first—and most important—imperative for any US military mission.
	5.4 Centrally Controlled Flexibility	The unique flexibility of airpower requires that limited resources be centrally controlled by the senior airman in theater, who can direct those resources to the highest-priority location or task. For maximum efficiency and effectiveness, all US military aviation assets should be centrally controlled, not held in reserve for service-specific agendas. In general, centralized control of assets, distributed as needs dictate, is the preferred method for managing resources.
Means	**5.5** Technology and Identity	The Air Force was created to exploit a disruptive new technology and has an abiding faith in the potential for new technologies to change the face of warfare. These technologies naturally attract the loyalty and identity of the airmen who operate them. Due to length and complexity of research and development processes, the nation must invest today to have a world-class Air Force tomorrow.
	5.6 Informal Collegiality	In the Air Force way of war, relatively few airmen experience the perils of combat; most who do are circumscribed by their machines. Consequently, operational culture is meritocratic and rank-agnostic, not hierarchical. Since most face-to-face interactions occur away from the battle zone, social dynamics in the Air Force should be respectful but collegial and informal.

Figure 5.1. A summary of the US Air Force's cultural beliefs about its preferred ends, ways, and means.

chapter 6

Getting There Fast

The Story of the Rapid Deployment Joint Task Force

> Our political system is in many ways poorly designed for the
> conduct of the foreign policies of a great power aspiring to world
> leadership.
>
> —George Kennan, *American Diplomacy*

For the past 25 years, operations in the Middle East have defined the rhythms of the American military. Shuttling through Kuwait, Iraq, Afghanistan and now Syria, many members of today's US military know little else but continual rotations to the desert. Across this vast span of time and sand, United States Central Command (CENTCOM) has been the military giant directing US military operations. Unlike European Command and Pacific Command, which have been in place since World War II, Central Command is a relative newcomer in the American military pantheon. For the early decades of the Cold War, the Middle East languished as the neglected hinterlands of European and Pacific Commands—both had bigger concerns elsewhere. Until the creation of CENTCOM in 1983, the US military did not have a robust combatant command dedicated to the now-dominant region. The story of its initial creation offers a compelling case of civil-military relations in action.

As an empirical application of principled agent theory, this chapter focuses on the creation and development of the Rapid Deployment Joint Task Force (RDJTF)—the organizational precursor to CENTCOM. The case study highlights the period from President Jimmy Carter's 1977 presidential directive to prepare deployable forces for global contingencies through the establishment of CENTCOM on January 1, 1983. During that six-year span, the RDJTF lived its short embattled life, from conception to birth to its ultimate transition to a combatant command. The RDJTF served as a critical bridge between a time when the United States had *no* military command focused on the Middle East to a time when the US military has focused on little else.

The RDJTF joined the American military structure in 1980 to address a strategic conundrum. How could the US military deter or repel a Soviet invasion of Persian Gulf oil facilities, without regional bases or new military forces, while still meeting alliance commitments in Europe and East Asia? Without any good answers, the American defense community clamored for the least bad option it could find. The result was the RDJTF, a military organization steeped in controversy from cradle to grave. The conventional wisdom and prevailing histories of the RDJTF tend to indict the US military on two notable charges.[1] First, the military services appear to ignore quite deliberately an August 1977 presidential directive to create a rapid deployment force.[2] The services evidently had no interest in or motivation to create the force, the thinking goes, so they simply did nothing. The second common critique is that once the civilians put enough pressure on the military to generate action, the Army and Marine Corps locked horns in an interservice rivalry, wrestling for control of the fledgling RDJTF.[3] From ignoring President Carter to petty interservice squabbling, this appears to be a case of strikingly poor civil-military relations.

The evidence and analysis marshaled in this chapter challenge the conventional wisdom. Drawing on previously classified data from eight archival sites, amplified by interviews with several key figures, this case study reveals the military services' behavior to be more complex and principled than existing analyses suggest. The case of the RDJTF is one in which political ambiguity, competing demands, limited resources, and genuine differences of strategic thought all collided to create suboptimal political compromises. In this difficult instance of crafting national strategy, the road of faithful military compliance was not a well-marked path from which the services deliberately veered to go their own way. Instead, the pathway of compliance was highly uncertain, steeped in an ambiguity that defied easy answers or straightforward solutions. The evidence here suggests that the military actors were not making calculated cost-benefit decisions about whether or not to carry out a straightforward request. Consequently, the military agents' behavior cannot be easily explained or appraised with a traditional agency model. Instead, the analysis finds a more satisfying explanation with a new principled agent approach that incorporates the cultural predispositions of the services, the temporal dynamics of policymaking, and the effects of political ambiguity on the civil-military interaction.

The chapter begins with a brief history of the US security approach to the Middle East since World War II, highlighting the role and purpose of the military's Unified Command Plan. It then considers the essence of the strategic problem facing the United States in 1977 and hypothesizes how the Army and Marine Corps might respond in the light of their cultural beliefs explained in earlier chapters. The narrative then unfolds, covering three periods. First is the period from August 1977, with the signing of Presidential Directive 18 (PD-18), to August 1979, when Secretary of Defense Harold Brown provided an initial update on what the Department of Defense (DOD) had done to comply with PD-18. The second period extends from Secretary Brown's decision to create a joint task force in October 1979 through the end of the Carter administration in January 1981. And, finally, the third period covers the beginning of the Reagan administration in 1981 through the formal establishment of USCENTCOM in January 1983. Each of these three narrative sections evaluates the extent to which the civil-military interactions reflect the aggregate predictions of the principled agent model.

Geopolitical Background and Military Command Structure

In the late 1970s, the United States clung to a fragile security structure in the Middle East, with seemingly no conventional military capability to advance its interests in the region. How did that happen? And more importantly, how could the United States design a responsive, mobile, and robust military force to counter Soviet aggression 10,000 miles away from America's shores?

For decades after World War II, the United States and the United Kingdom worked together to advance Anglo-American interests around the world, with American involvement increasing as British presence waned. As its imperial structure dissolved, the United Kingdom found it increasingly costly and unsustainable to stay engaged in the Middle East, Indian Ocean, and key areas in the Mediterranean. After successive withdrawals from India, Greece, Turkey, Egypt, Kuwait, and Yemen, Prime Minister Harold Wilson announced in January 1968 that all British troops would withdraw from east of the Suez by the end of 1971.[4] The inexorable British retreat from the Middle East thus left a security vacuum in an increasingly unstable region.

Filling the void, the Americans incrementally stepped forward as the British backed out. Following the British departure from Egypt and the 1956 Suez crisis, for example, President Dwight Eisenhower pledged support for the region, deploying Marines to Lebanon in 1958 under the aegis of the Eisenhower Doctrine's commitment to the Middle East.[5] After the British announced their final withdrawal from the region in 1968, President Richard Nixon adopted the "twin pillar" strategy of relying on Iran and Saudi Arabia as staunch regional allies. With its standing postwar commitments in Europe and the Far East, the United States had devoted only limited attention and resources to the Middle East. By relying on British and regional allies, America maintained a modicum of stability at a discounted rate. But as the British slowly left, the United States had to shoulder more of the burden. As one commentator summarized it, "the entire postwar history of American strategic interaction with the region can be seen as an attempt—under circumstances of limited military resources—to cope with successive British retreats from Greece and Turkey (1947), Egypt and the Arab East (1957), and the Persian Gulf (1971)."[6]

In concert with shifting international commitments, the US military's global command arrangements likewise evolved. During World War II, the American and British forces had divided the world into geographic regions of responsibility to unify command authority in each theater of operations.[7] After the war, the US military crystallized this arrangement in the first Unified Command Plan (UCP), approved by President Harry Truman on December 14, 1946.[8] To this day, the UCP divides the world geographically and functionally into unified commands, comprising forces from two or more of the military services. The four military services organize, train, and equip the requisite forces that are employed operationally by the unified commands. These unified commands—led by their respective combatant commanders, formerly called commanders-in-chief (CINCs)—serve as the US military's main warfighting organizations.[9]

Throughout most of the Cold War, the four major geographic commands specified in the UCP were European Command (EUCOM), Pacific Command (PACOM), Atlantic Command (LANTCOM), and Southern Command (SOUTHCOM). EUCOM and PACOM, with their abundance of forces and important security commitments, clearly dominated the US military landscape. Despite being headquartered in Germany and Hawaii, respectively, EUCOM and PACOM shared formal responsibility for the Middle East according to the UCP. EUCOM's area of responsibility included most of the Middle Eastern landmass over to Afghanistan; PACOM held responsibility for all the water in the region, as well as the Asian landmass from Pakistan to the east. While the UCP split the Middle East between the two commands, the region was clearly not the priority for either one. An intractable question thus arose and persisted: how should the US military organize in peacetime and deploy in wartime for crises outside its alliance commitments to the North Atlantic Treaty Organization (NATO), Japan, and Korea? Indeed, the authors of the history of the UCP noted that "no issue connected with the UCP provoked more debate than unified command of deployable general-purpose forces based in the continental United States."[10]

After a series of service-centric attempts to design deployable general-purpose forces, the DOD established US Readiness Command (REDCOM) in January 1972. Readiness Command replaced the fledgling US Strike Command (STRICOM), which had attempted to merge Army and Air Force units in an integrated command. Much like its predecessor, REDCOM's assigned missions included "providing a general reserve of combat-ready forces to reinforce other unified commands, conducting joint training and exercises with assigned forces, and developing recommendations to the Joint Chiefs of Staff regarding doctrine and 'techniques for the joint employment of forces assigned.'"[11] With a focus on training and not employing, REDCOM languished as a rather weak unified command. The Navy and Marine Corps did not have forces assigned to REDCOM, so the command was limited to the joint readiness of only Army and Air Force units. Furthermore, the military services had statutory responsibility for training their forces, which further diminished the role and prestige of REDCOM.[12] By the mid-1970s, therefore, REDCOM occupied a tenuous orbit in the constellation of military unified commands. As one observer noted, REDCOM was stuck as "a unified command without assigned forces, a joint command limited in its doctrinal formulation to the operation of two services, a limited contingency force without a specific region of responsibility, [and] an organization of loosely-connected forces plagued with erroneous notions of force flexibility to match a vague, yet global mission."[13]

As President Carter took office, the US military's ability to respond to military crises in the Middle East was clearly suboptimal, both organizationally and materially. EUCOM and PACOM shared formal responsibility for the region, but were focused on Europe, Korea, and the Pacific. REDCOM had a mission to train and deploy US-based general-purpose forces to support other geographic commands, but was limited in its scope and effectiveness. Furthermore, all three command headquarters (Germany, Hawaii, and Florida) were many thousands of miles from the Persian Gulf region and ill-equipped to provide on-site command presence. Muddling through had worked to a point, but changing times soon called for a new approach.

By 1977, the combined effect of several geopolitical and military trends loomed dangerously. The Middle East had clearly become a region of critical strategic significance for the United States and its allies. Western civilization was addicted to Persian Gulf oil, with no clear or viable alternative sources. Historically, the United States and the West had relied on Great Britain to underwrite security in the Middle East, but with the British presence in steady abeyance, the US had to fill the vacuum. American military command arrangements, however, treated the Middle East as a peripheral theater, with no formal alliance networks, basing, or logistical infrastructure to enable a meaningful military response. Meanwhile, the Soviet Union appeared both motivated for and capable of rolling south into Iranian oilfields, seizing the strategic terrain, and holding the West hostage to its demands. Together, these trends conspired to create a complex strategic problem for Carter and his national security team.

How Might the Military Respond?

With the basic context in place, the discussion now briefly suspends the historical account to consider the predictions made by principled agent theory. More specifically, this discussion predicts the general shape of the Marine Corps' and Army's policy preferences in the light of their enduring cultural beliefs. To apply the framework *ex ante*, the analysis stipulates the general contours of the strategic problem, and then deduces the implications of each service belief for each element of the policy debate. Revisiting Alexander George's work on operational code, this analysis asks: for this particular issue of creating a rapidly deployable force, what are the "diagnostic and choice propensities" that each service's cultural beliefs are likely to create?[14] The argument here recognizes that final decisions always involve contingent factors in the policy environment, but this code of beliefs helps to provide the "pre-strategic preferences" an actor brings into a debate.[15] Using a dyadic approach, each belief is isolated against each policy issue in turn, assessing how belief a will shape the interpretation of issue x. The implications of two different beliefs might therefore predict different preferences on the same issue, in which case the framework anticipates a mixed reaction.

Generally speaking, the following parameters shaped the strategic requirement. In its essence, the mission was to provide or create a conventional military force to handle non-NATO contingencies worldwide, with a focus on the Middle East. The guidance focused on using general-purpose, nonnuclear forces that were not already committed to Europe or East Asia. These forces needed to be rapidly deployable, available on short notice to meet sudden crises. Moreover, they needed to be prepared for conflicts ranging from small brushfires up to a full Soviet invasion of Persian Gulf oil fields (i.e., Iran). Finally, such forces had to prepare to perform the mission without any military bases in the Persian Gulf region and without regional allies inclined to provide them.

To meet this general policy requirement, the discussion in this chapter focuses on three questions faced by civilian and military leaders in creating and executing this policy. First, which components of the US military should comprise this response force? In other words, should the mission be given to a single service or to multiple services in a joint framework? Second, and most controversially, what type of command entity should be established? Should this mission be given to an existing unified command? Or should a new geographic command be created to focus on Southwest Asia? Third, how should the military services make forces available to whatever command entity is established? Should they be formally assigned to the command, or just made available when needed? Should specific units be identified, or just generic capabilities? The case study focuses on these three general questions.

As such, this chapter does *not* focus on the normative questions that dominated the press coverage and editorials of this period. As the RDJTF was created and developed, myriad critics questioned whether the fledgling force could accomplish its putative mission.[16] James Schlesinger, former secretary of defense, penned a particularly memorable editorial entitled "Rapid(?) Deployment(?) Force(?)," in which he argued that the nascent force was neither rapid nor deployable nor much of a force.[17] Rather than engaging these debates, I focus here on the military services' efforts to help create and then implement those policies, however infeasible they may have been.

Given their enduring cultural beliefs, how might the Army and Marine Corps respond in shaping and implementing this evolving policy? A hypothesis matrix (fig. 6.1) maps the Army's six cultural beliefs onto the three focus areas described above, as well as a general category.[18] Several highlights deserve comment. First, the Army's self-conception as an apolitical servant of the nation (4.1) suggests that the Army will exhibit a cooperative civil-military posture, will engage in little if any advocacy with Congress, and will work hard to carry out whatever is decided. Second, the Army's self-appraisal as the nation's indispensable last line of defense (4.2) indicates that the service will not be particularly concerned with the security of its institutional position and will focus on concentrating sufficient mass and logistical sustainment to *finish* rather than just begin a war. The third Army belief in the matrix (4.3) concerns its preferred way of battle: using technology and firepower to win full and complete victories. This belief points to a likely preference for creating a military organization with sufficient mass, firepower, and command structure needed to win, not just to send a political signal.

Fourth, the Army's dependent posture on the other services and its persistent concern with synchronizing and coordinating combat units (4.4) suggest that the service will favor a full four-service approach to the problem, as well as a command arrangement that clarifies the chain of command and enhances unity of command. The Army's fifth belief, concerning the manpower requirement of expanding rapidly in wartime (4.5), implies that the service will show a keen interest in manning the new force, particularly the guard and reserve requirements that might accompany it. Finally, the Army's belief in organizing its forces in fixed, enduring units (4.6) predicts a unit-centric approach to fielding the new force, with a preference for keeping designated units intact and assigned to the force, rather than creating ad hoc task forces on a case-by-case basis.

The Marine Corps hypothesis matrix (fig. 6.2) predicts a different institutional response. First, the Marines' historical role as the nation's fast-acting warriors from the sea (3.1) has several implications across this policy space. The Marines can be expected to emphasize their capacity to send calibrated political signals, to respond quickly to global crises, and to *seize* new military bases by force, when needed. Similarly, this self-conception is likely to inspire the Marines to emphasize the degree to which this supposedly new mission requirement has been the Corps' historical specialty. This belief also suggests the Corps' employment preference will be according to its Marine Air-Ground Task Force (MAGTF) concept, in which the closest Marine forces get task-organized into tailored packages to meet a particular threat, rather than identifying specific units ahead of time.

Second, the Marine Corps' precarious institutional position (3.2) suggests that the Corps will be very alive to any potential threats to its domain or any duplication of its mission. Consequently, given that elements of the proposed rapid deployment mission overlap with the Marine Corps' jealously guarded domain, expect a determined effort to eliminate the threat. This belief predicts that the Marines will try either to make this initiative go away entirely or to take it over completely. While these first two beliefs are likely to dominate the Marines' response, the other three beliefs may affect the margins. The warrior-minded Corps (3.3) can be expected to handle whatever is thrown at

ARMY POLICY PREFERENCE HYPOTHESES

Belief	General approach	Which components of the US military should comprise the response force?	What type of command entity should be established?	How should the military services make forces available to this new entity?
4.1: Apolitical Servants of the Nation. *Faithful extension of American people. Members of profession of arms.*	Cooperative civil-military posture; little, if any, engagement or lobbying with Congress.			
4.2: Land Force of Last Resort. *The Army is an indispensable last line of defense, prepared to take more blame than credit.*	Not concerned with its institutional position or security; focused on finishing, rather than starting a war.	Focus on bringing forces with sufficient mass and logistical sustainment to finish a war.		
4.3: The Army Way of Battle. *Use technology and firepower to win total victories. Minimize political interference.*		Bring enough mass and firepower to win the war, not just send a political signal.	Create entity for battlefield effectiveness, not for political signaling.	

Belief		
4.4: Synchronizing the Fragments. *Waging war requires coordination, control, and synchronization.*	Support full joint effort with all services participating in integrated fashion.	For unity of command and coherence of effort, establish separate unified command for Persian Gulf region.
4.5: Fielding an Army: Regulars and the Militia. *Sufficient manpower is job #1. Army must be ready to expand.*	Both active duty and guard/reserve forces may be required.	For major conflict with Soviet Union, manpower will be critical factor. Be prepared to call up reserves.
4.6: Soldiers, Units, and Leaders. *Soldiers are building block. Designated units serve essential organizational and heraldic function. Leaders should have muddy boots.*	Create fixed organizational entity with dedicated and established units.	Focus on specific, designated units, not ad hoc structures.

Figure 6.1. The US Army's policy preference hypotheses on the key issues at stake in creation of the Rapid Deployment Joint Task Force. Each hypothesis is posited individually as a logical deduction of how each belief (numbered as in chapter 4) interacts with each policy issue.

MARINE CORPS POLICY PREFERENCE HYPOTHESES

Belief	General approach	Which components of the US military should comprise the response force?	What type of command entity should be established?	How should the military services make forces available to this new entity?
3.1: Warriors from the Sea. *An amphibious maritime force, deployed on naval ships, prepared to secure an American beachhead wherever directed.*	Focus on the Marines' constant global presence as part of the fleet; emphasize ability to respond flexibly to crisis, big or small.	Marines have been a rapidly deployable force since their inception in 1775. Mission should be—or at least can be—Marines only.	A minimalist and flexible command entity should be created that can draw swiftly from the Fleet Marine Forces.	Forces should be task-organized for particular missions, in keeping with the Marine Air-Ground Task Force concept (MAGTF).
3.2: Survive to Serve. *As the smallest of the services, the Marine Corps must vigilantly defend and promote its role in America's defense.*	Expect the Marines to be very concerned about defending their institutional position and mission; expect willingness to engage Congress and the American public as needed to defend its place.		Nothing should be created that remotely duplicates the statutorily protected roles and mission of the Marine Corps.	

Belief		
3.3: Elite Warrior Identity. *Being a Marine is an identity, not a profession. Marines run toward the sound of the guns and take care of their own.*	Marines can and will handle anything you throw at them.	
3.4: Faithful Stewards of the National Trust. *Marines are frugal warriors, making do with less, improvising, and taking care of their equipment.*	Expect willingness to make the best of any situation; expect willingness to improvise as needed to get job done.	
3.5: Every Marine a Rifleman. *All Marine Corps efforts coalesce in support of the Marine infantryman.*	Focus on getting battle-ready Marines into the fight. Heavy equipment and fancy toys are luxuries. Marines are essential.	The type of command entity is less important than getting Marine infantry into battle swiftly and aggressively.

Figure 6.2. The US Marine Corps' policy preference hypotheses on the key issues at stake in creation of the Rapid Deployment Joint Task Force. Each hypothesis is posited individually as a logical deduction of how each belief (numbered as in chapter 3) interacts with each policy issue.

it; the frugal Corps (3.4) will make it work on a shoestring; and the infantry-minded Corps (3.5) will emphasize getting rifle-bearing Marines into battle over any other tactical concern.

The chapter's conclusion revisits these hypotheses to assess how well the services' revealed preferences aligned with these culturally informed predictions.

Creation and Implementation of Presidential Directive 18: January 1977–August 1979

Within weeks of his inauguration in January 1977, President Jimmy Carter directed his National Security Council (NSC) to begin a wide range of strategic studies for the new administration. One of these studies included a "Comprehensive Net Assessment and Military Force Posture Review," overseen by National Security Advisor Zbigniew Brzezinski and actively led by Harvard political scientist Samuel Huntington.[19] In his net assessment, Huntington identified several potential crises; his most salient conclusion found that "from their viewpoint the Soviets would be hard-pressed to find a better spot than Iran for a crisis-confrontation with the U.S."[20] Brzezinski reviewed Huntington's assessment, together with the DOD's force posture review, and found a striking lack of US military capability to respond to the Soviets in Iran. Consequently, he recommended creating "a highly responsive, global strike force" to be prepared for short-notice deployments to non-NATO contingencies.[21]

Brzezinski's recommendation soon took the form of policy. On August 24, 1977, President Carter signed PD-18, entitled "U.S. National Strategy."[22] The directive focused primarily on the US-Soviet relationship, which appeared likely "to be characterized by both competition and cooperation" in the coming years. The directive also included a section on global contingencies that focused attention outside NATO commitments. Importantly, it specified that "the United States will maintain a deployment force of light divisions with strategic mobility independent of overseas bases and logistical support, which includes moderate naval and tactical air forces, and limited land combat forces."[23] This seemingly simple declaration, which would prove to be quite complex in execution, was the first tangible step in the creation of the CENTCOM giant.

Signed by President Carter, PD-18 became official national policy, and key officials soon began discussing it publicly. In September 1977, Secretary of Defense Harold Brown declared that the United States needed to complement its NATO-focused troops in Europe with a flexible and responsive force for other contingencies, to include "a limited number of relatively light land combat forces (such as the three Marine divisions and some light Army divisions); moderate naval and tactical air forces; and strategic mobility forces with the range and payload to minimize our dependence on overseas staging and logistical support bases."[24] In March of the following year, President Carter affirmed this requirement in a speech at Wake Forest University. Carter emphasized that the United States would support regional allies in the Middle East, while also maintaining forces of its own to handle crises. He acknowledged that the "Secretary of Defense, at my direction, is improving and will maintain quick deployable forces—air, land, and sea—to defend our interests throughout the world."[25]

The requirement for "a deployment force of light divisions" was therefore established policy, confirmed publicly by the president and secretary of defense. But this was not the only policy competing for attention. In addition to PD-18, Carter had signed a series of presidential directives pledging the United States to work toward nuclear nonproliferation and conventional arms control. Additionally, the new administration's first year focused on a second round of talks on the Strategic Arms Limitation Treaty (SALT II), arms control in the Indian Ocean region, a treaty to return control of the Panama Canal to Panama, and the historic Camp David peace agreement between Egypt and Israel.[26] To the extent that the administration focused on strengthening defense, the attention clearly went to European and NATO commitments. Forces in Europe were in very poor condition, and NATO's ability to mass forces swiftly to repel a Soviet invasion of central Europe had been called into question by the Army's Hollingsworth report in 1976.[27] Consequently, the main focus of the Defense Department's efforts, even as specified in PD-18, was on rebuilding and strengthening its NATO forces.

While the administration tried to focus on Europe and a peaceful accommodation with the Soviet Union, disturbing developments in the Middle East called for renewed attention. The Soviet Union was projecting power in Ethiopia, Yemen, and Afghanistan, while US ally Iran began seething with anti-shah and anti-US sentiment. In March 1979, one of Brzezinski's weekly reports to the president included a 13-page report entitled "Comprehensive Net Assessment 1978," detailing the NSC's most recent appraisal of the strategic balance with the Soviet Union. The assessment noted that within the previous two years, the Soviets had gained important footholds in Ethiopia, Afghanistan, and South Yemen, while the United States had been focusing its attention on Europe. Further, the assessment warned, "despite the emphasis in PD-18 on the need to enhance U.S. strategic mobility and to develop a quick reaction force, the unfavorable trend in power projection continues."[28]

Two key NSC meetings in May and June 1979 reinforced this renewed focus on the US military's ability to respond quickly to Mideast crises. First, on May 11, the principals agreed that "the Saudis have lost confidence in the US ability to help them manage their security problems, and that an important objective in our future plans is to reverse that perception."[29] Consequently, they discussed various strategies for strengthening US capability in the region, to include increasing American naval presence, prepositioning equipment at regional bases, and generating "the rapid capability to respond to requests for military assistance." A second round of important NSC meetings, held on June 21–22, 1979, concluded that "the Persian Gulf region has become a region ranking barely behind Northeast Asia and Europe in strategic importance."[30] The background papers prepared by the Defense Department for these NSC meetings conveyed an "acute anxiety based on the perception of vulnerability: US interests in the area are extremely vital; the potential threats to them are immediate and powerful; US capabilities in the area, under stress, are very weak."[31]

Carter and Brzezinski were both eager to learn what steps the DOD had taken to address its acute anxiety. On July 9, 1979, Brzezinski sent a memo to Secretary Brown asking for an update on the "Persian Gulf Contingency Forces."[32] Brzezinski reminded Brown of President Carter's clear directive in PD-18 to maintain a light deployment force, and he wanted to know what the DOD had specifically accomplished toward that end. Brzezinski followed up with a second memo to Brown on August 3, 1979, levying another request for an update.[33] President Carter was apparently underwhelmed by the military's efforts on the issue. His hand-written notes in the margin of a Brzezinski memo read: "I don't see that any progress has actually been made."[34]

What Had the Department of Defense Been Doing for Two Years?

Although the data are indeed limited, some evidence exists of DOD efforts to carry out the PD-18 requirement. The Pentagon conducted a deliberate strategy review in the summer of 1978, and the Joint Chiefs of Staff (JCS) sent its summary report to the secretary of defense in September 1978.[35] In its report, the JCS affirmed three major national interests in the region: ensuring access to oil, preventing "an inimical power or combination of powers from establishing hegemony," and defending the continued existence of the state of Israel.[36]

To secure those interests, the Joint Chiefs made a series of recommendations for an expanded military presence in the region by increasing deployments of US naval and Marine forces, improving facilities on the island of Diego Garcia in the Indian Ocean, and securing base-access agreements with Oman, Saudi Arabia, and Djibouti.[37]

The DOD's attention on the Persian Gulf increased significantly with the rising turmoil in Iran. After the shah was deposed, Secretary Brown met with the JCS in January 1979 to hear its plan for protecting Persian Gulf oil fields. Cobbled together by EUCOM, the plan was "rudimentary at best."[38] The deputy assistant secretary of defense for international security affairs, Robert Murray, recounted that the plan called for "all of the Army, all of the Air Force, most of the Navy and all of the Marines Corps, and they still couldn't tell you what the outcome would be."[39] Needless to say, Murray noted, "the secretary was underwhelmed." Secretary Brown personally visited regional allies in the Persian Gulf in February 1979, and on his return he tasked the JCS to draft a plan to improve US military presence in that critical region.[40] Without access to local bases, the JCS could do little more than recommend an extensive series of wargame exercises with regional allies, which might maintain a thin but continuous US military presence in the region.[41]

While the JCS reviewed national strategy and responded to Brown's requests, the military services took their own steps to implement the PD-18 guidance. The Army, for example, began developing a "unilateral corps" for rapid response to non-NATO emergencies. In June 1979, the outgoing chief of staff of the Army, General Bernard Rogers, noted that "the Army has always had . . . what we call the heavy/light corps, which was a spectrum of forces from a platoon of rangers all the way up to a three-division corps, with supporting forces, of about 100,000. We are designing what will be known as the unilateral corps, and it will be a spin-off from that heavy/light corps." When asked if the unilateral corps was just an idea or a plan, Rogers replied, "It is decided to do this. Now the Army intends to do this, and the Defense Department . . . also will ensure that the other Services have a capability along the same lines."[42] In a television interview three days later, Secretary Brown confirmed the four-service nature of the developing forces.[43]

Pulling together these various joint and service-centric efforts, Brown sent Brzezinski a formal reply to his memos in August 1979. He summarized the DOD effort by noting that "we have made some progress in the last two years; but the programs we have instituted since August 1977 are just now beginning to take effect, and most of our work is before us. Major changes in defense posture take five or more years—all the more reason for us to get on with it."[44] Brown attached several amplifying documents with details of the department's work. The first detailed the various forces that had been programmed for the so-called Rapid Deployment Force. The Army's forces included the 18th Airborne Corps headquarters, the 82nd Airborne Division, the 4th Mechanized Division, and the 194th Armored Brigade. The other three services listed only notional capabilities to include an undesignated Marine Amphibious Force, three carrier battle groups, and six Air Force flying wings.

A second attachment to Brown's memo included details on the various infrastructure-support improvements at Diego Garcia in the Indian Ocean. These efforts included improved fuel storage, a deeper anchorage for more ships, an expanded pier, and improved airfield facilities to include more ramp space and better maintenance structures. The last component of Brown's submission to Brzezinski included a background paper entitled "US Capability to Respond to Limited Contingencies."[45] The paper recognized the PD-18 requirement for a non-NATO contingency force, but identified a central problem in meeting that requirement: "very little of our earmarked contingency force can be *quickly* brought to bear in a Mideast crisis." The paper identified the lack of sufficient airlift to get to a distant theater of operations, the bottleneck of getting adequate logistics support to the Persian Gulf, and the fact that most of the Army's fast-response equipment was already prepositioned in Europe.[46] To address these challenges, the background paper noted several DOD initiatives to improve airlift capability and to rely on allies for increased sealift, but the net result was the same: the US military could not get far enough fast enough with sufficient force to stop a Soviet invasion of the Persian Gulf.

Assessing the Military Response

For this initial two-year period, what is a responsible appraisal of these civil-military interactions? Applying the four-square typology of principled agent theory (see fig. 1.2), the first step determines whether this is a case of implementing a more or less coherent policy (i.e., whether the period tends to occupy square I or square IV of the figure). To assess the relative coherence of the policy, the framework evaluates the clarity, consistency, and feasibility of what the military was being asked to do.

How clear was the policy requirement in Carter's August 1977 presidential directive? Unsurprisingly, the members of the National Security Council who were involved in creating the policy viewed the requirement as being quite clear. In his 2006 history of the period, for example, Brigadier General William Odom, who worked with Brzezinski and Huntington at the NSC, remarked straightforwardly that "PD-18 ordered the Pentagon to create a Rapid Deployment Force (RDF) for the Gulf region." From that clear appraisal, Odom argued that the "the Pentagon essentially ignored the directive to set up an RDF."[47] Given his role in the process, Odom's perspective is understandable, but the actual policy requirement was not so clear-cut. The language of PD-18 specified that "the United States will maintain a deployment force of light divisions"; the specific policy directed a force to be *maintained*, not created in the way Odom suggested. Furthermore, a formal entity known as the "Rapid Deployment Force" was not part of the conversation until 1979. Robert Komer, the undersecretary of defense for policy during this period, later noted the requirement for an RDF was "far too general and had failed to set in motion specific planning guidance."[48]

Similarly, the policy to create a rapid deployment force had little external consistency with the surrounding policy environment. The ecosystem of other demands served to distract from rather than reinforce a move to create an RDF; limited attention and resources were simply focused elsewhere. In fact, President Carter himself did not give much personal attention to a rapid deployment force until the latter half of 1979. Historians Frank Jones and Steven Rearden both correlate the tepid response to PD-18 with Carter's lack of attention. "Brzezinski and his staff could do little to advance [the RDF] beyond the conceptual stage," writes Jones, "because the president had no interest in it and did not view it as a priority."[49] Rearden assessed President Carter to be "a reluctant supporter to begin with," who "gradually lost interest in the idea."[50]

President Carter clearly had many other priorities competing for his attention; so did the military. The PD-18 specification to maintain light divisions for rapid mobility was one of many policy requirements levied upon a thinly stretched military force. Rebuilding and strengthening NATO forces comprised the top policy guidance for the DOD. Moreover, PD-18 shared a crowded policy space with other Carter administration efforts on SALT II, nuclear nonproliferation, and arms control efforts around the world but particularly in the Indian Ocean region. An NSC staff member at the time noted that "the new policies discouraging arms transfers and nuclear non-proliferation were applied indiscriminately in ways that weakened the emphasis upon enhanced strategic capabilities called for in [PD-18]."[51] The resulting policy confusion motivated an apt cartoon that hung on the walls of the Joint Staff's policy and plans directorate (J-5) in the summer of 1979. The cartoon depicted two American military generals arguing on the battlefield, one with a set of plans to defend Persian Gulf oil fields, the other with plans to attack them.[52]

Finally, the low feasibility of the policy prescription made compliance problematic at best. In the course of its strategic reviews, the JCS identified the lack of strategic airlift and sealift as critical factors that made full and complete implementation of the RDF impossible. Moreover, the PD-18 guidance did not have any associated budgetary initiatives or increases, making robust implementation essentially impossible without affecting force structures for NATO commitments.

Overall, the specific tasks the military was expected to perform in this phase were relatively unclear, at odds with competing policies, and difficult to achieve under the best of circumstances. As a case of civil-military relations, this period therefore falls within square IV of figure 1.2: implementation of a low-coherence policy. As the framework suggests, in this policy space the military agent is generally motivated by *how* to comply, not whether to do so. In figuring out the *how*, principled agent theory predicts that the services will fall back on culturally conditioned interpretations of what the policy requires.

So at this point, is this an example of poor civil-military relations, as conventional wisdom suggests? Clearly, the military response did not meet the full satisfaction of various elements within the executive branch. And it is certainly true that the Joint Chiefs did not create a new rapid deployment force with alacrity when PD-18 was signed. But that does not appear to be a responsible standard by which to evaluate the response. While the services did not act quickly to implement this aspect of PD-18, they prioritized their efforts in Europe in accordance with other elements of the very same presidential directive. Moreover, as the discussion above demonstrates, the JCS and the services did take various actions to strengthen US military capability in the Persian Gulf region.

Furthermore, as the military prioritized its attention and funding on Europe, it did maintain rapidly deployable forces for short-notice contingencies—however insufficient they might have been. The Army's 82nd Airborne Division airlifted by the Air Force, together with the Marine Corps deployed with the Navy, constituted an existing capability to meet the intent of the presidential directive. Testifying to the Senate in March 1980, senior defense official Walter Slocombe emphasized this fact: "First of all, while the terms 'rapid deployment forces' and 'power projection' are relatively new additions to the jargon, the military missions they signify are not new at all. The United States has been in the rapid deployment and power projection business for a long time. If you doubt that, I would suggest you ask the US Marine Corps, which five years ago celebrated its 200th anniversary."[53]

In summary, this initial phase of the RDJTF story does not offer easy categorizations of working or shirking. There is little evidence of a military agent deliberately shunning the work prescribed by the civilian principal. Instead, the military agent had the complex task of adjudicating competing demands, in an arena of limited time, attention, and resources. Working out the requirements of one policy entailed limited effort applied to another. In fact, a fair reading of the evidence suggests that the military worked surprisingly hard to carry out this challenging policy. Instead of being an instance of poor civil-military relations, the opposite may in fact be the case.

Creating and Implementing the Rapid Deployment Joint Task Force: August 1979–January 1981

To create a rapid military response for the Middle East, the DOD had to tackle the seemingly mundane element of organization. Who should own the mission? Geographically, EUCOM, PACOM, and REDCOM had different degrees of organizational interests in the Middle East. Functionally, the mission seemed to require both the responsiveness of the Marine Corps and the staying power of the Army. So should an existing unified command take on the mission? Or should the DOD create a new unified command, or perhaps give the mission entirely to one of the services? These difficult questions defied easy answers, consuming time and attention from civilian and military leaders alike.

In June 1979, Secretary of Defense Brown had sent the JCS a memo directing it to evaluate the command arrangements for the Middle East and Persian Gulf region.[54] To answer Brown's memo, the Joint Staff's plans and policy directorate (J-5) collected various inputs from the services and unified commands.[55] In compiling these inputs, staff officers in the J-5 realized that the right solution to the command arrangements depended on how one framed the problem. If the central issue involved defending sea lanes for safe passage of oil tankers, then it should be a PACOM mission. If the core problem was terrestrial defense and logistical sustainment, then EUCOM should have the lead. Finally, if the real problem was phased, orderly, and joint deployment, then perhaps REDCOM should own the new mission. Taking these views into account, the Joint Chiefs sent a 3–2 split-opinion memo to the secretary of defense in August 1979. The chairman of the Joint Chiefs, the chief of staff of the Army, and the chief of staff of the Air Force favored assigning the Middle East mission to REDCOM, with support from EUCOM for security assistance and contingencies. The chief of naval operations and commandant of the Marine Corps held a different view; they favored creating a joint task force (JTF), administratively under REDCOM, but with autonomy to "plan, exercise, and deploy forces to the Persian Gulf region."[56]

In addition to this input from the JCS, Secretary Brown gathered counsel from his key staff. The new undersecretary of defense for policy, Robert Komer, strongly supported the idea of a separate JTF focused on the Middle East. "When you have a new job to do," Komer argued, "you set up a new organization to do it—that's a fundamental principle of bureaucratic success."[57] Like Komer, Deputy Assistant Secretary of Defense Robert Murray believed the Middle East required a separate military command, but thought that creating a JTF was the right intermediate step. The situation required immediate action, and there was not time "to take apart the UCP"; creating a joint task force was "a reasonable starting point."[58] Taking these views into account, Secretary Brown issued his guidance to the JCS in October 1979. Heeding the views of the Navy–Marine Corps team and his top civilian advisors, Brown directed the JCS to establish a joint task force by March 1, 1980, with global responsibilities, but with an initial focus on "planning for rapid deployment force operations in the Middle East and Africa."[59] President Carter's general guidance in PD-18 thus took concrete form in Brown's October 1979 guidance. How, then, would the services go about implementing the policy?

Initial Implementation of the JTF Guidance

With an established directive to create a new joint task force, the Joint Chiefs started to work out the details. For whom should the JTF work? Where should it be based? And what forces should be part of it? When General Volney Warner, commander-in-chief of Readiness Command, heard about Secretary Brown's guidance, he immediately thought REDCOM was the natural choice to command and lead the new JTF. "That sounds as if Readiness Command should be in charge of this," Warner recalled thinking, "because that is what our mission is, to ensure the readiness of joint forces, maintain a headquarters to command them, and be prepared to deploy forces, headquarters, or both, to reinforce other unified commands at their request."[60] Warner also recalled speaking with Chief of Staff of the Army General Edward "Shy" Meyer about REDCOM taking the lead role, and Meyer agreed that it was an obvious fit for REDCOM.[61]

Warner and Meyer, however, were only two of many voices. In a staff memo prepared for the chairman of the JCS in early November 1979, the services shared their views on how to implement Brown's guidance. By that point, the proposed JTF had a name, the Rapid Deployment Joint Task Force, or RDJTF.[62] The Navy and Marine Corps opposed giving such formal recognition to a mere task force and also "objected to the implicit requirement that all Services assign forces to the JTF."[63] The Marine Corps proposed that the RDJTF be specifically linked to a particular geographic region or contingency, rather than giving it a global charter for any crisis that arose. Finally, the Army took issue with the force-structure model proposed by the Navy and Marine Corps, who wanted to tailor specific task forces in real time as crises required. Instead, in view of the demanding mission proposed, the Army wanted each service to identify units to form the pool from which the RDJTF would draw.

In late November 1979, the Joint Chiefs of Staff "approved the establishment of the Rapid Deployment Joint Task Force (RDJTF) Headquarters to be located at MacDill AFB, Florida, as a separate subordinate element of Headquarters, USREDCOM."[64] During peacetime activities such as planning, training, exercising, and preparing to deploy, this new RDJTF was to be under the operational command of General Warner at REDCOM. When the RDJTF deployed for an actual contingency, the commander of the RDJTF would then report to whichever unified commander had responsibility for the crisis location. The RDJTF had the initial task of planning for operations in the Middle East and Africa, but was on the hook for other regions as well, when directed by the Joint Chiefs.

The November 1979 decision memo made one other notable stipulation. Near the end of the memo, the JCS directed that "the RDJTF headquarters will include a small liaison staff established in the Washington, D.C., area." This Washington Liaison Office (WLO) was the brainchild of senior civilian leaders such as Brown, Komer, and Murray, who were convinced that the policy action was in Washington, that the best intelligence information was in Washington, and that the Middle East represented a very dynamic and politically sensitive region.[65] By creating a WLO in the Pentagon, the civilian leaders and JCS could keep a close eye on the RDJTF, ensuring it remained responsive to emerging political and military requirements. In practice, the WLO gave the RDJTF a direct foothold in the policy community that its new parent command (REDCOM) did not have.

In response to the Joint Chiefs' memo to create the RDJTF under REDCOM, the Marine Corps worked hard to ensure a prominent place at the table. First, the Marines were tasked with trailblazing the RDJTF with one of their 50,000-person Marine Amphibious Forces. In a December 1979 press conference, Marine Major General P. X. Kelley announced that the Marines "had been ordered to organize a 50,000-man spearhead for President Carter's Rapid Deployment Force."[66] During the press conference, Kelley acknowledged that while the RDJTF was not a Marine-only outfit, Marines were uniquely equipped to lead the way. "If you want to place a well-balanced unit" in a remote area, Kelley said, "we offer this better than most."[67] The commandant of the Marine Corps, General Robert Barrow, advocated for the Corps in a letter to the chairman of the JCS, Air Force General David Jones.[68] Barrow reminded the chairman that the Corps' "role as this nation's force in readiness is as important today as it was twenty-seven years ago," apparently referring to the 1952 Douglas-Mansfield Act that etched the Marine Corps force structure into law. Furthermore, Barrow emphasized that the Marine Corps offered a "small, highly mobile, efficient, combat-ready striking force, which could be deployed rapidly as this nation's 'first strike' capability . . . I want to ensure that these forces are properly utilized."[69]

Barrow also took up his case with Deputy Secretary of Defense Graham Claytor, petitioning for a Marine officer to be placed in charge of the RDJTF. "You know how many people on Capitol Hill and so forth think that this should be a Marine show," Barrow told Claytor. "If you really want to put the final polish on it, and make it look like it's going to amount to something, send a signal that a Marine is in charge."[70] Barrow's sense of congressional support for the Corps was apparently well founded. In December 1979, a group of 104 House members signed a letter to President Carter urging him to create a worldwide Marine military rescue force.[71] In the coming months, key senators endorsed the Corps not just as the *lead* element of the RDF but as the *entire* RDF. On March 6, 1980, Senator Gary Hart gave a floor speech arguing that "the entire Rapid Deployment Force mission should be assigned to the Marine Corps, rather than being split between the Army and the Marines as presently planned."[72] Barrow's efforts paid off, as Secretary Brown selected Marine Major General P. X. Kelley for a third star and command of the new RDJTF.

Congenital Birth Defects

In late February 1980, Chief of Staff of the Army General Edward Meyer, called Colonel Carl Stiner to his office.[73] Meyer summarily promoted Stiner to brigadier general and told him he had a job for him to do: he was going to work for P. X. Kelley to help establish a new joint task force. Stiner was on a plane to Tampa two days later, and sent an official message to the Pentagon activating the Rapid Deployment Joint Task Force on March 1, 1980.

Shortly after Stiner got the lights on, Kelley arrived from Washington and started assembling personnel from all four services to compose the RDJTF headquarters. The RDJTF was not a new military force per se, but a head-quarters element to provide command and control of forces from all four services when called to a crisis. As Kelley explained during one of his first congressional hearings as its commander, the RDJTF was "neither a separate nor discrete category of forces . . . The concept calls for a 'reservoir' of capabilities and units within the country and from this reservoir, primarily from CONUS bases, we would then tailor our forces for a specific contingency."[74]

From the start, however, the policy parameters established by the JCS and the Office of the Secretary of Defense made the RDJTF's early life quite diffi-cult. The Joint Chiefs had created the RDJTF as both separate from and sub-ordinate to REDCOM. This ambiguous policy compromise spurred friction between the RDJTF's attempts to be separate and REDCOM's attempts to keep it subordinate. General Warner at REDCOM believed that since a new task force had been created within his unified command, he had responsibility for its direction and execution. He also had strong feelings that REDCOM's char-ter was weak and that the RDJTF offered a vehicle for revitalizing REDCOM as a meaningful command. Warner thought that an empowered RDJTF within REDCOM could finally bring together the capabilities of each service into a meaningful four-service contingency response force.[75]

Warner's strong feelings prompted a flurry of communication to Secre-tary Brown and the Joint Chiefs of Staff. Within weeks of the RDJTF's formal activation, Warner sent multiple communiques to the secretary of defense, including an April 1980 memo to recommend that Brown make clear to all parties that the RDJTF was subordinate to REDCOM in all matters of pre-deployment planning, exercises, personnel, and budgeting.[76] Warner also pressed his case with the Joint Chiefs, emphasizing that command relation-ships between the RDJTF, REDCOM, and the other unified commands "must be clarified to permit the RDJTF to smoothly function within and through the unified command structure rather than establish a duplicative and competitive structure."[77]

Particularly odious to Warner was the existence of the RDJTF's Washington Liaison Office. "This sort of a liaison office," Warner discovered, "began to circumvent Readiness Command, and dealt direct with the RDJTF, giving orders, guidance, and direction."[78] Of course, the WLO's direct dealings with the RDJTF were part of its charter and purpose, as established by civilian authority. From Warner's point of view, however, the WLO filled the critical communications function that Readiness Command, by law, was supposed to fill. Warner argued to the Joint Chiefs that the WLO "establishes a special planning relationship with HQ RDJTF which bypasses the chain of command in which planning guidance from the JCS should pass through me to HQ RDJTF."[79] In short, Warner viewed the WLO as an affront to the unified command structure, a violation of the chain of command, and a duplicative staff structure that prevented REDCOM from exercising its proper command over the RDJTF, as directed by the Joint Chiefs.

While Warner pushed to subordinate the RDJTF more fully under REDCOM, Kelley tried to make the RDJTF concept work despite its tangled lines of authority. Kelley believed that the RDJTF's separate status communicated an important political signal of US commitment to the Persian Gulf region, and the WLO served an essential role in allowing the RDJTF to respond to the fluid direction of the National Command Authority (NCA).[80] In response to Warner's efforts to subordinate the RDJTF more clearly under REDCOM, Kelley sent a memo to Warner explaining his position. "It is my professional view," he wrote, "that the Washington Liaison Office is essential to the future success of the RDJTF . . . Moreover, while I admit that such an element may not be in keeping with more conventional traditions, I believe it responds to the desires of the NCA. If we are to provide timely and effective responses to the direction of the NCA and/or JCS, the Washington Liaison Office is essential to the process."[81]

Interservice Rivalry?

During this challenging two-year period, the US military grappled with internal disagreements about the best way to organize and create rapid deployment forces for the Middle East. The evidence presented above, however, offers a more complex story than mere interservice rivalry between the Army and the Marine Corps, as most histories of the period describe it. Instead, the primary axis of conflict seems to have been the incompatible relationship between the

RDJTF and Readiness Command. Given the command arrangements specified by the DOD and the JCS, organizational conflict was inevitable. The RDJTF was technically subordinate to REDCOM for all pre-deployment activity, but its geographic charter gave the RDJTF operational responsibilities for the Middle East that REDCOM *did not have*. In the view of Brigadier General Dale Vesser, head of the RDJTF's WLO, this contradiction created the main source of conflict, as Warner attempted to get involved in operational matters for which he had no responsibility.[82]

In late 1980 and early 1981, the conflict between Warner and Kelley spilled into the press, which resulted in the various descriptions of fractious interservice rivalry between the Army and the Marine Corps. While Warner was indeed an Army officer and Kelley a Marine, the Army–Marine Corps axis of conflict appears to be overdrawn. Compared with the RDJTF-REDCOM tension, far less evidence exists of a heated service-level feud between the Army and Marine Corps. None of the lead players in the RDJTF-REDCOM tension (Warner, Kelley, Stiner, and Vesser) could recall receiving any input from their respective service chiefs. When asked whether the Army and Marines were arguing over control of the RDJTF, Chief of Staff of the Army General Shy Meyer replied, "If there's going to be an argument, it's going to be a one-sided argument, because the Army is not going to argue with the Marines over this issue."[83] Meyer insisted that with 16 Army divisions, 3 Marine divisions, and an operational need for airborne, air assault, and light infantry forces, the mission required all the services; each would have plenty to do.

Several years later, Meyer recalled that the principal source of argument with the Marine Corps was not control of the RDJTF but rather "a power projection issue."[84] Since the primary obstacle to employing the RDJTF was transporting troops and equipment far enough and fast enough, the military and the DOD pursued an entire suite of mobility initiatives: a new aircraft for strategic airlift, maritime prepositioning ships, and a new fleet of fast sealift ships. Meyer believed the prepositioning strategy lacked flexibility, because all the gear was preloaded and thus not subject to adjustment. "We were much better off," Meyer reflected, "with all the divisions we have, with all things we have to do throughout the spectrum of warfare, to have a more flexible power projection force in the conventional arena." In sum, Meyer insisted that the debate hinged on identifying optimal means for strategic mobility, and "the arguments were not so much between the Army and Marines."[85]

Characterizing these disagreements as interservice rivalry misrepresents the nature of the debate. Interservice rivalry connotes services jockeying for prestige, mission turf, or dollars—fighting destructive internal battles instead of focusing on external ones. Such rivalries are often at odds with productive civil-military outcomes.[86] But in this case, the evidence portrays responsible military actors faithfully muddling through the contradictions of the policies given to them. The case reveals principled military agents carrying out assigned missions, clashing with one another as they did so.

Civil-Military Assessment

As discussed earlier, a principled agent framework makes general predictions about the military services' policy preferences in the light of their prevailing cultural beliefs. From the evidence cited above, thus far, the hypotheses outlined in figure 6.1 find a solid measure of support. The Army seemed to be cooperative in its civil-military posture, lobbied its position little if any, and did not appear to be institutionally threatened by the policy. It focused on flexible mobility initiatives to bring sufficient mass and firepower to any potential conflict, supported a full joint effort, favored (initially) a full unified command for the Middle East, and designated specific units for inclusion in the RDJTF reservoir of forces.

The Marine Corps' preference hypotheses likewise find support during this period. As predicted, the Marines were spirited in their defense of statutorily protected roles and missions; in fact, they enjoyed the vocal support of Congress to shore up those defenses. A large constituency within the Marine Corps even appeared willing to turn down funding and equipment for maritime prepositioning ships, fearing that such a task would detract from their core mission of amphibious assault.[87] The Corps also appeared ready and eager to own the RDF mission in its entirety; when a fully joint effort was mandated, Marines secured a prominent place at the table.[88] Next, the Marines were more attuned to the nuances of political signaling than their Army counterparts, as suggested by their maritime disposition. Finally, the commandant of the Marine Corps continually advocated for a command entity that was flexible and minimalist, that reported directly to the JCS/NCA, and that did not duplicate the roles and function of the Marine Corps.

The principled agent framework also makes predictions about the probable form of military behavior in varying political conditions. Like the first period in this case study (creation and implementation of PD-18), this two-year period occupies square IV of figure 1.2, where the military must carry out policy prescriptions that are relatively unclear, inconsistent, or infeasible. As predicted by the theory, the services did indeed respond differently to the civilian guidance, but those disagreements were adjudicated primarily within military structures, not civil-military ones. Informed by their unique belief structures, the services held differing conceptions of what compliance and sound strategy looked like. Overall, the aggregate impression of this period is one of intramilitary disagreement over the optimal strategy for *complying* with an ever-clearer civilian policy. The weight of military effort is toward compliance; the by-product of that compliance was acute intramilitary disagreement, to the frustration of their civilian principals.

The most compelling evidence for compliance is the military's acceptance of a seemingly impossible mission. As President Carter made increasingly muscular declarations about US commitments in the Middle East, the nation did not have the military capability to back up the rhetoric. Carter was acutely and uncomfortably aware of this fact. In December 1980, Carter confided to his NSC staff: "Entirely for the privacy of this meeting. It is hopeless to believe that we can match the Soviets with conventional forces in Iran. We simply cannot do it."[89] This fact was clearly not lost on the military forces tasked to execute the impossible policy, who nonetheless worked hard to make it happen. General Kelley understood that the RDJTF was a commitment device—a political signal. The purpose of such a force was not to defeat the enemy, but to stake a claim. For the military members working hard to serve as a global tripwire, this appears to be an unusually committed form of compliance. Once again, the overall tenor of civil-military relations in this period depicts a military agent grappling with how best to comply, not making a material calculation of whether or not to do so.

Transition from RDJTF to USCENTCOM: January 1981–January 1983

When Ronald Reagan entered the White House in January 1981, his national security team inherited a pile of intelligence and policy information from Carter's outgoing staff. Within the National Security Council, Brigadier General William Odom ensured that the new NSC staff clearly appreciated the wisdom of creating a new unified command for the Middle East.[90] In the previous months, Odom had urged President Carter to order a change to the Unified Command Plan, even drafting a memo to Brzezinski on election day with one last attempt. Once the election was over, Odom wrote, "a Unified Command should simply be ordered by the President . . . No study is needed."[91] Carter chose not to do so, and the action passed to the Reagan team. In February 1981, several weeks into the new administration, Odom sent the new national security advisor, Richard Allen, a memo with clear words on what needed to happen. "Our own military command and control for the [Persian Gulf] region is in a shambles," Odom observed, "and the JCS is institutionally incapable of improving it. The inter-service quarrels, particularly on the 'Unified Command Plan,' are paralyzing. The big ones will not be settled without direct orders from the President which are delivered in unambiguous words."[92] Allen's military assistant, Major General Robert Schweitzer, followed through with this advice and took the issue straight to President Reagan, ensuring that the RDJTF, the Middle East, and the UCP were on the new president's radar. In turn, Reagan delegated to Secretary of Defense Caspar Weinberger the lead role in deciding the fate of the RDJTF and the US military posture in the Middle East.

Military Advice on the Evolving Policy

In the months that followed, the service chiefs, General Warner, and General Kelley all had ample opportunity to express their views to Secretary Weinberger on the proper future of the RDJTF. The tense working environment at MacDill clearly merited a change of some kind. Should the RDJTF stay within REDCOM, but with improved working parameters? Should the RDJTF shift to EUCOM or PACOM, which already had some geographic responsibility for the Middle East? Or should the RDJTF be an autonomous entity—possibly a unified command—working directly for the JCS? These questions dominated public and private debates and even became the subject of congressional inquiry.

The chief of staff of the Army, General Meyer, articulated a consistent Army position in congressional testimony, in various staff documents, and later in his oral history interviews. Broadly, Meyer favored a robust four-service approach, with flexible options for strategic mobility, moving eventually toward a full unified command for the Middle East—but with an interim step of moving the RDJTF under EUCOM's authority. Testifying before the Senate Armed Services Committee (SASC) in late January 1981, Meyer emphasized that "the Army can't go to war alone. I am not sure that any of the services can go to war alone . . . I believe that we must look across all of the services to insure a composite ability to carry out whatever contingencies this Nation expects us to meet."[93] At the close of the hearing, in response to a question about the Army's proper role in the RDF, Meyer's written answer (for the record) was equally ecumenical: "Each Service has unique force capabilities that are essential to the Rapid Deployment Force concept . . . In short, it is the combination of unique Service capabilities tailored for the specific situation at hand that is the strength of the RDF concept."[94]

Later in the SASC hearings, Meyer outlined his view on the proper future of the RDJTF as a unified command. When asked about the wisdom of creating a new unified command for the Middle East, Meyer replied, "A unified command would have significant military advantages: establish unity of command, enable optimum command and control . . . From a military standpoint, there would be few, if any, disadvantages."[95] As an interim solution, however, Meyer supported placing the RDJTF under EUCOM until a command headquarters could be established in the region.[96]

The commandant of the Marine Corps, General Robert Barrow, articulated a different view. In his public testimony to Congress, Barrow consistently pressed for sequential military operations led by the Navy–Marine Corps maritime team. Instead of insisting that all four services participate in every operation, Barrow argued for giving the lead to the capable and forward-deployed force that has always performed that role: Navy ships carrying warrior Marines. If a given task exceeded the Marines' capability, they could call in reinforcements from the other services. Joint operations should be sequential rather than simultaneous, Barrow suggested. During a January 1981 SASC hearing, for example, General Barrow testified:

> First, we are convinced that there is considerable commonality between what is termed 'RDF' and the congressionally mandated roles and functions of the Marine Corps. Indeed, when PD-18 and the initial Secretary of Defense guidance on the Rapid Deployment Force (RDF) were published, we took the position that today's Marine Corps precisely fits that definition. We have never altered that position. We also happen to believe that the Indian Ocean / Persian Gulf region is ideally suited for employing Naval power. If a land campaign ensues, Naval forces are especially suited to either provide the total response in the case of minor contingencies, or to serve as the spearhead for a larger force in the event of Soviet involvement.[97]

Based on this logic, Barrow favored getting rid of the RDJTF altogether and transferring responsibility for Middle East contingencies entirely to Pacific Command, "who already has the major in-being presence there in the form of naval forces."[98] Since the United States lacked military bases in the Middle East, Barrow argued that leaning heavily on naval forces as first responders made the best strategic sense. In the end, Barrow summarized his critique of the entire RDF (or RDJTF) concept by saying, "it is regrettable that we have something called the Rapid Deployment Force. There is no such animal; it is a label without a product. There is no way you can get there rapidly."[99]

General Warner at REDCOM consistently pressed for strengthening the unified command system rather than creating ad hoc joint task forces to deal with various crises as they arose. Consequently, he favored a long-term transition to a new unified command for the Middle East, once a regional command headquarters could be found. In the interim, Warner argued for a revitalized status quo, with Readiness Command operating as a robust four-service global response force. In fact, Warner delivered a three-page letter to Secretary Weinberger in January 1981, on Weinberger's first day in charge of the Pentagon, with a list of six suggested actions for his new boss.[100] His recommended actions included revitalizing the unified command plan, consolidating various ad hoc task forces under REDCOM, abolishing the Washington Liaison Office of the RDJTF, and giving CINCs input into the budget process.[101] Warner followed up with another letter in early March 1981, as Weinberger solicited inputs on the future of the RDJTF.[102] In this letter, Warner once again emphasized the importance of working *through* the unified command system and not around it.

Finally, the commander of the RDJTF, Lieutenant General Kelley, offered still another view. In his SASC testimony, Kelley argued for strengthened unity of command, giving a commander "direct access to the forces he would command in combat," and a strengthened role for the part played by the RDJTF in national security.[103] In short, Kelley recommended transitioning the RDJTF into a unified command.

The Secretary's Decision

Taking all these options under consideration, Weinberger opted for a hybrid. His April 1981 press release read: "The Secretary of Defense announced today that over a period of three to five years the Rapid Deployment Joint Task Force (RDJTF) should evolve into a separate unified command—with its own geographic responsibilities, Service components, forces, intelligence, communications, logistics facilities and other support elements."[104] Weinberger decided to transition the RDJTF into a unified command slowly, keeping the status quo in the meantime. The press release concluded: "For the time being, relationships among the present unified commands will not change, and the RDJTF headquarters will continue to be located at MacDill Air Force Base in Florida. Nor will its mission change. The RDJTF will continue to have a potential for world-wide deployment, but its major focus will remain on South-west Asia."[105]

General Warner at Readiness Command clearly did not agree with the decision and summarily retired from the Army in frustration—though, curiously, his parting shots were directed at the JCS, not at his civilian bosses.[106] The service chiefs did not particularly agree with the decision either, but they had the task of executing it. They submitted their initial transition plan to Weinberger in May 1981, which included a three-stage evolution over an 18-month period.[107] The first stage lasted through the fall of 1981 and preserved the status quo—the RDJTF remained under the operational command of REDCOM. The second stage began in October 1981, when the RDJTF moved out from under the authority of REDCOM and became a fully independent joint task force, reporting directly to the secretary of defense through the JCS. The third phase involved the final transition into a full unified command, with a target date of January 1, 1983. While thorny issues surfaced in the transition—most notably, where to draw the boundaries around the new command's geographic area of responsibility—the transition proceeded as planned.[108] On schedule, the RDJTF was inactivated on December 31, 1982, and US Central Command was established in its place the following day. After 1,036 days of contentious existence, the RDJTF was history.[109]

Civil-Military Assessment

How well do the service preferences and civil-military interactions in this final period align with the principled agent framework? The Army's position remained largely consistent with the previous phase, and thus accorded quite well with the theoretical hypotheses. The Army did not seem to engage in external advocacy, while Meyer continued to push for a full four-service organization and an eventual unified command. Further, the Army's support for a transitional phase for the RDJTF under EUCOM was consistent with a focus on long-term sustainment and logistical flow. As explained by a Joint Staff paper in 1981, the Army favored putting the RDJTF under EUCOM, "recognizing that the major flow of men and equipment from CONUS to the region would be through EUCOM's area of responsibility and into the major states traditionally within EUCOM's purview (e.g., Egypt, Saudi Arabia)."[110]

The Marine Corps' position likewise strengthened in this third phase, with General Barrow articulating increasingly clearly the Marine Corps view. The Marines clearly favored a Marine-first, and possibly Marine-only, approach to contingency operations—a view consistent with the Marines' maritime orientation toward national security and their institutional proclivity for guarding their flanks. The Marines' focus was getting to the fight first, establishing a beachhead of American presence, and then assessing the situation from there. Further, Barrow remained attuned to the calibrated political signals afforded by Marine amphibious forces deployed globally on Navy ships. Finally, the Marine Corps displayed a keen sensitivity to the interests of Congress and the American people. Emblematic of the Corps' approach during this period, Barrow assured the SASC in January 1981 that, most importantly, "we continue to be deeply conscious of the expectations you and the public at large have in terms of being ready to go on short notice. That is deeply embedded in the Marine consciousness; it always has been and always will be."[111]

The civil-military interactions continued to reverberate in a low-coherence environment, as military agents advised on and pursued options for how best to comply with a challenging strategic mandate. The Marine Corps did indeed push hard for a Marine-centric approach to Middle East contingencies, as a bureaucratic explanation would predict. But the Marine view had both logic and evidence on its side, with a legitimate strategic rationale for why such an approach was the best way to link the desired ends of national policy with limited means. The Army was *not* pushing for an Army-centric or Army-only approach and was not interested in defending its flanks or protecting its mission—a difference in attitude predicted and explained by the principled agent framework.

In summary, the evidence in this period suggests that the main military disagreements derived from different approaches to a complex strategic problem. Bureaucratic interests may indeed have been present, but they do not tell the whole—or even most—of the story. The crafting and execution of a complex military strategy was not a straightforward matter of compliance or disobedience. These issues teemed with ambiguity, uncertainty, and political judgments. The evidence here suggests a larger conclusion that intramilitary disagreements do not necessarily constitute reflexive interservice rivalry, but can be seen as legitimate strategic debates informed by competing first principles.

Conclusion

This chapter has traced the arc of American military strategy in the Middle East from President Jimmy Carter's directive in August 1977 through President Ronald Reagan's establishment of US Central Command in January 1983. For the first two years, Carter's directive saw little concrete implementation, as higher-priority events and limited resources diverted attention elsewhere. For the next two years, the Rapid Deployment Joint Task Force secured a tentative and contentious foothold in the Middle East, organizationally if not materially. Finally, the last two years witnessed the transition of the RDJTF from the subjugated stepchild of Readiness Command into an independent entity and, eventually, a full unified command.

This case study of civil-military relations examines why the military agents responded as they did to the initiatives of their civilian principals. The evidence marshaled here challenges the conventional wisdom—a wisdom that indicts the military for dragging its feet, ignoring a presidential directive, and then nearly ruining the president's plan in a petty contest for control. Like most stories of political intrigue, a deeper look reveals that the story is not so simple.

In this difficult case of civil-military interaction, the evolving civilian policy reached into the uncertain domain of military strategy—a messy process of applying prudential judgments to align ways and means with political ends. Although civil-military and intramilitary friction suffused the narrative, it appears that, by and large, the military was trying to figure out where to go, not how to go its own way. Within this ambiguous policy environment, the services did indeed have different preferences for how the policy should unfold. How closely did their preferences accord with the hypotheses offered at the beginning of the chapter?

Figures 6.3 and 6.4 revisit the policy preference hypotheses of the Army and Marine Corps. Hypotheses in bold found strong support in the data, those in plain text had some support, and those in italic found little to no support in the available evidence. A skeptical reader may well object that this congruence is contrived, as the *ex ante* predictions could have been made with full knowledge of the case. It is true that the congruence procedure is at risk of malpractice, like any social scientific method. But two brief responses can be made. First, methodologically, the preference hypotheses were made in good faith as soon in the research process as the central issues became clear. Each hypothesis attempted a responsible juxtaposition of the belief with the issue; the finding that several hypotheses end up unsupported by the data reflects this honest effort. Second, if the hypotheses appear contrived merely to suit the case, what would a more responsible deduction look like? A skeptic can do his own congruence analysis, making reasonable deductions about the likely implication of each belief for each issue, then compare the two deduction patterns against one another to see which passes the higher reasonableness standard. I argue that such an exercise would reveal that the hypotheses here are indeed a defensible treatment of the ideas and issues.

Overall, most of the Army's hypotheses had strong or some support (fig. 6.3), particularly the service's overall posture of nonthreatened engagement, its support for a full unified command, its designation of specific units for the RDJTF, and its advocacy for a full four-service solution. The Army did, of course, engage in some intramilitary disagreements, but its civil-military posture remained generally cooperative and pliant.[112]

Figure 6.4 considers the Marine Corps hypotheses, and likewise finds generally good support for most of the predictions. As discussed throughout the chapter, the data strongly support the Corps' focus on its maritime presence, its capacity to go first and go solo, its engagement with Congress and the American people, and its efforts to guard its domain by preventing any duplication of its mission by an external actor. While basic differences between the Army and the Marine Corps may not be obvious to an outside observer, the portraits sketched earlier in the book exposed the many ways in which these two organizations differ culturally. Those differences, in turn, translated into different responses to the evolving civilian policies seen in this case.

The theory and evidence amassed in this case study yield several conclusions. First, the initial two-year phase is not a simple story of the military ignoring the president. Instead, the analysis affirms that a new civil-military policy often enters a cluttered and chaotic policy environment, which challenges a military agent to comply faithfully with competing demands. In this case, the PD-18 requirement to "maintain a deployment force of light divisions" interacted and competed with other initiatives such as SALT II, nuclear nonproliferation, arms control, and rebuilding NATO forces. Furthermore, the explicit military priorities established by the president and secretary of defense were on Europe, not the Middle East. Any evaluation of military shirking or noncompliance, therefore, should be alive to the possibility that such shirking is merely the by-product of complying with a higher priority.

A second insight emerging from this initial two-year phase reflects the importance of robust civil-military dialogue before a decision is made. The PD-18 requirement sprang from the analysis and conclusions of civilian staffers on the NSC, without formal military input. As a result, the policy-drafters had little appreciation for the magnitude of the task imposed on the policy-implementers. Not until the summer of 1979, two years after PD-18, did NSC staffers start to meet with the Joint Staff to discuss the RDF policy.[113] Through these meetings, the staffers slowly began to understand the magnitude of the requirement that PD-18 had levied. Only then did they realize that the logistics of projecting a capable force—rapidly or not—over thousands of miles was well beyond the military's existing capability. Lawful civilian authorities have the right to create whatever policies they choose, but this case highlights that full compliance with some policies may be structurally unattainable in the short run.

A third insight finds that the quality of military compliance often correlates with the quality of the policy itself. Due to political expediency and the nature of political compromise, certain policies issued to the military may have contradictions woven into their original fabric. The RDJTF's early years epitomize this phenomenon. As Robert Murray observed, Secretary Brown made a logical decision to create a joint task force rather than a unified command because *something* needed to happen; creating a JTF was much faster than changing the Unified Command Plan.[114] Furthermore, the JCS had logical reasons for situating the RDJTF under the peacetime authority of Readiness Command, and Secretary Brown had logical reasons for creating a Washington Liaison Office for the RDJTF. These policy components, logical in isolation, combined to create an illogical product. One senior Pentagon official observed that "the conflict is built in, almost as if somebody set out to say, 'let's see if we can make this thing awkward or maybe even unworkable.'"[115] In fact, to resolve the impracticalities of the policy, some officials in the DOD wanted certain elements in the military *not* to carry out their assigned responsibilities. As one senior official commented, "the working arrangement was that on paper Readiness Command had some responsibility; in practice, it wasn't supposed to exercise those responsibilities."[116] In other words, the job of particular military agents was not to do their job; working was shirking, and vice versa. Clearly, conventional agency categories of working and shirking fall short of a satisfying explanation in this case.

Finally, this case reinforces the true insight in the book's opening story of the four services securing the building in four different ways. Crafting and executing difficult military strategy is an exercise in uncertainty. Framing the problem, gathering resources, and deciding on operational approaches all require prudential judgments—there are no right answers or clear paths of compliance. Consequently, a policy directive to create and execute military strategy naturally animates the different belief patterns of the four services. Given their unique histories and operational requirements, the four services approach the framing, resourcing, and tackling of problems in different ways. The Army and Marine Corps in this case responded differently to the strategic problem

ARMY POLICY PREFERENCE FINDINGS

Belief	General approach	Which components of the US military should comprise the response force?	What type of command entity should be established?	How should the military services make forces available to this new entity?
4.1: Apolitical Servants of the Nation	• Cooperative civil-military posture • **Little if any engagement/lobbying with Congress.**			
4.2: Land Force of Last Resort	• **Expect the Army not to be concerned with its institutional position or security.** • Focus on finishing, rather than starting a war.	**Focus on bringing forces with sufficient mass and logistical sustainment to finish a war.**		
4.3: The Army Way of Battle		**Bring enough mass and firepower to win the war, not just send a political signal.**	*Create entity for battlefield effectiveness, not for political signaling.*	

	Support full joint effort with all services participating.	For unity of command and coherence of effort, establish separate unified command for Persian Gulf region.	
4.4: Synchronizing the Fragments		**For unity of command and coherence of effort, establish separate unified command for Persian Gulf region.**	
4.5: Fielding an Army: Regulars and the Militia	Both active duty and guard/reserve forces may be required.		For major conflict with Soviet Union, manpower will be critical factor. Be prepared to call up reserves.
4.6: Soldiers, Units, and Leaders		**Create fixed organizational entity with dedicated and established units.**	**Focus on specific, designated units, not ad hoc structures.**

Figure 6.3. The US Army's policy preference findings. Hypotheses with strong support in the available evidence are in **bold**; hypotheses with some support are in plain type; and hypotheses with no meaningful support in the available evidence are in *italic*.

MARINE CORPS POLICY PREFERENCE FINDINGS

Belief	General approach	Which components of the US military should comprise the response force?	What type of command entity should be established?	How should the military services make forces available to this new entity?
3.1: Warriors from the Sea	• **Focus on the Marines' constant global presence as part of the fleet.** • **Emphasize ability to respond flexibly to crisis, big or small.**	**Marines have been a rapidly deployable force since their inception in 1775. Mission should be—or at least can be—Marines only.**	*A minimalist and flexible command entity should be created that can draw swiftly from the Fleet Marine Forces.*	Forces should be task-organized for particular missions, in keeping with the Marine Air-Ground Task Force concept (MAGTF).
3.2: Survive to Serve	• **Expect the Marines to be very concerned about defending their institutional position and mission.** • **Expect willingness to engage Congress and the American public as needed to defend its place.**		**Nothing should be created that remotely duplicates the statutorily protected roles and mission of the Marine Corps.**	

3.3: Elite Warrior Identity		Marines can and will handle anything you throw at them.
3.4: Faithful Stewards of the National Trust	• Expect willingness to make the best of any situation. • Expect willingness to improvise as needed to get job done.	
3.5: Every Marine a Rifleman	**Focus on getting battle-ready Marines into the fight. Heavy equipment and fancy toys are luxuries. Marines are essential.**	*The type of command entity is less important than getting Marine infantry into battle swiftly and aggressively.*

Figure 6.4. The US Marine Corps' policy preference findings. Hypotheses with strong support in the available evidence are in **bold**; hypotheses with some support are in plain type; and hypotheses with no meaningful support in the available evidence are in *italic*.

of projecting power to the Middle East. On balance, those differences were predicted by the cultural typologies of each service, representing service interpretations of *how* to comply rather than material calculations of whether to do so.

Principled agent theory offers new ways of predicting and explaining the civil-military interactions in the creation and development of the RDJTF. The framework predicted service preferences on the basis of enduring cultural beliefs, and then explained patterns of civil-military interactions with its three-axis expansion of traditional agency theory. The framework attempts to merge cultural predispositions with principal-agent calculations, recognizing that bureaucratic self-interest naturally comingles with culturally informed preferences. In other words, military leaders are apt to view and pursue the national interest through the prism afforded by their long-standing service culture. Whereas a bureaucratic politics model views the services as predictable black-box actors clamoring for fixed pots of mission turf, power, and money, the principled agent approach argues that the services have unique, service-specific preferences for *both* the national interest and the security of their service—two categories that tend to overlap closely in the minds of senior military leaders. Each service tends to appraise the "good of the nation" and the "good of the service" in a way that conflates the two concepts, and these appraisals look quite different from one service to the next. Understanding the full texture of American civil-military relations therefore requires an empathic appreciation of each service's pervasive beliefs about its ends, ways, and means.

The next chapter carries these ideas further, presenting a complementary case from the top left square of the four-square principled agent typology. In debating the Goldwater-Nichols legislation of 1986, civil and military actors put *preparatory agency* dynamics on full display.

chapter 7

Getting to Yes

Passing the Goldwater-Nichols Act of 1986

Each service holds certain parochial beliefs dearly. These ideas may
not be rational by some criteria, but that is irrelevant.

—Admiral William J. Crowe, *The Line of Fire*

In September 1986, when Congress sent a hard-fought bill to the White
House, Representative Les Aspin effused: "This is one of the landmark laws
of American history. It is probably the greatest sea change in the history of the
American military since the Continental Congress created the Continental
Army in 1775."[1] The Goldwater-Nichols Department of Defense Reorganization Act of 1986 remains the law of the land and a major force in US military
organization and policy. As a case study of civil-military interaction, this chapter examines the fractious four-year period from 1982 to 1986 that led to its
passage. During that time, key actors sparred over a fundamental question
of national security: how should power be distributed within the defense establishment? When it finally passed, the act made the chairman of the Joint
Chiefs of Staff (CJCS) the principal military advisor to the president, created
the position of vice chairman, took steps to enhance the quality of officers
assigned to the Joint Staff, and strengthened the authority of the unified and
specified commanders over their service components. These provisions endure, casting a long shadow over modern military history.

This chapter provides a second empirical test of principled agent theory.
The discussion here by no means provides a complete legislative history of
Goldwater-Nichols—other works capably recount the unique alignment of
events and actors that enabled such comprehensive reform.[2] Instead, it focuses
more narrowly on specific actors and variables within the story, while remaining true to the wider narrative. The chapter specifically highlights the actions
of the Army and Navy and offers an explanation for their responses to various

reorganization proposals—why they were similar at times, and why they often differed.

This case offers a useful complement to that of the Rapid Deployment Joint Task Force. While the latter focused primarily on advising and implementing low-coherence policies, the passage of Goldwater-Nichols animates other dimensions of principled agent theory. This case generally inhabits square II ("preparatory agency") of figure 1.2, with military agents offering pre-decisional advice to their civilian principals on reasonably coherent policy issues. Under these conditions, the argument expects civil-military actors to negotiate the specificity, imminence, durability, and enforceability of a debated policy, while pursuing more implementation slack for disfavored policies and less slack for preferred ones. The four-year debate culminating in Goldwater-Nichols puts these dynamics center stage.

The Goldwater-Nichols debate offers a rich but finite period for civil-military analysis. Between 1982 and 1986, many different proposals were introduced, discarded, and eventually approved, and the debates covered several related but distinct areas. Looking at these multiple issues allows us to hold the environmental factors constant and ask why some issues prompted conflict while others did not. The story also shows meaningful variation in the services' behavior, as the Army and Navy at times responded differently to the same policy proposals. This variation is compelling because the Goldwater-Nichols case does not involve issues in which bureaucratic theory expects much variation or disagreement among the services. The Army and Navy were not fighting over limited dollars or over acquiring major weapon systems or assigning roles and missions. Without these conventional bureaucratic issues in play, the diversity of service responses is more puzzling and in need of explanation.

After situating the Goldwater-Nichols debate in its historical context, I summarize the key issues at stake, with analytic deductions about the likely fact and form of Army and Navy responses to those issues. The three narrative sections are organized around major congressional hearings, as these provide valuable opportunities to assess and compare the publicly stated preferences of the Army and Navy throughout the four-year period. The first period begins in February 1982, when the dormant issues of defense organization came back to life, culminating in a major round of congressional hearings in the spring and summer of that year. The second period covers the summer and fall of 1983, when two more rounds of hearings were held before the House and Senate. The final narrative section evaluates the period from publication of the Senate Armed Services Committee (SASC) Staff Study in October 1985 through the final stroke of President Ronald Reagan's pen in October 1986.

Background on Defense Reform

The substantive issues that dominated the defense reform agenda between 1982 and 1986 descended from equally spirited contests in the post–World War II era. When the United States entered World War II in December 1941, the US military had few robust mechanisms to coordinate action between the various services. The War Department and Navy Department operated independently, with few organizational or procedural channels for coordination. The Joint Chiefs of Staff (JCS) did not yet exist, and the main institutional vehicle for aligning the activities of the military services was the intermittently effective Joint Board, comprising four senior officers each from the Army and Navy.[3] The impetus for creating the formal Joint Chiefs of Staff came from mirroring the British military, whose Chiefs of Staff Committee accompanied Winston Churchill to the Arcadia conference in December 1941 through January 1942.[4] During the conference, the US military merely adopted the British model and created the "Joint US Chiefs of Staff," later shortened to the now familiar Joint Chiefs of Staff.[5] From then on, the JCS operated with de facto authority conferred by President Franklin Roosevelt, but he never formally established the JCS with a specific charter or mandate.[6] The JCS operated as a type of super-cabinet for Roosevelt, conferring with him directly and frequently on matters of grand strategy, effectively bypassing the civilian service secretaries structurally positioned between the military chiefs and the president.[7]

As World War II progressed, the Joint Chiefs looked ahead to the postwar world and the organizational structure it would require. At a JCS meeting in November 1943, Chief of Staff of the Army General George Marshall initially proposed unifying the War and Navy departments into a single department of national defense.[8] The War and Navy departments had operated as autonomous cabinet-level departments for more than 150 years, with no common superior below the president himself.[9] Marshall's suggestion launched decades of bitter debate about the wisdom of unifying the military departments into a single organization. The services volleyed proposals back and forth. The Army pushed for an organizational structure equipped for unified action, while the Navy insisted on an independent structure for naval affairs.

The core issues centered on the distribution of power among the various participants in the national defense structure: the JCS, the military departments, the commanders-in-chief (CINCs) of the unified and specified commands, the civilian secretaries, the president, and Congress.[10] In December 1945, President Harry Truman weighed in forcefully on the debate, calling for a unified defense establishment, a single civilian defense secretary, and a single military chief of staff. "The President, as Commander-in-Chief, should not personally have to coordinate the Army and Navy and Air Force," wrote Truman. "He should be able to rely for that coordination upon civilian hands at the Cabinet level."[11] Following years of highly contentious debate, the services, Congress, and the president eventually hammered out their differences, and Truman signed the National Security Act on July 26, 1947.[12]

The National Security Act, like many pieces of major legislation, was the imperfect offspring of political compromise, not a pure expression of coherent discourse. With so much at stake, and with impassioned views on all sides of the issue, some of the compromises made to pass the bill weakened its intent. "Ironically," argues political scientist Amy Zegart, "the very importance of the Joint Chiefs of Staff guaranteed it would be poorly designed to serve the national interest."[13] The act created the National Military Establishment, headed by a new secretary of defense who received authority to "exercise general direction, authority, and control over such departments and agencies."[14] The act also created the United States Air Force as a separate military service, changed the War Department to the Department of the Army, and stipulated three separate cabinet-level service secretaries over the Departments of the Army, Navy, and Air Force. Finally, the act formally created the JCS and designated the Joint Chiefs as the "principal military advisers to the President and the Secretary of Defense." To support the JCS, the legislation provided a Joint Staff with no more than 100 officers.

From the beginning, the National Military Establishment suffered from the weaknesses inherent in its creation. In December 1948, Secretary of Defense James Forrestal provided his first report to Congress and lamented the structural weakness of his position, despite his putative authority.[15] President Truman agreed with Forrestal and petitioned Congress to update the law to give the defense secretary more formal authority. After forcing Congress to act by submitting a reorganization proposal of his own, Truman signed an amendment to the National Security Act on August 10, 1949. The amendment created the Department of Defense (DOD) in place of the National Military Establishment and subordinated the service departments as military departments within the DOD; it removed the word "general" from the secretary of defense's "direction, authority, and control" over the department; it increased the size of the Joint Staff from 100 to 210 officers; and it created the position of chairman of the Joint Chiefs of Staff to serve as a nonvoting presiding officer, without military command authority, and to serve as a liaison between the president and the JCS.[16]

Despite the intentions of the 1949 amendment, the defense establishment still suffered from inherent deficiencies immune to legislative tinkering. When President Dwight Eisenhower came into office in 1953, he identified a root cause of the enduring dysfunction. Eisenhower recognized that the four services held most of the political power, and the institutions designed to integrate the service perspectives had too little power to do so effectively. He therefore spent his political (and military) capital treating four prevailing symptoms of this core issue.[17] First, the chairman lacked independent authority over the other members of the JCS. Second, the JCS members had a built-in conflict of interest since they were "dual-hatted": they wore one proverbial hat as chief of their service and another as a member of the joint JCS body. Third, the service staffs dominated the operation of the Joint Staff, preventing the formulation of a cross-cutting joint-service perspective. And fourth, the CINCs of the unified and specified commands had limited power and authority over the service components under their command.

After achieving modest changes in a 1953 amendment, Eisenhower succeeded in his push for more extensive reforms in 1958. Signed into law on August 6, 1958, this third major amendment to the National Security Act continued the power shift toward a stronger central executive—and away from the services.[18] The secretary of defense was given power to change the services' roles and missions, subject to a congressional veto. The power to create unified and specified commands moved from the JCS to the president, through the secretary of defense, "with advice and assistance of the JCS." Unified commanders received "full operational command" of assigned forces, and the act specified the chain of command running from the president to the secretary of defense to the CINCs. It gave the military services responsibilities for "organizing, training, and equipping" forces for the unified and specified commands. To lessen the counter-pressures created by "dual-hatted" service chiefs, the amendment said service chiefs could delegate management of their services to their vice chiefs, freeing up the chiefs to focus on joint JCS duties. The revised act repealed the CJCS's symbolic lack of vote in JCS deliberations and clarified that the chairman outranked all other military officers but still did not have command authority over military forces. Finally, the law increased the size of the Joint Staff from 210 to 400 officers.

In sum, the series of legislative changes between 1947 and 1958 attempted to reconcile fundamental political questions. Should power and influence be centralized for efficient conduct of military operations, or should it be spread widely to create diverse counsel and prevent consolidations of power and perspective? Such questions rooted in first principles rarely have definitive answers, only contingent ones that achieve temporary political compromises. Consequently, these issues resurfaced periodically in the years that followed, without major legislative update. Figure 7.1 summarizes the discussion thus far and captures the evolution of these issues across the four notable legislative updates.

Issues and Predictions

Before getting into the specific twists and turns of the Goldwater-Nichols story, the following discussion offers some theoretical predictions about how the Army and Navy might respond in the debates, based on the alignment of their cultural beliefs and the issues at hand. What were the core issues that sparked such recurring and heated interest?

Even after the Eisenhower reforms of 1958, recurring symptoms of organizational dysfunction plagued the national military structure. With each passing decade and each change of political party in the White House, yet another weighty commission studied the issues of defense organization and emerged with similar conclusions. One of the last and most comprehensive studies, chaired by Richard Steadman, occurred during the Carter administration. The Steadman report, published in 1978, echoed familiar themes from decades of commissions and studies.[19] Five of its main conclusions aptly summarize the central issues revisited during the Goldwater-Nichols debates.

First, the Steadman report found that the committee structure of the JCS, headed by a weakly empowered chairman, was largely incapable of offering sharp, incisive, and nationally oriented advice to civilian decision-makers. Most civilians found *individual* advice from the members of the JCS to be valuable, but its corporate advice was forged in the fires of committee compromise, resulting in lowest-common-denominator options. Such bland do-no-harm proposals amounted to little more than "nonaggression treaties among the various services."[20] In many cases, semantics triumphed over substance.

Second, the Steadman report recognized that the service chiefs filled an institutional position with nearly insurmountable conflict of interest: "A Chief cannot, for example, be expected to argue for additional carriers, divisions, or air wings when constructing a Service budget and then agree in a joint forum that they should be deleted in favor of programs of other Services. In doing so he would not only be unreasonably inconsistent, but would risk losing leadership of his Service as well."[21]

Third, the study found the quality of the Joint Staff could be improved—both the caliber of the officers serving there and the usefulness of their staff products. At the time, the Joint Staff coordinated its position papers through a tortuous color-coded staffing maze known as the "flimsy/buff/green/red stripe" process, with a different color for each level of the four-layered puzzle.[22] "I was at the Pentagon probably all of four months," one staff officer recalled, "and some action officer came sprinting into my office from the Army staff, saying he had a flimsy that was going to go instant green at 1400 unless we can purple it, and my task was to help him figure out how to purple it. Of course, I hadn't the foggiest idea what he was talking about."[23] Not only was the process cumbersome, but the extensive involvement of each service staff gave the military services a de facto veto over any joint policy.

The services were also critiqued for not sending their best officers for duty on the Joint Staff. This observation had a long historical precedent, and various attempts to increase the officer quality had generally failed. The clearest attempt to incentivize inclusion of high-quality officers on the Joint Staff was a directive issued in December 1959 by Secretary of Defense Thomas Gates, which levied a requirement that "all officers . . . will serve a normal tour of duty with a Joint, Combined, Allied or OSD [Office of Secretary of Defense] Staff before being considered qualified for promotion to general or flag officer rank."[24] This internal DOD policy, however, went largely unheeded as the services obtained exceptions to the policy and eventually ignored it altogether.[25]

Fourth, the Steadman report echoed the findings of earlier studies that the warfighting commanders—the CINCs of the unified and specified commands—had insufficient power and authority over the service components assigned to them. Although the 1958 amendment gave the CINCs "full operational authority" over assigned forces, the services retained powerful influence over readiness, training, weapons acquisition, and budget. The service component commanders assigned to the unified commands worked for two (or more) bosses; in actual operations they reported to the CINC, while administratively they reported to their service chief, who still had primary influence over their assignments and promotions.

SUMMARY OF POLICY CHANGES: 1947–1958

	1947 National Security Act	1949 Amendments to the NSA	1953 Reorganization Plan No. 6	1958 DOD Reorganization Act
Unified Department	• Created National Military Establishment (NME)	• Changed NME to Department of Defense (DOD)		
Secretary of Defense	• Created position of secretary of defense (SecDef) • SecDef to exercise "general" direction, authority, and control, and establish "general" policies and programs • Authorized 3 special assistants to the SecDef	• Created position of deputy secretary of defense (reclassifying undersecretary of defense created by 2 April 1949 legislation) • Eliminated the word "general" from SecDef authority and control • Withheld power from SecDef to adjust the services' combatant functions	• Authorized an additional 6 assistant secretaries • Created position of Office of Secretary of Defense (OSD) general counsel	• Gave SecDef authority to change service combatant functions, subject to congressional veto • Assistant secretaries of defense given authority over military departments, when explicitly authorized by SecDef
Joint Chiefs of Staff (JCS)	• Created JCS, comprised of service chiefs from Army, Navy, and Air Force • Created Joint Staff (JS), limited to 100 officers	• Created position of chairman of the JCS (CJCS), to serve as nonvoting agenda-setter and liaison • JCS members given right to appeal to Congress on any issue • Increased size of JS to 210 officers	• Commandant of the Marine Corps member of JCS on issues related to the Corps (per 1952 legislation) • CJCS given authority to approve JS members, and to manage JS directly	• Repealed CJCS's lack of vote • Specified CJCS as highest-ranking military officer, but not military commander • Specified that CJCS must inform SecDef or president when JCS not unanimous • Increased JS to 400 officers

Military Services	• Created US Air Force • Made Army, Navy, and Air Force all executive departments, headed by civilian secretary • Gave service secretaries direct access to present reports or recommendations to president or budget director	• Created military departments instead of executive departments • Service secretaries no longer in cabinet or on National Security Council • Service secretaries had right to appeal to Congress (but not president or budget director)	• Specified military services' role to "organize, train, and equip" forces for unified commands • Gave vice chiefs full authority over services when so delegated by chief
Unified Commands	• Unified commands created by JCS		• Unified commands created by president or SecDef (with advice and assistance of JCS) • Unified commanders given "full operational authority" over assigned forces
Chain of Command	• Based on Key West Agreement (21 April 1948), a member of the JCS served as executive agent to the unified commands	• Key West Agreement modified by DOD Directive 5100.1 • Specified military department, not JCS member, as executive agent	• Formally runs from president to SecDef to unified commands • DOD Directive 5100.1 specifies that link from SecDef to unified commands runs through JCS

Figure 7.1. Summary of legislative changes to the distribution of political power within the US defense establishment from 1947 to 1958.

A fifth issue concerned the chain of command from civilian decision-makers to military forces in the field. The 1958 amendment specified the chain of command from the president to the secretary of defense to the CINCs. By DOD directive, however, the transmission from the secretary of defense to the CINCs went *through* the Joint Chiefs of Staff. Consequently, though the corporate JCS did not create orders, it was in the key position of communicating them—an ambiguity used for advantage. The Steadman report argued that a "committee structure is not effective for the exercise of military command or management authority."[26]

Given the five issues outlined above and the service beliefs discussed in chapters 2 and 4, how might the Navy and Army respond to a rekindled debate? Following the deductive "congruence procedure" described by Alexander George, the analysis here considers how the services' cultural beliefs might inform their sense of these particular issues.[27] As described in chapter 6, the argument recognizes that final decisions always involve contingent factors in the policy environment, but codes of belief "provide the basic framework within which the actor approaches the task of attempting to process available information and to engage in rational calculation in pursuit of his values and interests."[28] This dyadic approach isolates the deductive implications of each belief for each policy issue. Consequently, two different beliefs could imply different reactions to the same policy, as the discussion here substantiates. In such cases, the composite hypothesis predicts a mixed reaction from the service.

For the Navy, the first element in its service culture (2.1) is the belief that naval forces offer a unique and essential instrument of national power (fig. 7.2).[29] In the Navy's view, naval power is not a subset of *military* power, but comprises a different category altogether. In the light of this belief, the service is likely to oppose moves that diminish the access of the chief of naval operations (CNO) to the president and secretary of defense, as an officer from any other service lacks the fluency to speak capably of the maritime domain. The third belief of Navy culture (2.3) reinforces this tendency, as the service believes that the operational environment at sea is a world apart, largely unknowable to outsiders. The Navy's fifth belief (2.5) likewise anticipates resistance to diminished access to civilian leaders. The Navy's professional and permanent fleet requires significant capital investment during times of peace, when major defense spending is often most difficult to justify. Consequently, Navy leaders need steady, undiminished access to civilian leaders in times of war *and peace*, to justify the need for sustained capital investments.

The Navy's fourth belief (2.4)—its accepted model of command leadership—

predicts support for some reform provisions and resistance to others. Navy command is built on decentralized trust, and the Navy emphasizes the critical linkages between responsibility, authority, and accountability. The service can be expected to support policies that maximize decentralized operations and empower subordinate commanders, such as giving CINCs increased authority and accountability to match their statutory responsibility. This belief in decentralization also suggests some support for streamlining the operational chain of command, thus reducing any unnecessary steps between the president and operational forces. Conversely, expect resistance from the Navy on policies that fail to show trust in the Navy as its own executive agent, such as any moves to direct internal personnel policies such as promotions and assignments to the Joint Staff.

Lastly, the Navy believes that it is not a garrison force that deploys when needed; it is a deployed force that returns to port when needed. The Navy's force of gravity flows in the direction of the sea, and the service regards sea duty more highly than shore duty; expect resistance to any attempts to redirect the Navy's finest officers from its deployed ships to its shore-based staff.

While the Navy appears primed to resist most reform provisions, the Army's array of cultural beliefs suggests a different institutional reaction (fig. 7.3). The Army's first cultural belief (4.1) involves a self-conception of the Army as a faithful and apolitical servant of the nation, with deep loyalty to the American people that can supersede loyalty to the Army itself. This belief carries a deep suspicion of any activity that might appear to be lobbying. Consequently, it predicts an overall level of support from the Army, or at least quiet and passive resistance to any unwelcome provisions.

The Army also sees itself as an indispensable land force of last resort (4.2), with a nontransferable job of finishing wars and tackling unwelcome assignments. With this secure view of its operating domain, the Army is less likely to feel threatened by reform legislation that might revisit the roles and missions of the services. Further, this belief suggests the possibility of some support for strengthening the CINCs who are tasked to perform and finish operational missions, as well as the possibility of grumbling but compliant support for being tasked to perform duty on a joint staff. This possible support may be counteracted, however, by the Army's sixth belief (4.6) about the most important job in the Army: leading troops in the field—the "muddy boots bias." The Army holds this belief strongly, which is likely to prompt its resistance (much like the Navy's) to any outside attempts to put the Army's best officers on a joint staff rather than in the field.

NAVY POLICY PREFERENCE HYPOTHESES

Belief	Overall attitude/ general issues	Strengthen CJCS as principal military advisor	Remove service chiefs from JCS	Strengthen CINCs power	Improve JS quality and incentivize JS duty	Streamline chain of command
2.1: An Armed Embassy of America. *Navy as unique instrument of national power.*		Since Navy power is unique, expect resistance to any diminished access to decision-makers.	Expect resistance to any move that reduces access of CNO to senior civilian leaders.			
2.2: America and Navy Prosper Together. *What's good for the Navy is good for America.*						
2.3: Survival through Enlisted Order and Commissioned Judgment. *Leaders must exercise judgment.*				Expect resistance to a non-Navy CINC having increased authority over navy assets.		

2.4: The Glory of Independent Command at Sea. *Trust ship captains to execute mission. Don't interfere.*	Expect resistance to increased intrusion into Navy affairs or micromanagement; expect support for decentralized execution.	Expect support for giving CINCs authority and accountability to match their responsibility.	Expect resistance to outside interference in internal Navy promotions and assignments.	Expect support for shortest chain of command from president to operational forces.
2.5: A Professional and Permanent Navy. *Maintain robust fleet in being. Navy always deployed, doing mission.*	Large capital investments require constant advocacy and explanation; expect resistance to reduced access to decision-makers.		Expect resistance to putting best officers in any shore or staff position instead of at sea.	
2.6: The Bigger the Better. *Build fleet around capital ships.*				

Figure 7.2. The US Navy's policy preference hypotheses on the key issues in the defense reform debates. Each hypothesis is posited individually as a logical deduction of how each belief (numbered as in chapter 2) interacts with each policy issue.

ARMY POLICY PREFERENCE HYPOTHESES

Belief	Overall attitude/ general issues	Strengthen CJCS as principal military advisor	Remove service chiefs from JCS	Strengthen CINCs power	Improve JS quality and incentivize JS duty	Streamline chain of command
4.1: Apolitical Servants of the Nation. *Faithful extension of American people. Members of profession of arms.*	Expect cooperative posture; willing to pursue national interest; expect minimal engagement with Congress.	Expect some support: need to generate national advice above service-level interests.	Expect mild support: not as threatened by diminished voice for chief of staff of the Army.	Expect some support: emphasis on national warfighting capability, less on service interests.		
4.2: Land Force of Last Resort. *The Army is an indispensable last line of defense, prepared to take more blame than credit.*	Since the Army understands its essential role, unlikely to feel threatened by legislative activity.			Expect support for strengthening warfighters who must perform and finish the job.	Expect mild support: Army accustomed to serving inglorious roles.	
4.3: The Army Way of Battle. *Use technology and firepower to win total victories. Minimize political interference.*	Expect resistance to political interference in warfighting.					

Policy issue					
4.4: Synchronizing the Fragments. *Waging war requires coordination, control, and synchronization.*	Expect support: centralizing policies enhance coordination and control.	Expect support: enhance unity of command.	Expect support: increase capacity to execute combined-arms joint warfare.	Expect support: need to strengthen capacity for coordinating service activities.	Expect support: chain of command enhances synchronized action.
4.5: Fielding an Army: Regulars and the Militia. *Sufficient manpower is job #1. Army must be ready to expand.*					
4.6: Soldiers, Units, and Leaders. *Soldiers are building block. Leaders should have muddy boots.*				Expect some resistance: best Army officers should be leading troops in the mud.	

Figure 7.3. The US Army's policy preference hypotheses on the key issues in the defense reform debates. Each hypothesis is posited individually as a logical deduction of how each belief (numbered as in chapter 4) interacts with each policy issue.

Finally, the best predictor of Army support for various reform initiatives is the Army's belief in the need to synchronize, coordinate, and centrally control operations. As a service that prizes combined-arms warfare, supported by the other services, the Army tends to favor centralizing policies that enhance coordination and control of warfighting elements. Consequently, expect some support for making the CJCS the principal military advisor to the president to strengthen the unity of command.[30] Similarly, expect support for strengthening the CINCs whose job entails coordinating joint warfare, as well as support for streamlining and clarifying the chain of command from the field to civilian decision-makers. Finally, the Army's belief in the wisdom of synchronization and coordination suggests there could be support for putting high-quality Army officers on the Joint Staff as a vehicle for improving joint integration.

With respect to overall civil-military interaction, this story of the Goldwater-Nichols Act focuses on the long advisory phase of the legislation, where the policy space seems relatively coherent—the issues at hand were long-standing and well understood, and the required path of military compliance was reasonably clear. Consequently, again, the case study largely inhabits square II of figure 1.2, in which military agents advise and debate with civilian principals on relatively coherent policies. Under conditions of preparatory agency, the framework argues that preference gaps and the anticipated implementation slack interact to generate various levels of military resistance or cooperation (fig. 7.4).

Most of the reform proposals involve self-executing redistributions of power, codified in durable legislation, which foreshadow relatively little implementation slack. Consequently, expect the Navy to have large preference gaps and little anticipated implementation slack, portending major conflict. For the Army, expect fairly small preference gaps with little anticipated slack, meaning that the Army will probably work to negotiate the details. Finally, principled agent theory also maintains that when the services have significant preference gaps with their civilian principals, they will negotiate for more implementation slack. They will seek to influence the specificity, durability, enforceability, and imminence of the policy, effectively moving the discussion from the left side of figure 7.4 ("major conflict") to the right ("negotiate to *avoid* the details"). The Navy might attempt such a strategy, working to shift its major conflict to a negotiation for more slack. The Army, however, is less likely to pursue a strategy of shaping the implementation parameters, as

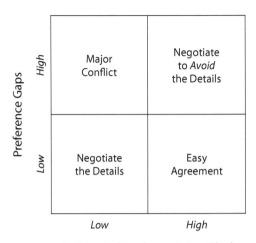

Figure 7.4. Hypothesized interactions between preference gaps and the anticipated implementation slack, which are most relevant during the advisory phase of more-coherent policies.

its predicted support for many of the policies suggests that the reduced implementation slack is less odious.

History Returns: 1982

By the time General David Jones was preparing to retire from the Air Force in 1982, he had served as a member of the Joint Chiefs of Staff longer than anyone before him—four years as chief of staff of the Air Force, and four more as chairman of the JCS.[31] During those eight years, Jones had suffered through all of the major issues identified above: his weak institutional position as chairman, the need for a vice chairman, the conflict of interest and overload of JCS members, the ineffectiveness of the Joint Staff, the dominance of service interests over joint interests, and the inability to give quality advice to senior civilian decision-makers.[32] At the start of his second two-year term as chairman in 1980, Jones had made defense reorganization a major personal priority.[33] In February 1981, he convened a group dubbed the Chairman's Special Studies Group, led by William K. Brehm, to review previous studies on military organization; analyze the effectiveness of the current joint system; consult service chiefs, CINCs, and senior military leaders; and make suitable recommendations in the light of any clear needs for change.[34]

As the studies group began its work, Jones drafted a journal article entitled "Why the Joint Chiefs of Staff Must Change," in which he chronicled the well-established deficiencies in the joint system and made several specific recommendations for change: strengthening the role of the chairman, creating a deputy chairman, limiting the involvement of service staffs in the Joint Staff workflow, and increasing the preparation and incentives for joint duty.[35]

Jones's frustrations were well known within the DOD, but he went public with his ideas in a dramatic way in February 1982. Appearing before the House Armed Services Committee (HASC) to discuss the upcoming budget, Jones took advantage of the platform to air his views on defense reorganization. After brief opening comments, he remarked:

> I look forward to testifying on the budget issues; however, there is one subject I would like to mention briefly here. It is not sufficient to have just resources, dollars and weapon systems; we must also have an organization which will allow us to develop the proper strategy, necessary planning, and the full warfighting capability. We do not have an adequate organizational structure today, at least in my judgment, and I have a much different perspective now, having served 4 years as Chairman, than during my time as a service chief when I was in a scramble for my service's share of the available resources.[36]

Jones went on to describe the weaknesses of the JCS "committee system" and emphasized that "the problem is not with people. It is with the system."[37] Echoing the recommendations in his journal article (which was soon to be published), Jones called for a strengthened chairman, limited involvement of service staffs on joint papers, strengthened CINCs, and greater training and incentives for joint duty.

In hindsight, it is clear that Jones's public testimony sparked the rekindled national debate about defense organization. A key staff member of the HASC appreciated its significance immediately.[38] Retired Air Force Colonel Arch Barrett had recently become a professional staff member on the HASC, having spent years of his professional and academic life studying defense reform. Within days of Jones's testimony, Barrett and his staff director, John Lally, approached the chairman of the HASC Investigations Subcommittee, Representative Richard White, and suggested the subcommittee hold hearings on the subject of defense reorganization.[39] White agreed, and over the span of three months and 38 witnesses, these hearings convened the most thorough analysis of defense organization since the Eisenhower administration.

HASC Investigations Subcommittee Hearings: April–July 1982

The subcommittee hearings began on April 21, 1982, with General Jones repeating his familiar critiques of the joint system.[40] Joining Jones on the first day of testimony was the chief of staff of the Army, General Edward "Shy" Meyer. Meyer had just published a bold article in the April 1982 edition of *Armed Forces Journal International.*[41] In his article, he pushed the reform agenda even further than did Jones, arguing that "the changes urged by General Jones, while headed in the right direction, do not go far enough to correct what ails the JCS."[42] To address the deep problems in the JCS system, Meyer suggested that the service chiefs wear only one hat—running their services. In turn, he proposed replacing the JCS with a body of full-time military officers with advisory duties only: a group of four-star generals and admirals, with no service responsibilities, on their final tour of active duty. In his HASC testimony, Meyer doubled down and restated these same recommendations: "I don't believe you can tinker with the issues any longer; tinkering will not suffice."[43]

Chief of Naval Operations Admiral Thomas B. Hayward testified strongly against these proposed reforms. In Hayward's view, the structure was essentially sound, and any deficiencies were the result of personalities, not the system. Hayward took serious exception to the suggestion that the dual-hatting of the service chiefs somehow compromised the integrity of their views or their ability to offer national-level advice. "I am deeply offended," he testified, "by the slanderous criticisms which one frequently and commonly hears about the Joint Chiefs of Staff being an ineffective group of parochial service chiefs." He went on, "While I am a naval officer first, I am also well aware of my obligations and responsibilities as a member of the Joint Chiefs of Staff."[44] Hayward concluded his comments with what he regarded as the main issue at hand: "When the Chief of Naval Operations is no longer the principal naval adviser to the Commander in Chief, which is the recommendation, but that one individual [i.e., the chairman] is the principal military adviser to the Commander in Chief, I say that is a dangerous way to go."[45]

Hayward's defense of the status quo received strong support from two other prominent Naval officers: former CJCS Admiral Thomas H. Moorer and former CNO Admiral James L. Holloway III. Like Hayward, Moorer emphasized that the arrangement of the boxes on the organizational chart mattered less than the quality of the officers who filled those boxes. The chairman, first of all, "has all of the authority within the uniformed organizations he is willing to take."[46] Any deficiencies in the chairman's ability to do his job were the fault of the chairman, not the structure. Second, Moorer dismissed the conflict of interest involved in dual-hatting: "If an officer cannot find time to handle both his service duties as well as his joint duties, then he is not qualified for either job." He concluded with a final plea: "my recommendation is a very simple one: leave the organization alone."[47] Any necessary changes were internal staff issues, he asserted, not matters for legislation.

Next was Admiral Holloway, who revisited many of the arguments he had made two years earlier in a defense journal article.[48] Holloway defended the quality of advice offered by the JCS, asserting that it was not poor but unwanted: "Now, the fact that the chiefs are accused of giving bad advice is, in my view, largely a euphemism which says that the chiefs have given us advice which was not the answer that we wanted to hear."[49] He then criticized the proposal to make the CJCS the principal military advisor, arguing that such a move would inhibit the breadth and expertise of counsel offered to the president. Holloway asked, for example, "If you didn't have a naval officer as chairman, or as vice chairman, who is going to talk about aircraft carrier operations in the Indian Ocean?"[50]

Finally, in May 1982, the former undersecretary of the Navy, R. James Woolsey, appeared before the committee and suggested that the Navy's esoteric self-conception informed its opposition to many proposed reforms. Woolsey relayed a comment from a retired naval officer about the Navy's relationship with the other services: "I think we understand them far better than they understand us."[51]

While the panel of Navy witnesses provided relatively little variation in viewpoint, the Army witnesses were more divided. Meyer clearly stood in the vanguard of Army support for reform, joined by Generals Andrew Goodpaster, Donn Starry, and Maxwell Taylor. Two other retired Army officers, however, registered opposition to legislative intrusion into internal military affairs. General Lyman Lemnitzer, former CJCS, and General Harold Johnson, former chief of staff of the Army, both urged caution in considering any major reform of the national defense. Speaking of the conflict of interest for dual-hatted service chiefs, Johnson argued that it was a problem but could be overcome with the right attitude. While he was chief of staff, Johnson noted, he had told his team that "we don't take Army positions in the Joint Chiefs of Staff meetings. We first look at what is good for the country, and what is good for the country is going to be good for the Army." He continued, "I believed then, and I believe now that if you look at the interests of the country as paramount that the service interest will be taken care of in due course."[52]

Additional Evidence

By the end of the hearings in July 1982, 38 witnesses had testified, offering a wide range of views and sparking a great deal of Washington debate. While these hearings offer the most thorough and focused venue for evaluating the early views on defense reform, other evidence from the period reinforces the general trends.

In April 1982, as the HASC hearings were about to begin, CNO Admiral Thomas Hayward forwarded a secret concept paper to Secretary of Defense Caspar Weinberger. The paper had originally been sent to the other members of the JCS in January 1981 in an effort to reassert the Joint Chiefs' prominent role in the councils of power. "My experience of the past two and a half years," the memo to the JCS began, "leaves me with the frustration that the Joint Chiefs, as a corporate body, still do not have the requisite influence on major security issues as intended by the National Security Act of 1947, or to the degree that is in the best interest of our country."[53] Hayward detailed a variety of shortcomings in the joint process, but concluded that the effectiveness of the Joint Chiefs largely hinged, first, on their "access to the President and the Congress"; next, on their "assertiveness in presenting their views"; and finally, on "the quality and timeliness of those views."[54]

Within the Department of the Navy, Secretary of the Navy John F. Lehman took a lead role in opposing any reorganization of the Defense Department. In fact, he tasked retired Marine Corps Brigadier General J. D. Hittle to keep a watchful eye on any maneuvers and issues related to defense organization.[55] From 1981 to 1983, Hittle sent Secretary Lehman a series of memos, updating him on the state of play. In a memo dated October 1981 and labeled "Very Personal," Hittle noted ominously the work of the Brehm committee established by General Jones, which was "examining possible ways to increase the chairman's authority."[56] Suggesting that "this whole operation is loaded with potential trouble for the Navy and Marine Corps," Hittle advised Lehman to direct the CNO and the commandant of the Marine Corps to make sure that their coequal chairman of the JCS did not get away with anything.

Once the proposals by Jones and Meyer became public in the spring of 1982, Hittle increased the fervor of his opposition. In a memo apparently drafted by Hittle for Lehman to send to Secretary Weinberger, he responded to the various points in the Jones and Meyer proposals. Among his various critiques: "The proposals would destroy the JCS system that combines authority with responsibility" and "are a raid on the constitutional principle of civilian control of the military." Similarly, "the Jones proposals would be needlessly disruptive, and would weaken support for the President's budget." And in a particularly colorful tone, Hittle ended his ghost-written memo with this recommendation: "Reject summarily the proffered Jones lame-duck legacy of needless turmoil, antagonism, and disruption of military planning at our seat of government."[57]

With Hittle's encouragement, Secretary Lehman began engaging pro-Navy advocates on Capitol Hill. Most importantly, Lehman worked with SASC chairman John Tower, who happened to be a senior enlisted sailor in the Naval reserves.[58] Lehman's engagement with Tower ensured that the Senate did not follow the HASC's lead in passing any reform bills, which effectively kept the issue sidelined.[59] In its lame-duck session in December 1982, the SASC held just one day of hearings with four witnesses, which was attended by only four senators, three of whom had a direct personal tie to the Navy.[60]

While evidence of the Army's wider position and response is not abundant, there are several indications of Army views outside the scope of congressional testimony. First, the US Military Academy at West Point sponsored a conference in June 1982 on the topic of defense reform. Each year, the Social Sciences department at the academy sponsored a senior leader conference to stimulate discussion on important topics.[61] In 1982, amid the larger interest in reform spurred by Generals Jones and Meyer, the department chose defense reform as its plenary topic, marshaling a wide array of views, most of them supportive of reform.[62]

A second piece of evidence exists in a briefing book prepared by the Army staff in July 1982.[63] One of the documents in the binder focuses on the substantive criteria that should govern any debate about defense reorganization. The first criterion was to "improve ability to wage war / meet requirements of CINCs," and it specified various subpoints that emphasized giving operational commanders the necessary support to accomplish the mission, enhancing unity of command, and crafting doctrine "attuned to joint operational requirements." The second and third criteria focused on "better, more timely military advice" and "allocat[ing] resources more wisely; us[ing] resources more efficiently." Overall, these criteria emphasized warfighting results and military effectiveness and were broadly supportive of the intent of the reforms.

Chiefs Unite: 1983

A second key juncture in the defense reorganization story occurred in the summer and fall of 1983, when new rounds of hearings by both the House and the Senate revealed a fresh dynamic in play. Back in the summer of 1982, the major political players had offered a wide array of preferences in response to General David Jones's call for reorganizing the national military structure. By 1983, however, the JCS had conducted its own internal review of the situation, and the testimony offered in congressional testimony looked somewhat different than it had the previous year.

As the HASC hearings concluded in the summer of 1982, three new members joined the JCS. Most important, General John Vessey took over from Jones as chairman. Vessey was hailed by President Reagan as "a soldier's soldier." Starting his career as an enlisted Army private, followed by a battlefield commission on the Anzio beachhead in 1944, with decorations for valor in World War II and Vietnam, Vessey clearly had deep credibility across all ranks and services.[64] Joining Vessey as new members of the JCS were Admiral James Watkins as CNO and General Charles Gabriel as chief of staff of the Air Force.

With a new group of faces around the table, the JCS took its own internal look at defense reform in the summer and fall of 1982. Vessey emphasized repeatedly that the Joint Chiefs would consider this issue themselves, without the dogmatic input of the "staff theologians."[65] This emphasis reflected one of Vessey's broader initiatives as chairman: "to engage the Chiefs in their duties as Chiefs."[66] Vessey did not want the chiefs to bless the staff work coming up from below; he wanted them to set strategic direction and drive the issues from above. Such top-down strategic initiative ultimately resulted in better products, Vessey argued: "If you could get the Chiefs to examine the issue before their staffs got them into concrete, where they had to posture in front of their own people, we usually came up with pretty good answers."[67]

Without an extensive staffing process informing these discussions, there is little evidence to capture the substance of the JCS review. Given the other dynamics in play, however, it seems likely that the review was not exhaustive. General Meyer later called the review "superficial," largely driven by the delicate balance of personalities in the group.[68] Only a few months earlier, Meyer had been publicly supportive of radical, far-reaching reform. With Vessey as chairman—a fellow Army officer who had just worked for him as vice chief of staff—Meyer believed his advocacy needed to change. Recalling their re-form discussions, Meyer noted that his fellow chiefs "didn't want to confront me, [and] I didn't want to confront them. So, it was a very superficial look at it."[69] Later, Meyer freely admitted that "I was leaving, and I didn't want to make Jack [Vessey]'s job any harder."[70]

From their internal review, the Joint Chiefs arrived at a set of modest rec-ommendations for change. In a November 1982 memorandum to Secretary Weinberger, Vessey relayed that they had "reached agreement that while there were flaws in JCS organization, other problems proceeded from relationships between OJCS [Office of the JCS] and OSD which over the years have ob-scured and diluted the military advice you and the President are by law enti-tled to receive."[71] With the real problems rooted more in staff overlap than JCS deficiency, the Joint Chiefs "concluded that sweeping changes to [the law] are unnecessary." Instead, they called for three minor changes to existing law: (1) increasing or eliminating the statutory limit on the size of the Joint Staff (then 400 officers); (2) increasing the length of a tour of duty for joint officers; and (3) inserting the CJCS into the chain of command between the secretary of defense and the CINCs to "organize the Department in peace as it will function in war." In addition to specifying these three changes, the chiefs explicitly rejected any calls to make the chairman the principal military ad-visor, to create a four-star vice chairman, to subordinate the Joint Staff to the chairman alone, or to replace the JCS with some other council of single-hatted advisors.

Secretary Weinberger forwarded the chiefs' recommendations to President Reagan and fully endorsed the JCS conclusions. Weinberger later acknowl-edged that Vessey and the JCS study had a "substantial impact on my think-ing, because I have enormous respect for General Vessey . . . He knows the whole situation. He was a battlefield commission at [Anzio]. He was an en-listed man, as I was."[72] In April 1983, the DOD submitted draft legislation to Congress, codifying the minor changes the JCS had proposed.

Second Round of HASC Investigations
Subcommittee Hearings: June 1983

When the Investigations Subcommittee started its next round of hearings in June 1983, the four service chiefs and the chairman of the JCS appeared together on the first day. Unlike previous hearings in which the chiefs each testified individually, the five members of the JCS submitted a common writ-ten statement, which General Vessey delivered for the group. In his statement,

Vessey reaffirmed that the JCS had ample room within existing law to effect necessary change. In fact, Vessey recited a litany of reforms already underway, noting the JCS's improved communication with the president and secretary of defense, the improved timeliness of its advice to the president, the increased participation of the CINCs in budget preparations, better strategic guidance to the CINCs, a new training program for Joint Staff officers, and tasking of the service professional schools to emphasize joint planning and operations.[73] In short, Vessey affirmed that change was needed and, more importantly, was already happening. The only areas needing legislative improvement were the three minor ones in the DOD-sponsored reform bill. Following Vessey's statement, all four service chiefs concurred and walked the party line, emphasizing repeatedly how well the current group made the system work.

The lockstep unanimity of the service chiefs frustrated members of the committee who knew the consensus was manufactured, not genuine. General Meyer, most notably, revealed clear inconsistency in his views from one year to the next.[74] His outspoken criticism of the JCS system in 1982 became muted solidarity with his fellow chiefs in 1983. When Representative Ike Skelton testified that same day, he highlighted how the united testimony of the Joint Chiefs provided compelling evidence of the very phenomenon that reformers decried: the JCS system created tepid, least-common-denominator solutions rather than genuine alternative views. When asked about the DOD-sponsored reform bill, Skelton observed that "it is the result of obvious compromise within the committee, within the joint system. I am disappointed, Mr. Chairman, that we do not have five testimonies before us today."[75]

When confronted about his apparent inconsistency, Meyer acknowledged that his support for the common JCS position was one of political feasibility. He expressed his belief that he had "a requirement to work within the art of the possible for what can and cannot be done."[76] As he would later admit, Meyer was about to retire and did not want to create unnecessary friction for Vessey. Meyer retired from the Army two weeks after the hearing.

Senate Hearings: Fall 1983

By the fall of 1983, the SASC was ready for its own hearings on defense organization. Before the hearings, however, several important events shaped the policy landscape. First, in July 1983, two more officers rotated into the JCS, as General John Wickham replaced Meyer as chief of staff of the Army, and General P. X. Kelley took over as commandant of the Marine Corps. The second crucial event occurred on October 23, 1983, when terrorists attacked the Marine barracks in Beirut, Lebanon, killing 241 American servicemen, 220 of whom were Marines.[77] The loss of these servicemen, coming on the heels of a congressional visit and in the context of a larger debate about military effectiveness, added fuel to the reformers' fire.[78] Just two days later, the US military launched Operation Urgent Fury, the invasion of the Caribbean island-nation of Grenada, conducted to protect American medical students and stabilize the political situation after a military coup.[79] On very short notice, the US military planned and executed a joint military operation that was generally hailed as a success. Several operational hang-ups and interservice problems, however, added fodder to the reformers' claims of joint military shortcomings.

Meanwhile, the SASC finally began to hold substantive hearings of its own. In November 1983, James Schlesinger, the former secretary of defense, and Secretary of the Navy John Lehman appeared before the committee. Schlesinger focused his testimony on the shortcomings of the JCS structure and the lack of cross-cutting national advice it generated. He observed that "the recommendations and the plans of the Chiefs must pass through a screen designed to protect the institutional interests of each of the separate services. The general rule is that no service ox may be gored." As a result of these institutional rules within the JCS, Schlesinger found, the "proffered advice is generally irrelevant, normally unread, and almost always disregarded."[80]

Secretary Lehman clearly had other concerns. At the start of his testimony, he professed a "strong personal bias toward judging individual performance rather than organizational structure and I think that it has been a fault of government over the last 30 years to concentrate too much on organization, charts, and structure rather than improving accountability and responsibility." Emphasizing that civilian control of the military is best preserved by having a variety of views—to wit, maintaining the statutory role of the CNO as the principal naval advisor to the president—Lehman dismissed any efforts that would shuffle organizational charts but "add nothing to the simplicity of authority."[81]

Later in November, the four service chiefs testified before the SASC, and each departed little from the institutional script the JCS had recited the previous June. General Wickham testified that he fully supported the earlier testimony of General Vessey and highlighted the number of reforms already underway. Admiral Watkins likewise endorsed the DOD's position, focusing his critiques on congressional over-management and the importance of decentralized relationships built on trust. "Good people overcome the shortfalls of most any organization," Watkins testified. "The basic organization is not the problem." General Gabriel concurred, noting that the chiefs had "made good progress in the last year and a half, at least since General Vessey became Chairman." Finally, General Kelley professed that "the existing JCS structure is basically sound" and that personalities mattered more than organization.[82]

The weight of congressional testimony offered by the service chiefs in 1983—first to the HASC Investigations Subcommittee, then to the SASC—strayed very little from their crafted orthodoxy. The colorful variety of opinions that had headlined the hearings in 1982 faded into a drab uniformity, at least in the chiefs' formal testimony. Additional evidence indicates that this uniformity belied deeper divisions within.

Additional Evidence

The consistent testimony of the service chiefs in 1983 assured Congress that necessary reforms could happen internally, without additional legislation. Internal Joint Staff documents substantiate these claims, to a degree. A February 1984 Joint Staff memo specified that "improving the quality and timeliness of JCS advice and responsiveness to NCA [National Command Authority] are important goals which the Chiefs have given us and which require aggressive attention on our part."[83] The memo detailed various procedural changes designed to preserve a joint viewpoint against the tyranny of bland service-led compromises. Rather than accommodating every concession to the services, the action officers were charged "to preserve the clarity and crispness" of their best military advice.

During this period, the Army and Air Force also began work on a series of collective agreements and joint initiatives to improve their capacity to equip, train, and fight together in combat. In 1982, the Army had published its new operational field manual, codifying a new doctrine called AirLand Battle.[84] The Air Force had helped shape the development of AirLand Battle, and the two services moved forward to solidify that cooperation in 1983.[85] In April 1983, Generals Meyer and Gabriel signed a memorandum of understanding between the two services, affirming that "the Departments of the Army and the Air Force concur that the opportunities are right, the level of joint interest is high and that valid military requirements exist to initiate an agreement of inter-service cooperation in joint tactical training and field exercises based on the AirLand Battle doctrine."[86] In subsequent memoranda between Generals Wickham and Gabriel, the two services agreed on a common joint-force development process and distributed a detailed list of initiatives to enhance the services' capability to field an effective joint force.[87] Colonel Raoul Alcala led the Army's effort to craft the "31 Initiatives," and he believed the impetus for collaboration was certainly linked with the momentum on Capitol Hill pushing for reform. In Alcala's estimation, both Wickham and Gabriel saw good potential for change and wanted to get ahead of the congressional effort so that change could come on their terms, not by writ of a congressional staff member.[88]

Beyond development of the 31 Initiatives, the Army staff generally supported many of the reform proposals.[89] Colonel James Stefan coordinated the Army's response to defense reorganization from 1983 to 1985, and he briefed General Wickham on the current status of defense reorganization every one to two weeks.[90] Through these interactions, Stefan realized that Wickham was privately more supportive of reform than he could acknowledge in public. William Brehm, in the course of research for General Jones, found Wickham to have "positive and insightful views," making him a likely ally for defense reform.[91] Colonel Jack Wood, who worked for the vice chief of staff of the Army during this period, recalled that Wickham was privately supportive of reform.[92] Wickham was very loyal to his JCS relationships, Wood observed, and did not want to take a position that would jeopardize the effectiveness of the JCS team. Both Stefan and Wood assessed that the Army staff generally supported most of the reform proposals even as they recognized their chief of staff was constrained in his freedom to adopt their position.

The Navy's overall posture, however, remained steadfastly opposed to most reforms. In February 1983, retired Brigadier General Hittle sent Secretary Lehman another update memo, notifying him that Representative William Nichols had taken over as chairman of the HASC Investigations Subcommittee. Hittle's memo advised Lehman to instruct the CNO and the commandant of the Marine Corps to meet with Nichols, "the sooner the better," to "urge him not to resurrect" any reorganization bills that session. He concluded his memo with a cautionary tone: "We missed a Senate fight last session . . . by too thin a margin for comfort. Jones has not folded his tent show. Now is the time to stop another JCS reorganization fight, before any hearings are scheduled."[93]

Lehman concurred with Hittle's approach and maintained his own assault on pro-reform positions. Throughout 1983, for example, Lehman worked to shut down a project sponsored by the Heritage Foundation that would publish several pro-reform pieces. By embedding a Navy "spy" as a research fellow at Heritage and pressing his long-time friends and associates at the foundation, Lehman effectively blocked the publication of papers that supported reform positions.[94] During this same period, Lehman continued his own personal assault on what he perceived to be the real culprit: bureaucracy. Fighting against the trend to "centralize everything," Lehman recommended eliminating "6,000 bureaucrats in OSD who are accountable, essentially, to nobody."[95]

Interim Assessment

While the variation in service views (as presented in congressional testimony) seemed to diminish in 1983, this unified position masked deeper divisions between the Army and Navy. The Navy's preferences and political behavior had changed relatively little since the previous period. Its preferences remained opposed, and the specific objections remained linked to cultural predispositions toward privileged access to civilian principals, decentralized operations, the importance of individual performance over organizational structure, and the unity of responsibility, authority, and accountability.

The Army's preferences and behavior during this second period were more complicated. As represented by its chief of staff, the Army appeared to retreat from its robust support for reform. The internal JCS dynamics drove both General Meyer and General Wickham to support publicly the consensus view of the JCS and the DOD. While the chief's words and actions comprised the official Army position, the deeper attitudes and actions of the broader Army staff indicated steady, albeit quiet, support for reform. According to Army staff officers with privileged access to private beliefs, the Army staff and senior leaders generally held a supportive view of reform, and actions such as the 31 Initiatives represented a good-faith effort to change the DOD from within.

Evidence also shows the services operating in a preparatory agency environment during this time, negotiating the agency contract with their civilian principals in Congress. The JCS and the military services made an effort to enact meaningful reforms within the existing legislative environment, being eager to avoid widespread legislative changes. These efforts were motivated in part by a desire to be left alone by Congress, ensuring that any changes came from the inside, not the outside. But the dynamics of preparatory agency offer a complementary viewpoint. By enacting good-faith reform efforts internally, the JCS did not wholly object to the *substance* of certain reforms. Instead, the chiefs objected to the prospect of specific and durable legislation that would create a rigid, long-term agency contract. As a broader insight on civil-military interactions, we see that military agents may sometimes be more focused on the terms of the agency contract than on the policy substance itself.

How should one evaluate the actions of the Vessey-led JCS during this period? Within the elite circle of the Joint Chiefs, General Vessey's reform efforts appeared to be sincere, seeking to improve the current system to avoid the massive disruption of major reorganization. While this JCS-sculpted unanimity frustrated those in Congress pushing for reform, it did not seem to involve willful disobedience or agency shirking on the part of the chiefs. Instead, the corporate JCS position favored a conservative and pragmatic approach. General Vessey acknowledged the need for certain limited changes and worked to make such changes internally. This second period therefore includes a mixed bag of civil-military behavior from the JCS, as a small degree of cooperation with the policy's substance mingled with larger efforts to resist the policy's form.

Stars Align: 1985–86

As the debate moved into 1984, think tanks and academic audiences began debating the merits of defense reform. To ensure a balanced look at the issues, the Navy decided to conduct its own study. In the fall of 1984, CNO Admiral Watkins convened a study group "to undertake a thorough review of the several proposals for reorganization of the Joint Chiefs of Staff and to make such recommendations as panel members might deem appropriate."[96] The panel, comprising retired Navy and Marine Corps officers—to include Brigadier General Hittle—released its report in March 1985 and recommended "the Chief of Naval Operations place himself squarely in support of civilian direction and control of the national security organization."[97] In the panel's view, support of civilian control required the CNO to oppose proposals that would make the chairman the principal military advisor or would subordinate the Joint Staff to the sole control of the chairman. The group also recommended that neither the corporate JCS nor the chairman should be in the chain of command between the CINCs and the national command authorities, and recommended strengthening the role of the CINCs in resource allocation and readiness matters.[98]

As 1984 ended, a pivotal change in congressional leadership fueled the momentum for reform. Senator John Tower retired from the Senate and Senator Barry Goldwater took over chairmanship of the SASC in January 1985. Goldwater was in his final term in the Senate and joined forces with ranking member Senator Sam Nunn to make defense reform his top legislative priority.[99] Goldwater's interest in defense organization stretched back many years; in fact, it was the topic of his 1958 thesis at the Air War College, as part of his Air Force reserve duty. In his thesis, Goldwater had concluded that defense organization was "one of the most important problems facing our armed services."[100]

Senate Staff Study

As Senators Goldwater and Nunn fixed their sights on defense reorganization, they tasked staff member James Locher to devote his full attention to a thorough study of the subject. In the months that followed, Locher compiled an exhaustive 645-page report detailing the history and shortcomings of the US military organizational structure.[101] The study made 91 specific recommendations and charged that "under current arrangements, the Military Departments and Services exercise power and influence which are completely out of proportion to their statutorily assigned duties."[102] After describing the various deficiencies of the joint structure, the study listed its 12 most important recommendations, which included proposals to abolish the JCS and create a Joint Military Advisory Council in its place; to make the CJCS the principal military advisor to the secretary of defense on operational matters; to integrate the secretariat and service staffs; to establish in each service a joint duty career specialty; and to authorize the CJCS to run a personnel management system for joint duty.[103]

Locher's staff study was publicly released in October 1985 and ignited a firestorm of attention. The SASC scheduled a series of hearings to discuss the report's findings, with Secretary of Defense Weinberger scheduled to testify in mid-November, and the service chiefs in early December. In their preparation for the hearings, the Army and Navy took different approaches to evaluating the study.

The Army's response included a dedicated effort to review the study's recommendations. In late October 1985, one week after the staff study was published, Colonel J. C. Conrad of the Army Studies Group sent an internal memo to the vice chief of staff of the Army, General Maxwell Thurman.[104] Conrad expressed concern that the routine staff system for evaluating the study was likely to produce bland, status quo recommendations "in spite of the significant support for change on the [Army Staff]." He recommended that, instead, "the Army make a concerted effort to review major findings of the study with an open mind and the best talent available." Conrad suggested forming an ad hoc review committee of four to eight officers to take another look at the issues with fresh eyes. He closed the memo by noting that "there are clearly opportunities in all of this to improve our joint/combined war fighting capability."[105]

General Thurman then approached General Wickham, who agreed to create the kind of group Conrad had proposed.[106] The Army chartered a special review committee (SRC), consisting of six active duty officers and one Army historian, "to make an unbiased and open minded review of the validity of the major conclusions" of the Senate staff study.[107] The group's charter included special instructions to "look for positive directions in which Army can support constructive change" and clarified that the committee's conclusions "will not be constrained by preestablished Army/OSD positions."[108] Brigadier General Howard Graves instructed the SRC to "look at what the country needs. Let's get out of the green suit." Toward that end, Graves conceded that "the Army might have to sacrifice some of its special interests for the greater good."[109]

The SRC spent three weeks researching, conducting interviews, and drafting a briefing for General Wickham. In its final briefing slides, the SRC indicated its "guiding philosophy": "Jointness is essential for national security. Although personalities are critical, jointness should be promoted thru structure."[110] In all, the SRC made six key recommendations: "Support a comprehensive review of service roles and missions; strengthen the role of CJCS; improve quality and operation of joint staffs; strengthen capability to establish joint doctrine; increase the authority of and support to the unified and specified commanders; and enhance role of CJCS/JS [Joint Staff] in programmatic issues." The slides then provided details on the various recommendations, balanced by the associated political risks.[111]

The Navy's response to the Senate staff study looked rather different. Having already convened a select panel to study the issues, the CNO did not follow General Wickham's lead in creating a special ad hoc review committee. Instead, the existing Navy staff infrastructure reviewed the study—and found little to its liking. Deputy Undersecretary of the Navy Seth Cropsey had worked for Secretary Lehman since May 1984, and he spent much of his time on JCS reform issues.[112] Cropsey believed that the Navy's primary objection to the staff study (and reform in general) was the reduction in the breadth of advice the president would receive from a strengthened chairman whose elevated status could reduce the president's access to expert naval counsel. If the president did not hear from the CNO regularly, naval affairs and strategy ran the risk of being overlooked or misunderstood. Ultimately, Cropsey noted, such a reduction in the scope of advice would result in a loss of civilian control over the military: the president would receive less varied advice and might feel compelled to accept more narrowly conceived counsel.

Cropsey's regular update memoranda to Lehman during this period substantiate these concerns. After reading an advance copy of the Senate staff study in mid-September 1985, Cropsey sent Lehman a memo appraising the report. The memo indicted the study for its "rank amateurism and self-defeating management jargon," calling the study "its own worst enemy."[113] The CNO's uniformed Navy staff also provided strong critiques of the staff report. In a series of documents to prepare the CNO for his SASC testimony, an action officer noted that the staff report "reflects a gross misunderstanding of what the JCS system is and what and who does what and why." The staff documents then detailed a list of guiding principles on issues of defense organization, to include the belief that "authority cannot be separated from accountability and responsibility" and the assertion that "civilian control [is] an essential requirement and means in reality access to divergent opinions and views."[114]

SASC Hearings: November–December 1985

In November 1985, a month after the release of Locher's study, the next round of SASC hearings began. Among the first witnesses to testify was *retired* General Edward Meyer, who once again offered strong support for reform, echoing his original 1982 testimony: "In summary, reform of the mechanism which provides military advice and counsel to our civilian leadership is long overdue. Tinkering with the mechanisms will not suffice."[115] Admiral Thomas Moorer also remained true to earlier testimony opposing reform and took great personal offense at the staff study's critiques. Moorer ended his testimony by declaring: "it is people who make things happen, who make decisions and fight wars. It is not organizations."[116]

The service chiefs testified in December 1985, each providing separate testimony rather than joining in one corporate statement. Chief of Staff of the Army General Wickham testified first and staked out the most pro-reform position of any service chief since General Meyer's testimony in 1982. While noting that the report did not give proper credit to the many in-house reforms already enacted by recent chiefs, Wickham offered support for several proposals. His testimony laid down a surprisingly pro-reform marker for the day's hearings, notable to senators on the committee who later referred back to his proposals several times. Members of the Army staff's SRC found Wickham's public endorsement of their recommendations "gratifying" and thought he was a "good consumer" of their work.[117]

Admiral Watkins testified next and offered qualified support for several reform proposals previously endorsed by Secretary Weinberger. Watkins emphasized two attributes of the current system that should be retained: the diversity of views reaching decision-makers and civilian control of the military. He also joined Wickham in expressing frustration at the lack of credit given to recent chiefs for implementing reforms on their own. Watkins concluded, "it is those of us who serve today in the national security organization who should be and are the real reformers." Secretary Lehman testified on the following day and urged two fundamental principles, much like Watkins: civilian control of the military and the maintenance of balance between the branches, as intended by the nation's founding fathers. "The reforms," Lehman insisted, "should be built around a principle of accountability." The "principle of accountability" coursed through Lehman's testimony; later, he suggested that the guiding philosophy of reform needed to be "that human beings should be held accountable for their decisions."[118]

Ongoing Service Activity

By the fall of 1985, momentum for reform was building considerably. While the SASC held hearings, the House of Representatives also took significant action. On November 20, 1985, under Representative Les Aspin's leadership, the House passed H.R. 3622, a major JCS reform bill, with more than 115 sponsors and significant bipartisan support.[119] The House bill represented a strong legislative achievement and included nearly all of the major JCS-related provisions that ultimately ended up in the Goldwater-Nichols Act.

With increased attention on reform from both chambers of Congress and the White House, the Navy stepped up its level of activity to defeat or diminish the proposed reforms. In August 1985, Seth Cropsey sent Secretary Lehman a memo outlining a proposed strategy for influencing the newly constituted Packard commission, established by President Reagan. Cropsey recommended that Lehman ask Secretary Weinberger to call a sympathetic commission member, requesting him to "hit the ground running on the issue—establishing a strong, early presumption in favor of decentralization and civilian authority." Cropsey then encouraged Lehman to ask "those on the Commission who agree with us" to take the lead in building momentum in the right direction.[120]

In December 1985, Lehman and his department pursued a more aggressive tack. A memorandum for record drafted by Headquarters Marine Corps and forwarded to Lehman suggested pursuing a "strategy of laying the foundations for a Presidential veto of unacceptable legislation."[121] In January 1986, Lehman engaged key principals, dashing off short letters of concern prompted by the SASC's initial reform bill. In a letter to Secretary Weinberger, Lehman dismissed the "Goldwater-Locker[*sic*]-Dave Jones Bill" as a "blatant indictment on all that we have done the last five years" and "simply an updated return to McNamara."[122] In a similar note to Vice President George H. W. Bush, Lehman criticized the bill as "largely written by Dave Jones" and "heavily directed against the Navy CNO and Sec Nav." He closed by observing the "sad irony that Goldwater has become the unwitting tool of the liberal 'whiz-fogies'" and letting the vice president know the Navy was "going to battle stations."[123]

By early February 1986, the Navy had indeed gone to battle stations, several of which were on Capitol Hill. As one source in Congress commented, "The Navy has been dead set against this legislation. Lehman has been up here doing everything he can to undo it."[124] When the SASC started its committee markup of the draft reform bill on February 4, 1986, the Navy's opposition strategy soon became clear: "It was to be death by amendment, and Sen John Warner had clearly been designated as executioner."[125] Senator Warner had served as secretary of the Navy in the Nixon administration and was a reliable Navy supporter. The Warner-Navy team introduced one amendment after the next, bogging down the committee proceedings to remake the bill into something more favorable. Over the course of 14 markup sessions, the SASC considered 87 amendments, 50 of which came from Warner.[126] Navy Captain William Cohen, director of legislation in the Navy's Office of Legislative Affairs, confirmed that he and others in his office had been very active on Capitol Hill, primarily feeding key information to Warner.[127] Cohen's backchannel communications to Warner's office even prompted a letter from Goldwater to Weinberger specifically rebuking Cohen's tactics.[128]

On February 28, 1986, the Packard commission published its interim report and recommended several key reforms of the JCS structure, to include making the CJCS the principal military advisor to the president and strengthening the CINCs.[129] President Reagan acted quickly to endorse the commission's interim recommendations; he published National Security Decision Directive 219 on April 1, 1986, directing the DOD to implement whichever reforms could be accomplished under existing law.[130] In a subsequent message to Congress, Reagan again endorsed the Packard commission's recommendations and suggested legislation to make the CJCS the principal military advisor, to create a vice chairman, and to make the Joint Staff responsible only to the chairman.[131] Reagan further recommended strengthening the CINCs, but preferred to do so through executive policy rather than legislative action.

President Reagan's public support for defense reform did little to temper the Navy's vocal opposition. On May 5, 1986, Senators Goldwater and Nunn sent a letter to Secretary Weinberger rebuking Seth Cropsey for "unprincipled efforts to misrepresent this bill," efforts that comprised "an affront to the integrity of the national political process."[132] The senators highlighted that Cropsey's stance pitted him against the president's own stated position: "We find it intolerable that an official of the Department of Defense would misinform Members of the Senate in addition to working actively in opposition to the stated position of the Administration." Bloodied but unbowed, the Navy remained at battle stations. Two days after this letter, the Senate convened to vote on its reform bill, and Lehman attempted one last flanking maneuver. In an early morning meeting with Senator Warner, Lehman asked him to introduce an amendment exempting the Department of the Navy from the provisions in the bill. Warner's support for the Navy had its limits, and the senator declined.[133] The Senate passed S. 2295 on May 7, 1986, by a vote of 95–0.

For the next several months, the Navy continued its efforts to deflate the bill. Lehman's strong opposition to reform became so well known that his own mother weighed in. After reading about the ongoing clash with Goldwater, Lehman's mother—a strong Goldwater supporter—sent him a straightforward note: "John: I don't know what the dispute is, but you're wrong."[134] Disregarding his mother's counsel, Lehman fought to the finish. His personal files include a draft letter to President Reagan, apparently unsent, written as Congress prepared to send the president their approved bill.[135] The draft letter expressed numerous concerns with the conferees' approved bill, noted its departure from the president's message to Congress, and ended with this recommendation: "While a number of provisions of H.R. 3622 are good ones, others are so flawed as to erode our national security . . . In the absence of a line-item veto, we must urge you to reject H.R. 3622, and implement its positive recommendations by executive means." Reagan did not veto the bill. The president signed the Goldwater-Nichols Department of Defense Reorganization Act of 1986 into law on October 1, 1986.[136]

Period Assessment

A principled agent framework finds its strongest support during this third period of the defense reorganization narrative, and it anticipates the Army's strong support for reform. The service clearly supported several key reform provisions, and General Wickham's SASC testimony in December 1985 offered more support than any service chief had given since General Meyer in 1982. Moreover, the work of the Army's special review committee in November 1985 offers compelling evidence of the Army's thinking as a service. The SRC specifically endorsed many of the core reforms eventually codified in Goldwater-Nichols and provided the rationale for its recommendations. In recommending a strengthened Joint Staff, for example, the SRC explained that "the critical nature of joint responsibilities demands that joint staffs be of top quality."[137] Similarly, in arguing for strengthened CINCs, the SRC's report noted that then-current joint publications "inhibit unity of command and thus unity of effort at the warfighting level."[138] In both areas, the SRC's support and underlying rationale are predicted by the various elements of the Army's service culture.

Indeed, the very existence and conduct of the SRC validate the predictions made by the Army's cultural beliefs. The service's self-conception as an apolitical servant suggests an inclination to look beyond Army-centric interests to consider the national good. This willingness took shape in General Wickham's creation of the SRC and the direction given to the committee. The SRC was charged to "get out of the green suit" and look at what the nation needed; this ecumenical mindset clearly guided the conduct of the group.[139] The committee was not expected to validate existing Army positions or known biases of senior leaders. Dr. Edgar Raines, the military historian on the SRC, was impressed by the extent to which the committee's discussions were "broad gauged," "not parochial," and open-minded toward the good of the nation.[140] Members of the SRC found that in considering JCS reform in 1985, the good of the nation and the good of the Army were highly compatible goals.

The Navy's preferences and behavior are also explained by its cultural beliefs. Clearly, the Navy's preferences were generally opposed to reform, particularly to aspects of centralizing the JCS structure, diminishing the president's access to naval expertise, adding layers of bureaucracy, or adding career requirements that would keep sailors from being at sea. All of these were generally predicted at the outset by the Navy's service culture. The service's resistance was not an unthinking reflex to reduced autonomy, but a principled position rooted in long-standing Navy beliefs. John Lehman, in fact, emphasized that one of the fundamental problems with Goldwater-Nichols was its failure to recognize that the Army and Navy are "very very different *professions.*" The independence of the War Department and Navy Department from

1798 until 1949 was not an accident of history, in Lehman's view, but a distinction rooted in the Constitution, reflecting their core differences.[141] The Constitution gave Congress power to "raise and support armies" for two-year periods, but a more expansive power to "provide and maintain a navy."[142] References to the Navy's constitutional uniqueness surfaced regularly during these debates. A letter from a retired rear admiral to Secretary Lehman in May 1986, for example, exhorted Navy officials to "zero in on the unconstitutionality of so-called unification with standing land forces."[143]

The Navy did support isolated tenets of the proposed reforms, as anticipated by the service's command philosophy. Based on the Navy's model of decentralized command, anchored in trust rather than structure, the hypothesis matrix predicted support for a streamlined chain of command and for strengthening of the CINCs—both of which occurred. In his congressional testimony and later reflection, Lehman assessed the "only good thing" in the reform legislation to be strengthening of the CINCs by giving them stronger operational control of their component forces, realigning their authority with their responsibility.[144]

The predicted civil-military dynamics of "preparatory agency" also find intriguing support in this third period, given the increased inevitability of legislation. The Navy's large preference gap with the proposed policies was exacerbated by the policy attributes that portended reduced implementation slack in the future. Consequently, the durability, specificity, imminence, and enforceability of the policy proposals became negotiating points for the Navy, as it tried to shape the parameters of its pending agency contract. For example, the Navy resisted making changes through durable legislation; it continually pushed to create change through executive rather than legislative means. In his autobiography, Lehman referred to Goldwater-Nichols as a "permanent solution to a temporary problem," suggesting that much of the trouble was not just the law's content but its durability.[145] The specificity and enforceability of the new statutes likewise troubled the Navy, as suggested by Admiral Moorer's objection in October 1985 that the proposed reforms were counter to the National Security Act of 1947, which was "purposely ambiguous; we didn't want it to be rigid."[146] The new legislation established specific reporting requirements and enforceable provisions making joint duty a prerequisite for flag rank. Even though existing DOD policy—as set in a 1959 policy directive by Secretary of Defense Thomas Gates—established the same requirement, the new provision was particularly objectionable for the lack of implementation slack it afforded.

In summary, the principled agent approach predicted that the Army would have a fairly small preference gap and would negotiate the details, while the Navy would have a large preference gap and would enter into major conflict. These dynamics indeed played out: once legislation appeared inevitable, the Army shaped it, while the Navy fought it even harder.

Conclusion

When President Reagan signed the Goldwater-Nichols Act, he closed the curtain on a four-and-a-half year legislative drama. A remarkable alignment of events and personalities enabled such landmark reform. This conclusion briefly discusses the key provisions enacted by Goldwater-Nichols in the five areas central to this chapter's analysis and considers how well the principled agent theory fares in explaining the facts of the case, across the three periods, for the Army and the Navy.

Goldwater-Nichols made the following changes in the five focus areas of this case study.[147] First, the act strengthened the chairman of the Joint Chiefs of Staff in several ways, designating him "the principal military adviser to the President, the National Security Council, and the Secretary of Defense." It gave the chairman new responsibilities related to fiscally constrained strategic planning, logistics, joint doctrine, joint education, and budgets. The act also created the position of vice chairman as the second-ranking US military officer, to assist the CJCS as needed and to function as acting chairman in his absence.

Second, the act retained the service chiefs as military advisors to the president, maintaining their dual-hatted status as service chiefs and JCS members. The chairman was charged to consider the views of the other JCS members "as he considers appropriate" when presenting his counsel to civilian leaders.

Third, the act took steps to strengthen the Joint Staff by specifying subordination of the staff directly to the CJCS and by creating a new "joint officer personnel policy." These far-reaching provisions created a new category of "joint specialty officers" and mandated specific educational, duty, and promotion requirements—to include the provision that no officer could be promoted to one-star general or admiral "unless the officer has served in a joint duty assignment."

Fourth, the act significantly empowered the CINCs of the unified and specified commands, giving a CINC full authority to (among other things) "employ forces within that command as he considers necessary to carry out missions assigned to the command." The new law also made clear that subordinate commanders, particularly of the service components, were "under the authority, direction, and control of, and are responsible to, the commander of the combatant command."

Finally, Goldwater-Nichols clarified the chain of command (unless otherwise directed by the president) from the president to the secretary of defense to the CINCs. It also specified, however, that the president could direct that communications between civilian authorities (the president or secretary of defense) and the CINCs be "transmitted through the Chairman of the Joint Chiefs of Staff." Similarly, the act allowed the chairman to "oversee the activities" of the CINCs, but such oversight was not to be confused with command authority, which the chairman did *not* have. In sum, the CJCS and the CINCs gained significant power and authority, while the service chiefs and the military departments saw their status and influence reduced.

Assessing the Theory

This chapter has explored two key dimensions of a principled agent framework. First, the analysis argues that service culture provides the most satisfying prediction and explanation for a service's policy preferences in a given context. Second, the case study tested the dynamics in square II of the four-square typology (see fig. 1.2), in which military agents advise civilian principals on relatively coherent policy issues. Under these conditions, standard agency variables of monitoring, enforcement, and punishment are not yet activated; they are only hinted at by attributes of a proposed policy that convey the likely degree of future implementation slack. When a policy is being crafted, agents pay attention to the amount of future slack its provisions imply and then negotiate accordingly for their preferred amount of maneuver room. This appraisal of future implementation slack interacts with the preference gap to determine the character of the military service's overall response.

How well does the framework explain the preferences and behavior of the Navy in the four years leading up to Goldwater-Nichols? Revisiting the hypotheses made earlier, figure 7.5 assesses the degree to which they are supported by the available evidence; hypotheses strongly supported by the data are in bold, those with some or weak support are in standard type, and those with little or no evidentiary support are in italic. As discussed in chapter 6, a skeptic could argue that the congruence here is contrived, as the *earlier* predictions could have been made with full knowledge of the case. Again, each hypothesis attempted a responsible juxtaposition of the belief with the issue; the finding that several hypotheses are not supported by the available data reflects this sincere effort. Overall, the theory of preferences supplied by service culture performs reasonably well in predicting and explaining the array of preferences exhibited by the Navy. The six-part cultural typology for the Navy gets most of the predictions correct, not only in fact but in form—the rationale, logic, and rhetorical strategy.

The theory also helps to explain the Navy's overall posture of active resistance across the four-year period. Many of the defense reform proposals anticipated little future implementation slack, which made the Navy's opposition to the policy substance all the more fervent. First, the proposed policies were in the form of binding and durable legislation, which is difficult to overturn and carries the normative weight of being *the law*. Second, many of the policy proposals involved transfers of power that were largely self-executing, as newly empowered constituencies had substantive interests in their enforcement. For example, not long after Goldwater-Nichols became law, Arch Barrett visited the commander of Central Command (CENTCOM), Marine Corps General George Crist. The general's copy of Goldwater-Nichols was "dog-eared," given his keen interest as a CINC in understanding all of the new power and authority given to him.[148] Third, the policies were being crafted with great specificity that largely precluded self-interested interpretations. Finally, the policies took effect immediately, not in some future context. Thus the anticipation of little implementation slack, combined with a large preference gap, suggested the Navy would engage in major conflict—which in fact occurred.

The Navy's actions also support the hypothesis that agents negotiate not only the substance of a policy but the parameters of its future implementation. As much as possible, the Navy sought to enact change through less durable executive means; it pushed for transitional terms to push back the law's enactment; and it sought exceptions to specific and enforceable terms that could then be exploited for maneuver room. The service negotiated, for example, an exception to the four-year period of joint education and duty required for promotion to flag rank, based on the sea-duty requirements of its submarine force. In response, the law made an exception for "critical occupational specialties." The services, in turn, designated nearly *all* of their career fields as critical specialties to secure a service-wide exception to the law.[149]

The Army's response to the proposed array of policies is also explained well by a principled-agency approach. A revisited hypothesis matrix, in figure 7.6, indicates the extent to which the Army's policy preferences were correctly predicted by the theory. The theory gets many of these dyadic predictions

NAVY POLICY PREFERENCE FINDINGS

Belief	Overall attitude/general issues	Strengthen CJCS as principal military advisor	Remove service chiefs from JCS	Strengthen CINCs power	Improve JS quality and incentivize JS duty	Streamline chain of command
2.1: An Armed Embassy of America		**Since Navy power is unique, expect resistance to any diminished access to decision-makers.**	**Expect resistance to any move that reduces access of CNO to senior civilian leaders.**			
2.2: America and Navy Prosper Together						
2.3: Survival through Enlisted Order and Commissioned Judgment				*Expect resistance to a non-Navy CINC having increased authority over navy assets.*		

2.4: The Glory of Independent Command at Sea	**Expect resistance to increased intrusion into Navy affairs or micromanagement; expect support for decentralized execution.**	**Expect support for giving CINCs authority and accountability to match their responsibility.**	Expect resistance to outside interference in internal Navy promotions and assignments.	**Expect support for shortest chain of command from president to operational forces.**
2.5: A Professional and Permanent Navy	Large capital investments require constant advocacy and explanation. Expect resistance to reduced access to decision-makers.		**Expect resistance to putting best officers in any shore or staff position instead of at sea.**	
2.6: The Bigger the Better				

Figure 7.5. The US Navy's policy preference findings. Hypotheses with strong support in the available evidence are in **bold**; hypotheses with some support are in plain type; and hypotheses with no meaningful support in the available evidence are in *italic*.

correct, though certainly not all. The Army appeared to have more variation than the Navy in its revealed preferences, particularly between the public posture of its chief of staff and the less public views of the Army staff. While most historical treatments of Goldwater-Nichols focus on a united opposition from the Pentagon, this research offers a more complex and nuanced story. The chief of staff of the Army did indeed stand fast with his fellow chiefs on a number of issues, but his personal views and those of his staff were quite supportive of many reforms. This supportive posture is explained well by the Army's service culture, as many Army beliefs aligned with the spirit of the reforms. In fact, the Association of the US Army published a primer on Goldwater-Nichols in 1987 and reached this conclusion: "The emphasis on greater jointness is totally compatible with the primacy of land power concepts and the new changes merit full and vigorous support."[150]

While the Army's preferences are explained by its cultural beliefs, the service's overall response is explained by the interaction of a small preference gap with the anticipation of little implementation slack. In this configuration, the theory predicts a negotiation of details during the policy creation phase, which did occur. Once it became apparent that reform was going to happen, the Army sought to participate constructively to ensure that the right provisions were enacted. This observation should not be taken too far; by no means was the Army enthusiastically working hard to make the legislation happen. Rather, the overall pattern of activity by the Army during this advisory phase was one of honest input and quiet support.

Final Observations

A clear challenge in studying civil-military relations is identifying the relevant actors to study and evaluate. In any given case, specifying which civilians are interacting with which military leaders requires some simplifying assumptions and a bit of methodological license. This chapter's use of "the Army" and "the Navy" as characters in the story illustrates this challenge. Who actually constitutes the Army and reveals its institutional preferences? Within the available evidence, who speaks for the Navy? This challenge affects any civil-military study; a principled agent framework just foregrounds the issue and makes it explicit. Across the two case study chapters, the impact of service culture on policy preferences seems to hold best at the aggregate service level. The preferences of the *organization*, typically in the form of its headquarters staff, are most likely to conform to the beliefs of service culture. The preferences of any given individual are clearly much harder to predict reliably. Individual preferences are even more elusive when those individuals are subject to counter-pressures, such as a service chief serving on the JCS. The variation in Army preferences seen in the defense reorganization narrative provides a good example of this. The Army staff generally held views that were congruent with the service's cultural beliefs, while the specific preferences shown by Generals Meyer and Wickham were moderated by the pressures for uniformity within the JCS.

While principled agent theory does admirable work in explaining the aggregate patterns of this case, many of the historical details stand for the proposition that *personalities matter*. The motive force in the Goldwater-Nichols story comes from fortuitous alignments of people, places, and dispositions. General David Jones, as he prepared to retire from military service, decided to air his grievances before the HASC. Arch Barrett had just finished writing a book about defense organization, had just been hired by the HASC, and happened to be in the room when Jones went public. Representatives Nichols and Aspin, along with Senators Goldwater and Nunn, were all in committee leadership positions at the same time, all with a keen interest in defense reform—a topic without a voting constituency and thus of rare congressional interest. While no one can predict or theorize about such details, a principled agent framework works in an aggregate, probabilistic way to explain service propensities and broad patterns of behavior. By adding depth to the baseline agency model—incorporating service-level actors, across the policymaking timeline, with varying degrees of policy coherence—the principled agent model is more likely to catch the particular causal variables that explain why civilian principals and military agents act as they do.

ARMY POLICY PREFERENCE FINDINGS

	Overall attitude/ general issues	Strengthen CJCS as principal military advisor	Remove service chiefs from JCS	Strengthen CINCs power	Improve JS quality and incentivize JS duty	Streamline chain of command
4.1: Apolitical Servants of the Nation	**Expect cooperative posture; willing to pursue national interest; expect minimal engagement with Congress.**	**Expect some support: need to generate national advice above service-level interests.**	*Expect mild support: not as threatened by diminished voice for chief of staff of the Army.*	**Expect some support: emphasis on national warfighting capability, less on service interests.**		
4.2: Land Force of Last Resort	**Since the Army understands its essential role, unlikely to feel threatened by legislative activity.**			**Expect support for strengthening warfighters who must perform and finish the job.**	Expect mild support: Army accustomed to serving inglorious roles.	
4.3: The Army Way of Battle	*Expect resistance to political interference in warfighting.*					

4.4: Synchronizing the Fragments	**Expect support: centralizing policies enhance coordination and control.**	**Expect support: enhance unity of command.**	**Expect support: increase capacity to execute combined-arms joint warfare.**	Expect support: need to strengthen capacity for coordinating service activities.	**Expect support: chain of command enhances synchronized action.**
4.5: Fielding an Army: Regulars and the Militia					
4.6: Soldiers, Units, and Leaders				*Expect some resistance: best Army officers should be leading troops in the mud.*	

Figure 7.6. The US Army's policy preference findings. Hypotheses with strong support in the available evidence are in **bold**; hypotheses with some support are in plain type; and hypotheses with no meaningful support in the available evidence are in *italic*.

Conclusion

The fact remains that the services are not alike, that no wit of man can make them alike, and that the retention by each of its separate character, customs, and confidence is essential to the conserving of our national military power.

—Brigadier General S. L. A. Marshall, *The Armed Forces Officer*

The American military exists to defend both the sovereignty and the character of the United States. Called to protect the citizens, interests, and values of the nation, the US military must embody Plato's guardians: "fierce to their enemies but gentle to their friends."[1] It must offer professional expert counsel to its civilian superiors, even when its counsel is contrarian. And then it must salute smartly and work hard in good faith to carry out the policies chosen by the people's elected representatives, whoever they might be. The self-discipline required to thread this political needle is the hallmark of the American military professional.

The great self-discipline of the American military has contributed to centuries of generally healthy civil-military relations. For today's US military, a coup is something that happens abroad—it is practically unimaginable at home. But avoiding a coup is a low bar for political excellence; the American normative standard is, appropriately, much higher. The US system aims for civil-military excellence in both *process* and *product*: smart decisions, well made. Civilian and military leaders share responsibility for crafting effective national policy in ways that preserve the constitutional principle of civilian control. Both goals—sound policy and healthy process—deserve committed pursuit. Military agents should not dictate terms, however wise, to a civilian boss; nor should respectful relationships be nurtured to produce reliably bad policies. But when the twin goals of process and product compete, the democratic process should prevail. Civilians retain "the right to be wrong."[2]

This final chapter summarizes the ways in which a principled agent framework strengthens these core political principles. After situating the framework in a broader context, highlighting the purpose and ambition of a four-service portrait of American civil-military relations, I explain the framework's practical application: how today's political and military leaders, policy practitioners, and interested citizens can use a principled agent approach to advance better policy and process. The discussion then turns to several contemporary defense issues, from future strategy to the military personnel system, and suggests how the four military services are likely to respond. The book concludes with some implications of the framework for both theory and practice.

Within the broad arena of civil-military relations, this book focuses on fundamental questions of civilian control. For a given issue or policy, how closely does military behavior align with civilian intent, and which variables combine to shape these important outcomes? When military behavior departs from civilian intent, what are the responsible judgments to make or lessons to learn? Building on the solid foundation of agency theory, the principled agent framework provides a richer way to explain and appraise civil-military behavior. The expanded framework extends the baseline model in three directions (see fig. 1.1). It expands *temporally* to consider the interaction between pre-decisional advising and post-decisional execution. It expands *contextually* to evaluate how policies with greater or lesser coherence affect military behavior. And it expands *relationally* to appreciate each of the four military services as civil-military actors with their own cultural beliefs. By offering insight into the different cultures of the military services, the argument bridges part of the "civil-military empathy gap" described by Peter Feaver—a gap of understanding and trust, which injures both process and product alike.[3]

Trading theoretical simplicity for empirical richness, this framework complements existing theories of civilian control. While some theories go after big trends, others calibrate their lenses to see finer details. To explain nuanced military behavior, particularly in a civil-military context, principled agent theory falls in the latter category. It presents new variables to consider and identifies the conditions under which those variables most likely shape the narrative. Like most social scientific work, it is suggestive and probabilistic in navigating complex social interactions.

The framework does not pretend to eclipse all that has come before. It builds upon and extends the baseline theory—an extension made possible by the root strength, not weakness, of agency theory. Similarly, the framework does not reject all competing explanations but finds them incomplete. For example, the argument here claims that military behavior is often more principled than bureaucratic or rivalry explanations suggest, but stipulates that scrambling for dollars, missions, and prestige does, in fact, occur. When the services move in different directions, frustrating civilian intent, bureaucratic rivalry may indeed be *part* of the story, but it has long been proffered as the whole story. As the evidence in preceding chapters shows, there is more going on. In many cases, the services act as principled agents, not mere bureaucratic actors scheming for greater autonomy, money, or turf.

Applying the Framework

This book pushes agency theory in new directions, with a goal of providing practical insight for civil-military practitioners and interested citizens. The following discussion integrates the theoretical work related in chapter 1 and the empirical work in chapters 2 through 7. If civil-military interactions tend to follow the patterns described here, how can practitioners channel these tendencies toward the common good? What counsel does this framework provide to civilian and military leaders living out these dynamics every day?

The framework's normative counsel to the American military is consistent with well-established norms in the academic and professional military literature.[4] As the junior partner in an "unequal dialogue," the military serves as an expert nonpartisan advisor to and faithful agent of lawful civilian authority.[5] The military wields national coercive power, subject to civilian direction and oversight. Its job is to give professional counsel by offering meaningful military options, with associated risks and likely impacts—all rendered in a way that preserves civilians' decision-making latitude. After a civilian decision, the military agent must do what any subordinate is trained to do: carry out the boss's intent to the best of one's ability, adopting the policy as one's own. In a democratic system, the will of the governed should prevail; the military does its part by faithfully executing the lawful orders of those who embody the national will—whoever they might be.

Building on this normative foundation, the bulk of counsel in this framework is oriented toward civilian leaders who serve as senior partner in the civil-military exchange. Civilians have the responsibility of building an environment that cultivates diverse expertise, optimizes policy outcomes, and promotes constitutional values. Looking again at the four-square typology (fig. C.1), how can civilians steer these trends to good effect?

Principled Agent Framework

	Preparatory Agency	Traditional Principal–Agent Theory
High Policy Coherence	• Agents anticipate the slack in the proposed future compliance environment • Civil–military debate covers both the policy substance and the parameters of implementation slack • Military agents seek to lock in favored policies or create slack for disfavored ones II	• Civilian principals adjust the monitoring regime, preference gaps, rewards, and punishments to encourage military compliance • Military decision is largely *whether* or *how much* to comply with the stated policy I
Low Policy Coherence	III Principled Diagnosis • In ambiguous, complex, or cluttered policy environments, military agents diagnose the situation, aided by the lens of service culture • Civil–military interaction is marked by culturally conditioned problem definition	IV Principled Agency • Military behavior is marked by culturally conditioned interpretation of what compliance requires in a given context • Military decision may be more about *how* to comply, not a material cost–benefit calculation of whether to do so
	Advising	Executing

Figure C.1. Summary of principled agent hypotheses as the timeline and coherence of the policy vary.

The first insight for civilian practitioners is to recognize two broad contour lines shaping the civil-military policy space. *Temporally*, the dynamics of advising a policy differ markedly from those of executing it. *Contextually*, the coherence of a policy shifts the military agent's calculation from *whether* to *how*. When compliance activities are clear, agents generally calculate whether to enact them; when they are unclear, agents more likely consider how to enact them. Thus, within a given civil-military exchange, civilians should orient themselves on these axes. Is one looking for expert and diverse counsel on a pending decision, or faithful compliance with a set policy? If compliance is the goal, how clear, consistent, and feasible are the behaviors required of the military agent? Answers to these questions suggest where the debate sits on the principled agent map.

Civilian leaders seeking expert counsel during the advisory phase tend to benefit from diverse opinions and a deep bench of options. Varying ideas are a source of collective advantage. Starting, then, in square III of the figure: as a policy idea is introduced into dialogue, before the issues clarify, expect the four services to offer counsel informed by prevailing cultural beliefs. Each service's advice will include a contingent mix of national and service-level interests, with enduring cultural beliefs playing a key role in forming these early preferences.

As a debate matures and the central issues clarify, the dynamics tend to shift up toward square II—the domain of preparatory agency. A mature debate foreshadows the future compliance regime, so more detailed negotiations are expected. While pursuing favorable policies, military agents will also angle for implementation slack: the degree of specificity, imminence, durability, and enforceability in the policy instrument. Civilian leaders can capitalize on these dynamics to effect better public policy. When a policy breaks new ground, for example, and different interpretations of compliance may be worth testing, civilians can design sufficient implementation slack to encourage service-level variation in the future. They can make the prescription less specific or the policy instrument less durable to preserve breathing room for future change. Conversely, when a policy requires a single interpretation of compliance, less implementation slack promotes a more uniform response. Clearly written expectations, with enforceable provisions that take effect soon, will tend to shrink the services' interpretative space.

These elements of implementation slack also serve as useful negotiating capital. In principle, civilian leaders should not have to bargain with military agents; in reality, however, leaders of all stripes occasionally find it helpful to make concessions to those they lead. Implementation slack offers a way for civilian leaders to prevail on a policy's substance while conceding some of its maneuver space. In fact, implementation slack may be the hidden cause of a civil-military surprise. Civilians bracing for a clash might find military indifference instead, or they might stray into a fierce battle over a matter of presumed agreement. If an issue sparks more or less friction than expected, participants should look at the slack in the proposed policy: both types of surprise are likely to indicate gaping holes in the foreshadowed compliance regime. When the future slack looks high, agents foresee room to sidestep the burdens of a disagreeable policy, so they probably choose to keep their negotiating powder dry. For an advantageous policy, however, slack spells trouble. When agents strongly favor a particular outcome, expect them to negotiate away the slack to bind all parties to an enduring, specific, enforceable provision. Principals and agents who agree today work hard to ensure their successors have to agree tomorrow.

Once a debate culminates and the civilian principal enacts the policy, the civil-military dynamics shift from the left to the right side of figure C.1. When the decision is made, the military agent's mindset shifts from advice to execution. Ideally, the expert advisors who offer their best military judgment become the executive agents delivering their best military behavior. On the execution side, the patterns of military behavior vary as a function of the policy's coherence. To gauge this coherence, practitioners can ask: (1) Are the specific behaviors of compliance clear? (2) Are they consistent with other known policies? And (3) are they feasible? As the answers to these three questions trend toward yes, the dynamics follow the logic of traditional agency theory (square I). Better policies encourage better patterns of faithful compliance. In this traditional agency realm, military agents tend to calculate their actions based on the interaction among preference gaps, monitoring conditions, and expectations of rewards and punishments. This arena emphasizes the rational materialist elements of civil-military interaction, where military agents make cost-benefit calculations about whether (or how much) to comply with a stated policy.

As answers to the three questions trend toward no, the civil-military pattern shifts down to square IV—the world of principled agency. When it is not clear what "right looks like" or how to "get there from here," the services might begin to "secure the building." The services might move in four different directions, most likely in good faith, interpreting the policy in culturally conditioned ways. Ambiguity activates culture, which animates the differing beliefs and interpretations of the four services. If a civilian finds these varying patterns of compliance acceptable, or even helpful, then the ambiguity serves a noble purpose. New, untested, or provisional policies might benefit from beta-testing of different models of compliance. If the variation is not useful, however, civilian leaders can channel service behavior toward a common translation by clarifying with more-specific language what compliance should look like. They can improve the internal and external consistency of the policy so that fulfilling the aims of one policy does not require frustrating the intent of another. And they can improve the feasibility of a policy to strengthen the services' capacity to comply. The services are unlikely to march in lockstep to cross a bridge too far.

Contemporary Application

How might these principled agent mechanics apply to today's civil-military issues? This brief discussion highlights some key concerns in the current defense environment and considers how the four services might interpret and respond to those concerns. As the national security community discusses the best suite of policies for today's military, the four services will be major players, informing debates and carrying out policy. Without trying to chase the latest headlines, the discussion here considers how the services' approaches to salient issues might differ, all else being equal, on the basis of their cultural beliefs. I present these hypotheses fully aware that all else is never equal—other factors intrude into the decision space, and the services' approach to these issues will differ from the sketches made here. In civil-military policy-making, service culture is at work but does not work alone. A keen awareness of the services' cultural propensities is simply one part of understanding a complex social pattern, allowing insight into specific behaviors or identifying the cultural baseline from which other contingent factors will move the story.

Looking at some of the central debates underway in 2017, we see two sets of issues receiving significant attention—issues that curiously revisit themes highlighted in the two case study chapters. First, in the realm of crafting strategy, the former deputy secretary of defense Robert Work has led the department to pursue a "third offset" strategy to find dimensions of American military advantage against strong state powers. Many of the conditions informing the third offset discussion mirror those in place in the late 1970s when the Department of Defense (DOD) created the Rapid Deployment Joint Task Force (RDJTF). Second, various experts in the national security community are currently calling for an update to the Goldwater-Nichols Act. After 30 years of shaping American military policy, Goldwater-Nichols is being scrutinized to see whether its provisions still accomplish their intent. A basket of current policies and proposals related to organization, personnel, acquisition, and authorities revisit many of the core issues addressed back in 1986.

The Third Offset Strategy

Championed by then Deputy Secretary of Defense Robert Work, the "third offset" quickly became a popular phrase in the DOD. As Secretary Work described them, offset strategies seek to counter an adversary's quantitative or geographic advantage without trying to match tank for tank or plane for plane. Instead, clever combinations of technology, operating concepts, and organizational structures can offset a competitor's current investment. Done right, an offset strategy restores advantage, giving options to policymakers and strengthening "comprehensive strategic stability."[6] In the 1950s, the first offset strategy conceived of using battlefield nuclear weapons to offset clear

Soviet numerical advantages in Western Europe. In the post-Vietnam world of the 1970s, the budget-constrained United States embarked on another off-set strategy, capitalizing on the microprocessor revolution to build battle networks linking reconnaissance and strike platforms. Enabled by advances in radar-evading stealth and precision weapons, the second offset strategy built the American military that has dominated the world for the past 25 years.

Secretary Work frequently noted that today's strategic situation bears keen resemblances to that of the post-Vietnam era: the public is weary of a long irregular war, budgets are tight, most American forces are based in the continental United States, and competitor states have blunted the edge of military superiority that the US has long enjoyed. Russia and China, for instance, have caught up in the core technologies of the second offset—stealth and precision now abound. Both countries have poured money into so-called anti-access and area-denial (A2/AD) weapons such as advanced surface-to-air missiles and long-range ballistic missiles, designed to keep American forces out of the area, or at least out of the fight. Furthermore, these competitors have built weapons and technologies that target America's vulnerable dependencies in space and cyberspace. In short, Secretary Work argued, the United States can no longer double down on its existing paradigm. He has asked each of the services to find new ways of combining emerging technology, concepts, and organizations to regain coercive leverage.

The planning of a third offset strategy satisfies many of the conditions in which the services are likely to respond in culturally conditioned ways—square III in figure C.1. The high priority, extensive scope, and pervasive ambiguity of the third offset establish the conditions that animate service culture. The policy is clearly a priority for the DOD, and plenty of defense dollars are at stake. The policy spans the equities of all four services; it is a global initiative, touching every domain of war in every corner of the globe. And though the services may be competing for prestige and dollars, this is primarily a competition of *ideas*. The service with the best ideas about how to reclaim advantage will find its budget share and press coverage on the rise. Since very little about the third offset is prescribed, the current debate focuses on making sense of an ambiguous but threatening strategic environment. Questions are many and answers are few. In sum, these conditions define the arena in which service culture should play a powerful if tacit role. How, then, might the four services diagnose the stakes and begin making choices about how to respond?

The Navy's belief structure (see fig. 2.1) suggests several themes likely to emerge from the Navy staff. First of all, the vexing challenge of facing global threats with only US-based forces is hardly a problem; that is exactly what navies are for. The Navy is forward, showing the flag and showing its guns from the Baltic to the South China Sea to the Strait of Hormuz. While the other services may *talk* about China, the Navy sails at the leading edge of international tension, where principles of sovereignty, freedom of navigation, and international law take steel-hulled form. The Navy is exactly the force one needs to navigate the hybrid space between peace and war, especially when the next hotspot is unknown. Expect the Navy, then, to downplay the DOD's concern over the mismatch between global challenges and limited forces to meet them—as long as the Navy has sufficient ships to do its job. As a corollary, the Navy may emphasize the enduring mission of protecting international commerce, as shipping lanes must remain open no matter what the threat environment may be.

With respect to ways and means, the Navy is likely to pursue several of the technologies central to the third offset debate. As a force of warrior-diplomats, the Navy seeks a deliberate mix of revealing and hiding—proudly sailing certain ships while hiding others. Electronic warfare, deception, undersea operations, and cryptography have long been staples of naval operations. So, expect the Navy to pursue new ways of hiding, finding, and maneuvering within the undersea and electromagnetic spectrum, so as to strengthen its ability to appear only at the times and places of its choosing. In addition, autonomy and artificial intelligence (AI) are key ingredients in the "technological sauce" of the third offset.[7] A Navy ship may be prime real estate for machines to assume more of the scripted mechanical tasks currently handled by enlisted sailors. Expect less eagerness, however, about the transitioning of tasks accomplished by officers, whose judgment and experience are critical to the Navy's success.

Lastly, the Navy's approach to force structure might involve some common themes. The service must continue to press for shipbuilding expertise, infrastructure, and funding in all seasons. The next-decade fleet begins today, so expect continual engagement on the need for a strong industrial base and steady ship production. An interesting thread to watch will be the kind of ships the Navy pursues. With globally dispersed challenges and clear threats to capital ships such as aircraft carriers, one possible strategy would call for higher numbers of smaller, less-capable ships to provide presence, mixed with submarines that can still hide. If the Navy continues to orient its thinking and strategy primarily around aircraft carriers, this may indicate the lingering influence of an enduring bigger-is-better service culture. A shift away from carriers would be a major cultural (and operational) undertaking.

The Marine Corps' belief structure (see fig. 3.1) presents another approach to "securing the building" of the third offset. Expect the Marines, like the Navy, to see a great opportunity to tell the story of the service as America's ever-ready fighting force, afloat with the Navy across the globe. The challenging security environment of the twenty-first century is exactly why America needs and wants a Marine Corps. Always concerned about the viability of its designated mission, the Corps is likely to emphasize the continuing relevance of amphibious operations, particularly in an era of dispersed threats and fewer overseas bases. Marines may be quick to note that amphibious operations are more relevant than ever before; the more things change, the more they stay the same. With respect to specific investments, the frugal Marine Corps will probably act less like venture capitalists and more like opportunistic tinkerers. By inheriting secondhand equipment or refurbishing its own, the Corps seems more likely to develop new capabilities on old gear than to invest in complex tech-intensive systems of its own. Any investments and innovations it makes are likely to be committed to supporting 19-year-old Marines and their rifles; the clarifying focus of Marine Corps operations is unlikely to shift.

The DOD's current fascination with autonomy and AI could affect the Marine Corps in a couple of ways. Marines may find small autonomous machines (both airborne and terrestrial) to be cheap, prolific, and effective ways of doing job number one: supporting rifle-bearing Marines who find and close with the enemy. The Corps has historically been low-tech, but not anti-tech. Creativity and nonlinear thinking have kept the Corps viable for hundreds of years. Semiautonomous machines, partnered with young, digital-native Marines, might eventually secure a prominent place on the Marine Corps battlefield. A possible counterpressure, however, may arise from the centrality of the Marine identity. Being a Marine is a governing identity, not a job. Marines exert strong in-group pressures, so trust is high internally but low toward outsiders. Will semiautonomous machines make the cut into the high-trust Corps? They might. As the Marine Corps discovers the utility of semiautonomous machines in combat operations, the service might look for visible ways of bringing these Marine machines inside their circle of trust.

Finally, as the DOD focuses on "transregional, multidomain, multifunc-tion" threats, all the services will look for ways to think more holistically across the traditional seams and boundaries of their missions.[8] The Marine Corps will probably do this well internally; the Corps has historically thought and oper-ated as a multidomain, integrated force across sea, land, and air. Integrating space, cyberspace, and electronic warfare into internal operations may be eas-ier for the Corps than for the other services. But strong in-group trust, com-bined with a signature mission of being first to fight, may lead Marines to pur-sue an *autonomous* realm of intra-Corps multidomain integration. Integration across domains with the other services is likely to prove as difficult as ever.

The Army offers a third approach to thinking about the third offset, in-formed by its prevailing cultural beliefs (see fig. 4.1). Of all the services, the Army is most likely to consider carefully the national and civic implications of the strategic problem. As vulnerabilities in cyberspace expose more of American society to foreign interference, the Army may take a leading role in new thinking about defending the American people and their power grids, dams, and financial markets. The Army will probably be more attuned to the civil-military gap in American society, looking for ways to meet global chal-lenges while remaining closely linked with the American people. The service will certainly be preoccupied with manpower, ensuring that it maintains ac-ceptable levels of suitably trained soldiers across its active, guard, and reserve components. The trend toward autonomy and AI may be difficult for the Army to navigate in this respect. Machines can help relieve some of the ser-vice's inevitable manpower struggles, but the Army sees itself as the honorable steward of the profession of arms. Can machines steward that legacy? The Army is unlikely to shy away from fielding more machines on the battlefield, but it is the service most likely to struggle deeply with ethical reservations about doing so. Muddy-boot leadership will still be prized, even in a force with more code than blood.

In addition to autonomy and AI, the Army is likely to pursue a small num-ber of high-impact, closely coordinated technologies. During the era of the second offset in the late 1970s and early 1980s, the Army invested in its "Big Five" suite of systems: the Abrams tank, the Bradley fighting vehicle, the Blackhawk transport helicopter, the Apache attack helicopter, and the Patriot missile air-defense system.[9] These systems, fielded in large numbers, have been the materiel foundation of the Army for the past generation. The ser-vice might take a similar approach in the third offset, building a closely coor-dinated suite of widely proliferated systems. Whatever the Army chooses to build, it is likely to develop a companion doctrine or operating concept, which it will reinforce across the service with extensive training exercises. If any service codifies a new manual or handbook to promote standardization in its third offset initiatives, it is most likely to be the Army.

The Army is also likely to lead efforts to bridge the functional gaps and seams across the services and domains. Synchronized effort is an Army imperative. Ever the joint coordinator, the Army is most likely to lead any joint initiatives that synchronize multidomain operations across the services. As it does so, the Army may resist integration efforts that discard geographic lanes and boundaries as their central organizing principle. Geography and terrain are fundamental to how the Army thinks, organizes, and maneuvers. But the multidomain world of space, cyberspace, and electronic warfare does not easily conform to the logic of physical geography. So, while the Army may lead the way in integrating joint efforts, such integration will probably remain geographic and unit-based, despite the nongeographic and diffuse nature of key domains.

The Air Force belief structure (see fig. 5.1) presents a fourth way to make sense of the third offset opportunity. The Air Force boasts a long history of going "over not through" strategic problems, and it played a leading role in each of the first two defense offsets.[10] A pre-announced third offset represents a golden opportunity for airmen to do it again, to reclaim American leverage by mating new technologies with clever operational concepts. Given this close congruence between the opportunity and Air Force culture, airmen will probably feel internal pressure to "hurry up and innovate!" But the gap between cultural pressure and achievable reality may be difficult to bridge.

As the DOD pursues multidomain thinking—tearing down artificial boundaries between operating domains—the Air Force is well positioned to lead the way. The service has expertise in air, space, and cyberspace; integrating them conceptually and operationally is likely to be a major goal of the service in the years ahead. But the service may have an embedded challenge in doing so. While the Air Force writ large has expertise in air, space, and cyberspace, its excellence is vertically isolated. Very few people or units have actual experience in thinking or operating across the seams of the three domains. So expect the Air Force to experiment with new technologies, operating concepts, and organizational constructs that test different models of building cross-functional intuition across its silos of excellence. Given the relative fluidity of Air Force organizational traditions, the service seems likely to test out different approaches to solving a perennial organizational puzzle: how to develop both specialists and generalists. How can an organization grow deep expertise, with that expertise integrated widely across the organization? For the Air Force, the functional goal of this organizational experimentation may well be the creation of an ever-improving targeting machine. The service's default operational code revolves around picking the right targets, finding them, and then delivering the best weapon (or effect) against them. For airmen, the third offset may be largely focused on perpetual refinements to the service's targeting-reconnaissance-strike engine, fueled by big data, networks, and breakthroughs in machine learning.

The Air Force seems likely to put new technologies at the forefront of its third offset efforts. Most Air Force missions are predicated on sophisticated technologies performing highly technical tasks; the future of the service should sustain that trend. Autonomy and AI will no doubt play a major role, particularly in various aspects of building the targeting machine referred to above. In a more general sense, expect the Air Force to pursue game-changing technologies that support its fundamental beliefs about the right ways to use airpower. The service will most likely sustain its focus on the primary imperative of air superiority, the latent potential in strategic attack, and the enduring wisdom of centralizing the control of assets under the senior airman in an operation. Some of the technological trends shaping the future of war may well challenge the core logic in these fundamental beliefs. The logic of centralizing control of air assets, for example, flows from an assumed condition of scarcity. With limited numbers of expensive things, it makes sense to control them centrally. But a developing trend in technology could favor quantity over quality, with higher numbers of cheap, 3-D printed, swarming, autonomous flying agents. When the future battlefield is littered with cheap and disposable flying machines—performing the reconnaissance and strike roles once played by large, expensive, manned platforms—will the logic of centralized control still apply? If the premise gives way, will the conclusion change, or has the belief been reified into a self-evident truth?

In sum, the third offset movement appears ripe for service-level variation, even if the *third offset* label loses some of its cachet. Both ambiguity and opportunity are high—dollars and prestige will flow to the service that makes the most compelling case for new technologies, concepts, and structures. To make that case, the services will draw upon both tacit cultural beliefs and contingent opportunities in the policy space. Service culture may play a leading role in this unfolding drama.

The Defense Reform Debate

A second set of current debates orbits around personnel and organizational policies across the DOD, revisiting the themes of the 1970s and 1980s that led to the Goldwater-Nichols Act. Among the many issues being considered, three in particular deserve further discussion here. First, former Secretary of Defense Ashton Carter led an initiative called the "Force of the Future," directing the four services to refresh their approaches to recruiting, talent acquisition, talent management, and family-life accommodation.[11] Second, some in the defense community have argued for interagency reform to improve the processes and products governing the DOD's many interactions with other executive departments and federal agencies.[12] A third issue under review is the DOD's Unified Command Plan (UCP), the central organizing document that carves the world into geographic and functional combatant commands. In a world of transregional, multidomain, multifunctional threats, some experts question whether the current model carves the world at the proper joints. This discussion touches on these three issues and considers how the services might vary in their approach to each.

From his first day on the job, Secretary Carter made it clear that the DOD needed to improve its ability to recruit and retain twenty-first-century talent.[13] Through a series of policy directives, Carter asked the services to modernize their approach to personnel management without discarding the core ethos of the profession of arms. The policy decisions have since been made, and the services have moved into the implementation environment. While Secretary Carter made clear his intent, each policy leaves some room for the services to implement it in ways that make sense for each service—the arena of principled agency. In their efforts to rethink recruiting, acquiring expert talent, and managing that talent, how might the services approach these new initiatives?

In a November 2016 memo, Secretary Carter issued guidance on recruiting the Force of the Future. He outlined in his memo two initiatives aimed at strengthening the services' recruiting efforts. The first focused on "enhancing geographic, demographic, and generational access in military recruiting," and the second on "reinvigorating the Reserve Officers' Training Corps (ROTC) at 100 years."[14] Within the two initiatives, the memo outlined several focus areas for the DOD. As implementation of these focus areas begins, the services may reinvigorate their recruiting in different ways. The Army is likely to take a strong and eager interest, given its imperative focus on manpower. It will probably focus on quantity over quality, looking for sheer numbers across the active, guard, and reserve components. The Army will probably have the most comprehensive recruiting effort geographically, canvassing the country for able-bodied soldiers. Its message is likely to accentuate the close connection between the Army and the American people and will not shy away from highlighting the financial and professional benefits of serving the country.

The Marine Corps, however, is likely to remain true to its elite warrior identity and continue offering its one enduring incentive: *the opportunity to be a Marine.* Its elite image will remain in the foreground, emphasizing perhaps that a high-tech future will still require fearless warriors. Joining the "few and the proud" will most likely remain the main benefit hawked in any recruiting pitch. The Air Force might be the most willing to rethink its height, weight, fitness, or appearance standards for new recruits. Recognizing its need for cyberspace experts, for example, the Air Force may decide to take a chance on young, elite coders who come with tattoos, piercings, or girth that do not meet conventional military standards. Since the service already wrestles internally with the question of "who or what is a warrior?" it may lean in and embrace that conflict, redefining its warrior class altogether. Given the informal collegiality of its operations, the Air Force might accommodate these new definitions better than the other services.

A second focus area in Carter's Force of the Future is talent acquisition and management. How can the DOD bring in twenty-first-century skill sets that tend to flourish in private industry more than in military structures? The secretary asked the services to consider ways for citizens to enter at higher ranks, particularly for experts in critical fields—just as the services have historically done for doctors, lawyers, and other professionals. Could the same approach work for experts in data science, technology, innovation, or AI? Could professionals enter the service for just a short period of time, serving in a rank or pay structure completely different from today's officer and enlisted frameworks? Of the four services, the Air Force's service culture appears to be the most amenable to these ideas. The Air Force most naturally organizes and identifies around technical expertise; and it does so with an informal collegiality that has fewer cultural hang-ups about formal rank and hierarchy. The Marine Corps, on the other hand, does not have a tradition of importing professionals at higher ranks—it relies on the Navy for most of its professional services such as doctors and dentists. Marine Corps culture begins with a common baptism at recruit training or the officers' Basic School. If the Corps were to accept more lateral entry for key professionals, expect participation in the common baptism to be a firm requirement. Both the Navy and Army seem culturally disposed to hire professional experts as needed, but those lateral entries will most likely stay far away from the prestigious posts of command. Without years at sea or muddy boots, no expert could expect to contribute to the *main* effort of the Navy or Army.

A third area of focus in the Force of the Future centers on more flexible talent management within the services. How might the services make more customized use of their talent through flexible promotion opportunities? The secretary asked Congress for authority to allow the services to promote selected officers before it would otherwise be their turn. In today's lineal promotion system, officers selected for promotion pin on their new rank based on a sequential order determined primarily by current date of rank. Those officers selected early or "below the zone" are last in a promotion group to wear the new rank, since the "in the zone" selectees have more senior dates of rank. Secretary Carter asked Congress to change this policy, allowing the services to adjust the lineal order to "promote officers of particular merit first."[15] The four services might embrace this new authority differently. The Army and Air Force, in particular, seem likely to pursue this in different directions. Army culture is process-driven, structured, and keenly aware of rank— and of seniority within the same rank. Air Force culture is less hierarchical and more informal and is comfortable choosing both tactical and organizational leaders based on qualification and demonstrated merit rather than seniority. Consequently, the Air Force seems more likely to embrace and make full use of the new authority, while the Army will probably use it more sparingly and reluctantly—perhaps only for its most conspicuous warriors whose combat boots are especially muddy.

In addition to these three focus areas in the Force of the Future, the broader defense reform conversation has two other notable threads to discuss. The first is the growing demand for better interagency coordination. The pattern of military operations in recent years, particularly since September 2001, has included challenging reconstruction and stabilization efforts in Iraq and Afghanistan. While led by the military, these missions have pursued a "whole of government approach," bringing together competencies from across the US government. Reconstruction efforts abroad have included, among others, elements from the DOD; the Departments of State, Justice, Treasury, and Agriculture; the US Agency for International Development; and scores of nongovernmental organizations. Domestically, the daily policymaking process relies on regular interagency coordination, typically led by the staff of the National Security Council. Practitioners at home and abroad commonly lament the procedural and cultural barriers to effective interagency coordination, prompting calls for comprehensive interagency reform—a Goldwater-Nichols-like overhaul of the interagency domain.

Among the four services, the Army and Marine Corps have the most institutional experience on the ground over the past 16 years. Both have lived and breathed the interagency atmosphere, but their cultural profiles suggest different responses to calls for interagency reform. As it did with Goldwater-Nichols, the Army seems likely to support interagency reform in pursuit of centrally coordinated and synchronized processes. The Army marches to the beat of process, so the service would probably favor clearer procedures, rules, and authorities to determine who is in charge of what and when. Establishing lanes of operation, then coordinating laterally with those on one's left and right (geographically or conceptually), is central to the Army way. The Marine Corps seems less likely to run toward the sound of interagency gunfire. The service certainly has plenty of interagency experience and also pursues closely integrated operations, but the Marine way privileges the Marine Air-Ground Task Force (MAGTF), the Marine-only combined-arms phalanx. This observation does not suggest that Marines will necessarily oppose better joint or interagency reform, but the Corps is less likely to pursue it actively or feel a compelling need. While such concerns live at the Army core, for the Marine Corps they sit at the periphery.

The final contemporary issue to consider here is the Unified Command Plan, a work of striking geopolitical ambition that divides the surface of the Earth into military regions, each commanded by an American four-star flag officer. The current UCP carves up the world both geographically and functionally, as some commanders lead regions (e.g., European Command and Pacific Command) while others integrate common tasks across those regions (e.g., Transportation Command and Strategic Command). This division of labor has worked well enough for the past 70 years, but does it deal adequately with today's multidomain, transregional world? A nonstate group such as the so-called Islamic State is diffused across three geographic commands, with activities that animate core interests of at least three functional commands as well. In view of these challenges, some in the security community are calling for an overhaul of the UCP, questioning whether the dotted lines on today's map reflect the right boundaries—geographic or otherwise—between commands.[16]

The four services are likely to approach a UCP debate with strong feelings and different reactions. The UCP expresses a fundamental division of labor among the services, and leading these commands is a major index of power and prestige in the DOD. One of the Pentagon's key scorecards of power is the tally of which service's officers lead which combatant commands. Consequently, any UCP discussion will tend to stoke rivalry dynamics and some inescapable jockeying for preeminence. Beyond sheer rivalry, however, the cultural profiles help indicate how the services might respond. The very nature of the UCP determines that the services will have strong feelings; the principled agency framework suggests what those strong feelings might be.

The Army and Navy seem likely to oppose fundamental changes to the current UCP construct. The two services have had a long-standing geographic division of labor, with clear distinctions between land and sea interests. In particular, the Army has long held sway over European Command, while the Navy has dominated the blue-water territory of Pacific Command—perhaps the two most prestigious combatant commands. Giving up such influential posts will be difficult, especially when the services are already predisposed to think in the geographic terms that define those commands. The enduring character of geography provides cultural ballast to each service, bringing reliable continuity to changing times.

The Marine Corps and Air Force are more likely to favor a new construct for the unified commands. Both services tend to think more episodically than geographically. The Marine Corps organizes, trains, and equips to serve as a MAGTF, providing a ready-made Marine-only force wherever a crisis erupts. It thinks in terms of short-notice and short-run conflicts, where the Corps establishes a beachhead for heavier follow-on forces, if needed. The Air Force has different reasons to favor change. It tends to take a fluid view of geography—borders and boundaries are more to be crossed than reified. Airmen organize, train, and equip around missions in multiple domains—air, space, and cyberspace. These domains challenge terrestrial lines, conditioning airmen to approach the world in more nonlinear ways. Air Force missions tend to occur in temporal bursts, with forces—perhaps originating thousands of miles away from each other—packaged together contingently for a specific event. With an episodic, mission-oriented, multidomain way of war, where terrain is more footnote than reality, the Air Force is more likely to argue for a new construct oriented around missions, organized in joint task forces and across multiple domains.

In summary, these service-level hypotheses about the third offset and defense reform illustrate a contemporary application of principled agency. Of course, the actual moves, debates, and service responses of the future will no doubt deviate from the modest predictions made here. But as a demonstration of how to apply the cultural components of the framework, and as a first cut into the likely differences in approach across the four services, the discussion presented here serves an important purpose, no matter the future headlines.

Principled Agency for All

The analysis of civil-military relations presented in this book aims to provide novel yet practical insight for scholars, practitioners, and engaged citizens alike. For scholars of civil-military relations, it enriches agency theory by carefully stretching the baseline to reveal variables and outcomes unseen in the core theory. For practitioners of civil-military policymaking, both uniformed and civilian, the book paints a picture of who tends to think what, and how they might go about translating preferences into policy. These insights should prove useful in channeling common tendencies of belief and action toward the twin goals of sound policy and healthy process. For the American people, this project delivers a closer look at their military, the constitutive differences among the services, and some of the civil-military dynamics that animate the headlines. Engaged citizens who develop an appreciation of these factors can better steward their republic toward its constitutional vision.

The principled agent framework offers new ways to explain and appraise the dynamics of civilian control over the military. It highlights variables such as service culture and implementation slack that interact to effect important outcomes. While the framework is explanatory in nature, it rests on a strongly normative foundation. The purpose of this book is not merely to understand civil-military dynamics but to improve them. It seeks to arm practitioners with insights on principle and process so that they can craft effective security policy in ways that reinforce constitutional virtues.

In cultivating healthy civil-military relations, one variable appears to rule them all: *trust*. Civil-military relations thrive when trust is high; they wither when it erodes. Indeed, *any* relationship—even civilization itself—flourishes as trust builds. When both civilian and military leaders commit themselves to acting in good faith, exercising the constitutional process, and disciplining their actions to the proper duties of the roles they exercise, they inject trust directly into the bloodstream of the republic. When each side understands and appreciates the other's role and equities, empathy and trust grow stronger. As this happens, civilian and military leaders can discard suspicion of the other, thus emboldened to make better policies through healthier processes.

Ironically, this book leveraged principal-agent theory—usually predicated on opposing interests and distrust—to develop deeper empathy and trust among civil-military practitioners. If this goal of building trust can be achieved, a principal-agent perspective could become interesting but irrelevant. When trust is high, agency variables such as preference gaps, monitoring, and punishments fade from view. In a healthy relationship, trust beats agency every time.

In the end, trust and empathy are virtues we should all cultivate in a democratic republic. Clearly, these virtues strengthen civil-military relations and reinforce key practices such as civilian control over the military. But in a sense, all citizens in a representative democracy are under civilian control. To pursue a shared vision of human flourishing, each citizen chooses to subordinate his or her unbridled desires to the principles, procedures, and positions created by the Constitution. Subordinating the group with the guns is just a conspicuous case of something that applies to all of us. In whatever role we serve, each of us answers to another. The military submits to civilian control. Elected leaders submit to the public will, expressed through the ballot box. And citizens submit to one another and to constitutional virtues. In our republic as in our military, we should redouble our commitment to offer a principled voice to the process and then carry out our duty, whatever it might be.

Introduction

1. For a video presentation of Peter Feaver describing the empathy gap, see "Power Struggle—Peter Feaver," https://www.youtube.com/watch?v=WIU8rIOkkVo (accessed December 4, 2016).

2. Rosa Brooks, "Civil-Military Paradoxes," in *Warriors & Citizens: American Views of Our Military*, ed. Kori Schake and Jim Mattis (Stanford, CA: Hoover Institution Press, 2016), p. 39.

3. Ibid., pp. 39, 49.

4. Jim Golby, Lindsay P. Cohn, and Peter D. Feaver, "Thanks for Your Service: Civilian and Veteran Attitudes after Fifteen Years of War," in Schake and Mattis, *Warriors & Citizens*, p. 110.

5. Peter Feaver, *Armed Servants: Agency, Oversight, and Civil-Military Relations* (Cambridge, MA: Harvard University Press, 2003).

6. Plato, *The Republic*, trans. Richard W. Sterling and William C. Scott (New York: Norton, 1985), p. 71.

7. Samuel E. Finer, *The Man on Horseback: The Role of the Military in Politics* (London: Pall Mall, 1962), p. 4.

8. Alexis de Tocqueville, *Democracy in America*, ed. J. P. Mayer, trans. George Lawrence (New York: Harper & Row, 1969; New York: HarperCollins, 2006), p. 649. Citations refer to the HarperCollins edition.

9. Peter Feaver, "The Civil-Military Problematique: Huntington, Janowitz, and the Question of Civilian Control," *Armed Forces and Society* 23, no. 2 (1996): 167.

10. Feaver, *Armed Servants*. Feaver's work is the most thorough adaptation of principal-agent theory to civil-military relations, but his is not the first. Feaver builds on the work of other scholars, such as Deborah D. Avant, *Political Institutions and Military Change: Lessons from Peripheral Wars* (Ithaca, NY: Cornell University Press, 1994).

11. Kenneth A. Oye, *Cooperation under Anarchy* (Princeton, NJ: Princeton University Press, 1986), p. 23.

12. Ann Swidler, "Culture in Action: Symbols and Strategies," *American Sociological Review* 51, no. 2 (1986): 273–86.

13. Golby, Cohn, and Feaver, "Thanks for Your Service."

14. Alexander L. George, "The 'Operational Code': A Neglected Approach to the Study of Political Leaders and Decision-Making," *International Studies Quarterly* 13, no. 2 (1969): 190–222; Alexander L. George, "The Causal Nexus between Cognitive Beliefs and Decision-Making Behavior: The 'Operational Code' Belief System," in *Psychological Models in International Politics*, ed. Lawrence S. Falkowski (Boulder, CO: Westview Press, 1979); Nathan Leites, *The Operational Code of the Politburo* (New York: McGraw-Hill, 1951).

15. George, "Causal Nexus," p. 101.

16. Ibid.

17. Alexander L. George and Andrew Bennett, *Case Studies and Theory Development in the Social Sciences* (Cambridge, MA: MIT Press, 2005).

18. Carl H. Builder speaks of service "personalities" in his *The Masks of War: American Military Styles in Strategy and Analysis* (Baltimore: Johns Hopkins University Press, 1989).

19. Edgar H. Schein, *Organizational Culture and Leadership*, 3rd ed. (San Francisco: Jossey-Bass, 1989), p. 7.

20. This essay appears as an appendix in J. C. Wylie, *Military Strategy: A General Theory of Power Control* (Annapolis, MD: Naval Institute Press, 1989). First published in 1967 by Rutgers University Press. The essay originally appeared in the US Naval Institute *Proceedings* 83, no. 8 (August 1957): 811–17. Citations refer to the Naval Institute's 1989 edition.

21. Ibid., p. 150.

22. Victor H. Krulak, *First to Fight: An Inside View of the U.S. Marine Corps* (Annapolis, MD: Naval Institute Press, 1984), p. xv.

23. "Army Museum Listing," http://www.history.army.mil/html/museums/dir-links.html (accessed November 16, 2012). Ironically, the Army is the only service without a national museum. A national museum is currently being built. See http://thenmusa.org.

24. Wylie, *Military Strategy*, p. 72.

25. Andrew Bennett and Jeffrey T. Checkel, *Process Tracing: From Metaphor to Analytic Tool* (Cambridge: Cambridge University Press, 2015), p. 7.

26. United military opposition is the main impression in the authoritative history of Goldwater-Nichols: James R. Locher, *Victory on the Potomac: The Goldwater-Nichols Act Unifies the Pentagon* (College Station: Texas A&M University Press, 2002).

27. "Proposed Charter for DOD Organization Special Review Committee," in "HRC 321 Special Review Committee, Goldwater-Nunn" folder, Army Center of Military History, Fort McNair, Washington, DC.

28. Ibid.

29. Edgar Raines, "Memorandum for Record," 11 December 1985, p. 3, in "HRC 321 Special Review Committee, Goldwater-Nunn" folder.

30. To investigate the impact of service culture, this study required conditions in which cultural explanations had a strong but not uncontested likelihood of holding true. The study needed cases of civil-military policymaking that (1) applied to more than one service; (2) were not primarily about dividing a limited budget; (3) were not primarily about a decision to use military force; (4) focused largely on internal US dynamics, not international relationships; and (5) occurred after the Vietnam War but sufficiently long ago to be largely settled history. These criteria shaped a pool of cases in which the variables of interest had a reasonable opportunity to be seen and heard in a complex political history.

31. See, for example, Kathleen J. McInnis, "Goldwater-Nichols at 30: Defense Reform and Issues for Congress" (Congressional Research Service, report no. 44474, June 2, 2016), https://fas.org/sgp/crs/natsec/R44474.pdf (accessed January 2, 2017).

Chapter 1 · Principled Agent Theory

1. Samuel P. Huntington, *The Soldier and the State: The Theory and Politics of Civil-Military Relations* (Cambridge, MA: Harvard University Press, 1957), p. 83.

2. Ibid., p. 15.

3. Peter Feaver, "The Civil-Military Problematique: Huntington, Janowitz, and the Question of Civilian Control," *Armed Forces and Society* 23, no. 2 (1996): 160.

4. Samuel E. Finer offers a similar critique and argues that professionalism does not inherently lead to subordination as Huntington suggests. See Finer, *The Man on Horseback: The Role of the Military in Politics* (London: Pall Mall, 1962).

5. Peter Feaver, *Armed Servants: Agency, Oversight, and Civil-Military Relations* (Cambridge, MA: Harvard University Press, 2003).

6. For a review of principal-agent theory, see Gary J. Miller, "The Political Evolution of Principal-Agent Models," *Annual Review of Political Science* 8 (2005): 203–25.

7. Civil-military relations involve two-tiered delegation dynamics. The electorate serves as the first principal, hiring a political class as its governing agent. The political leaders, in turn, serve as principal to various subcontractor agents such as the military.

8. Feaver is quick to note that the term *shirking* has problematic connotations in a military context. He emphasizes that his use of these terms is in the strictly formal sense of principal-agent theory, not a pejorative evaluation of negligent or unprofessional behavior. Hawkins et al. use different terms to describe similar principal-agent phenomena. They use the term *agency slack* to describe agent behavior that departs from the principal's intent. In their framework, agency slack comes in two forms: shirking (minimizing effort) and slippage (shifting behavior toward the agent's preference, away from the principal's preference). See Darren G. Hawkins et al., *Delegation and Agency in International Organizations* (Cambridge: Cambridge University Press, 2006), p. 8.

9. This distinction, however, does not justify aggressive or disingenuous advocacy by the military for its preferred position. The relationship remains an "unequal dialogue" between a superior civilian and subordinate military. See Eliot Cohen, *Supreme Command: Soldiers, Statesmen, and Leadership in Wartime* (New York: Free Press, 2002). While offering professional expert advice, the military can still shirk relationally by taking advantage of its asymmetric expertise (i.e., offering half-truths) or compromising the relational integrity of its subordinate position. Ultimately, ideal military conduct during the advising phase involves walking the delicate line of providing informed advice, offered in honest good faith, without any unscrupulous attempts to overdetermine the outcome for the civilian.

10. This insight builds on James Fearon's work on ratifying international agreements. See James D. Fearon, "Bargaining, Enforcement, and International Cooperation," *International Organization* 52, no. 2 (1998): 269–305.

11. *Implementation slack* as used here should not be confused with *agency slack* as used by Hawkins et al. My use of *implementation slack* refers to embedded monitoring parameters in a policy, while *agency slack* refers to agent behavior that departs from principal intent.

12. This mechanism draws on the work of Xinyuan Dai and Beth Simmons. See Xinyuan Dai, "Why Comply? The Domestic Constituency Mechanism," *International Organization* 59, no. 2 (2005): 363–98; and Beth A. Simmons, *Mobilizing for Human Rights: International Law in Domestic Politics* (New York: Cambridge University Press, 2009).

13. The motto of the Air Corps Tactical School, the cognitive birthplace of the US Air Force, was *Proficimus More Irretenti*, "We Make Progress Unhindered by Custom." See Robert T. Finney, *History of the Air Corps Tactical School, 1920–1940* (Washington, DC: Air Force History and Museums Program, 1998), p. 5.

14. This understanding of culture comes from Edgar H. Schein, *Organizational Culture and Leadership*, 3rd ed. (San Francisco: Jossey-Bass, 1989).

15. This proposition is informed by the writings of John Boyd. For an overview of Boyd's life and work, see Grant T. Hammond, *The Mind of War: John Boyd and American Security* (Washington, DC: Smithsonian Institution Press, 2001).

16. Alexander L. George, "The Causal Nexus between Cognitive Beliefs and Decision-Making Behavior: The 'Operational Code' Belief System," in *Psychological Models in International Politics*, ed. Lawrence S. Falkowski (Boulder, CO: Westview Press, 1979), p. 101.

17. Aaron Wildavsky, "Choosing Preferences by Constructing Institutions: A Cultural Theory of Preference Formation," *American Political Science Review* 81, no. 1 (1987): 4–21.

18. For insight on adjustments to pre-strategic preferences in a decision-making environ-

ment, see Robert Dahl, "The Concept of Power," in *Political Power: A Reader in Theory and Research*, ed. Roderick Bell et al. (New York: Free Press, 1969); and Andrew Moravcsik, "Taking Preferences Seriously: A Liberal Theory of International Politics," *International Organization* 51, no. 4 (1997): 513–53.

19. On "bounded rationality," see Herbert A. Simon, *Administrative Behavior: A Study of Decision-Making Processes in Administrative Organizations*, 4th ed. (New York: Free Press, 1997).

Chapter 2 · Thinking Like a Sailor

1. This was the Navy's advertising slogan in 2012. See, for example, the main banners at "Navy.com," http://www.navy.com (accessed July 30, 2012).

2. See, for example, Russell F. Weigley, *The American Way of War: A History of United States Military Strategy and Policy* (Bloomington: Indiana University Press, 1977).

3. Roger W. Barnett, *Navy Strategic Culture: Why the Navy Thinks Differently* (Annapolis, MD: Naval Institute Press, 2009), p. xi.

4. These figures come from the Navy's own summary of its current maritime strategy, at http://www.navy.mil/maritime/display.asp?page=strglance.html (accessed August 8, 2012). The Navy cites the 70-80-90 rule: 70% of the Earth is covered in water, 80% of the world population lives on or near the coast, and 90% of international trade moves by sea.

5. Amy B. Zegart, *Flawed by Design: The Evolution of the CIA, JCS, and NSC* (Stanford, CA: Stanford University Press, 1999), p. 7. This insight from Zegart comports with an extensive political science literature on historical institutionalism. See Kathleen Thelen, "Historical Institutionalism in Comparative Politics," *Annual Review of Political Science* 2, no. 1 (1999): 369–404.

6. Journal of the Continental Congress, 13 October 1775, in *Naval Documents of the Naval Revolution*, ed. William Bell Clark (Washington, DC: Government Printing Office, 1966), 2:442.

7. Ian W. Toll, *Six Frigates: The Epic History of the Founding of the U.S. Navy* (New York: W. W. Norton, 2006), p. 15.

8. Alexander Hamilton et al., *The Federalist: A Commentary on the Constitution of the United States* (New York: G. P. Putnam's Sons, 1888), p. 63.

9. Rutledge quoted in Jonathan Elliot, ed., *The Debates in the Several State Conventions on the Adoption of the Federal Constitution* (Philadelphia: J. B. Lippincott, 1881), 4:299.

10. US Const., art. I, § 8.

11. Barnett, *Navy Strategic Culture*, p. 63.

12. In Navy parlance, a distinction is made between the *rank* of captain (the sixth officer rank, or O-6) and the *position* of captain. The rank of captain is earned over time by promotion through the lower ranks. The position, or title, of captain is an honorific for the commanding officer of a ship or submarine—which can be held by someone in a rank other than captain (O-6).

13. Kenneth J. Hagan, *This People's Navy: The Making of American Sea Power* (New York: Free Press, 1991), p. 94.

14. Max Boot, *The Savage Wars of Peace: Small Wars and the Rise of American Power* (New York: Basic Books, 2002), p. 51.

15. Hagan, *This People's Navy*, p. 148.

16. John H. Schroeder, "Matthew Calbraith Perry: Antebellum Precursor of the Steam Navy," in *Quarterdeck and Bridge: Two Centuries of American Naval Leaders*, ed. James C. Bradford (Annapolis, MD: Naval Institute Press, 1997).

17. United States Navy Department, *Annual Reports of the Navy Department* (Washington, DC: Government Printing Office, 1893).

18. Robert A. Hart, *The Great White Fleet: Its Voyage around the World, 1907–1909* (Boston: Little, Brown, 1965).

19. Even as late as the 1960s and 1970s, the Navy had unique authority and responsibility for diplomatic negotiation in securing port access in Bahrain and negotiating with the British over Middle East security arrangements. See Michael A. Palmer, *Guardians of the Gulf: A History of America's Expanding Role in the Persian Gulf, 1833–1992* (New York: Free Press, 1992), p. 94.

20. Michael S. Sherry, *The Rise of American Air Power: The Creation of Armageddon* (New Haven, CT: Yale University Press, 1987).

21. *Department of Defense Appropriations for 1963: Hearings before the Senate Committee on Appropriations*, 87th Cong. 766 (1962) (statement of Admiral John S. McCain, Jr.).

22. Peter Karsten, *The Naval Aristocracy: The Golden Age of Annapolis and the Emergence of Modern American Navalism* (New York: Free Press, 1972), p. 35.

23. Hamilton et al., *Federalist*, p. 65.

24. Ibid., pp. 254–55.

25. Ibid., p. 255.

26. Toll, *Six Frigates*, p. 43.

27. For the full text of the letter, see George Washington, "Special Message," 25 March 1796, in Gerhard Peters and John T. Woolley, *The American Presidency Project*, http://www.presidency.ucsb.edu/ws/index.php?pid=65517 (accessed October 14, 2016).

28. Hagan, *This People's Navy*, p. 190.

29. Alfred T. Mahan and John B. Hattendorf, *Mahan on Naval Strategy: Selections from the Writings of Rear Admiral Alfred Thayer Mahan* (Annapolis, MD: Naval Institute Press, 1991), p. 95.

30. Philip A. Crowl, "Alfred Thayer Mahan: The Naval Historian," in *Makers of Modern Strategy: From Machiavelli to the Nuclear Age*, ed. Peter Paret (Princeton, NJ: Princeton University Press, 1986).

31. Harold Hance Sprout and Margaret Tuttle Sprout, *The Rise of American Naval Power, 1776–1918* (Princeton, NJ: Princeton University Press, 1939), p. 203.

32. Karsten, *Naval Aristocracy*, p. 326.

33. *Department of Armed Forces, Department of Military Security: Hearings before the Committee on Military Affairs on S. 84 and S. 1482*, 79th Cong. 124 (1945) (statement of Admiral Ernest King).

34. "Our Flag Was Still There," http://www.ourflagwasstillthere.org (accessed August 2, 2012).

35. Barnett, *Navy Strategic Culture*, p. 24.

36. Donald M. Schurman, "Mahan Revisited," in *Maritime Strategy and the Balance of Power: Britain and America in the Twentieth Century*, ed. John B. Hattendorf and Robert S. Jordan (New York: St. Martin's Press, 1989), p. 106.

37. William P. Mack et al., *The Naval Officer's Guide*, 11th ed. (Annapolis, MD: Naval Institute Press, 1998), p. 82.

38. Eugene S. Ferguson, *Truxtun of the Constellation: The Life of Commodore Thomas Truxtun, U.S. Navy, 1755–1822* (Baltimore: Johns Hopkins Press, 1956), p. vi.

39. Karsten, *Naval Aristocracy*, p. 53.

40. Ibid., p. 52.

41. Elting E. Morison, "The War of Ideas: The United States Navy, 1870–1890," in *The Harmon Memorial Lectures in Military History, 1959–1987*, ed. Harry R. Borowski (Washington, DC: Office of Air Force History, US Air Force, 1988), p. 414.

42. Barnett, *Navy Strategic Culture*, p. 122.

43. Clark G. Reynolds, *Command of the Sea: The History and Strategy of Maritime Empires* (Malabar, FL: Krieger, 1983), p. 66.

44. Barnett, *Navy Strategic Culture*, pp. 14, 18.

45. Admiral Gary Roughead, "Memorandum for all Prospective Commanding Officers," 9 June 2011, ser. N00/100050 (Donnithorne's personal papers).

46. A commanding officer (CO) in the Navy could be the captain of the ship *or* the commander of a shore-based unit. While the focus of this discussion is on the legacy of shipboard command, the philosophy of at-sea command translates to the Navy's operations ashore.

47. Barnett, *Navy Strategic Culture*, p. 80.

48. Department of Defense, *The Armed Forces Officer* (Washington, DC: US Department of Defense, 2006), p. 87.

49. Ferguson, *Truxton of the Constellation*, p. vi.

50. Ship captains cannot, of course, do *whatever* they want on ship—they remain subject to Navy regulations, and the Navy has shown a consistent willingness to relieve ship captains for cause. Ship captains bear absolute responsibility for their ship and are thus entrusted with near-absolute authority, subject to Navy regulations.

51. The Navy's reverence for Jones came late, however. See James C. Bradford, *The Reincarnation of John Paul Jones: The Navy Discovers Its Professional Roots* (Washington, DC: Naval Historical Foundation, 1986).

52. Charles West Stewart, *John Paul Jones Commemoration at Annapolis, April 24, 1906* (Washington, DC: Government Printing Office, 1907), p. 16.

53. Samuel Eliot Morison, *John Paul Jones: A Sailor's Biography* (Boston: Little, Brown, 1959), p. 486.

54. United States Office of Naval Records and Library, *Naval Documents Related to the Quasi-War between the United States and France* (Washington, DC: Government Printing Office, 1935), p. 327.

55. Eric Larrabee, *Commander in Chief: Franklin Delano Roosevelt, His Lieutenants, and Their War*, 2nd ed. (Annapolis, MD: Naval Institute Press, 2004), p. 162.

56. Toll, *Six Frigates*, p. 414. With fitting irony, Toll comments: "It was strange that these dying words, comprising an order (not obeyed) to commit mass suicide, were subsequently adopted as the Navy's unofficial motto."

57. While today these terms have different meanings, *mines* and *torpedoes* were virtually synonymous during the Civil War period. James M. McPherson, *Battle Cry of Freedom: The Civil War Era* (New York: Oxford University Press, 1988), p. 761.

58. George Dewey, *Autobiography of George Dewey: Admiral of the Navy* (New York: Scribner, 1913), p. 50.

59. Laurin Hall Healy and Luis Kutner, *The Admiral* (Chicago: Ziff-Davis, 1944), pp. 174–75.

60. *Department of Armed Forces, Department of Military Security: Hearings before the Committee on Military Affairs on S. 84 and S. 1482*, 79th Cong. 539 (1945) (statement of Admiral William Halsey).

61. Department of Defense, *Armed Forces Officer*, p. 86.

62. I thank Richard Diamond (CAPT, USN, Ret.) for this insight.

63. Edwin B. Hooper, *The Navy Department: Evolution and Fragmentation* (Washington, DC: Naval Historical Foundation, 1978), p. 2.

64. Craig L. Symonds, "Defining an American Navy, 1783–1812," in *In Peace and War: Interpretations of American Naval History*, ed. Kenneth J. Hagan and Michael T. McMaster (Westport, CT: Praeger Security International, 2008), p. 27; Sprout and Sprout, *Rise of American Naval Power*, p. 58.

65. Sprout and Sprout, *Rise of American Naval Power*, p. 164.

66. Symonds, "Defining an American Navy," p. 27.

67. Christopher McKee, *A Gentlemanly and Honorable Profession: The Creation of the U.S. Naval Officer Corps, 1794–1815* (Annapolis, MD: Naval Institute Press, 1991), p. 156.

68. Symonds, "Defining an American Navy," p. 29.

69. Mahan and Hattendorf, *Mahan on Naval Strategy*, p. 168.

70. "U.S. Navy Active Ship Force Levels," Naval History and Heritage Command, http://www.history.navy.mil/branches/org9-4.htm (accessed August 7, 2012).

71. Hagan, *This People's Navy*, p. 226.

72. William Tuohy, *America's Fighting Admirals: Winning the War at Sea in World War II* (St. Paul, MN: Zenith Press, 2007), p. 29.

73. Thomas Hone et al., *American & British Aircraft Carrier Development, 1919–1941* (Annapolis, MD: Naval Institute Press, 1999); Stephen P. Rosen, *Winning the Next War: Innovation and the Modern Military* (Ithaca, NY: Cornell University Press, 1991).

74. Edward L. Beach, *The United States Navy: 200 Years* (New York: Henry Holt, 1986), p. 443.

75. Jonathan E. Czarnecki, "Confronting All Enemies: The U.S. Navy, 1962–1980," in Hagan and McMaster, *In Peace and War*.

76. Elmo R. Zumwalt, *On Watch: A Memoir* (New York: Quadrangle / New York Times, 1976), p. 60.

77. Ibid., p. 72; Thomas J. Cutler, "Elmo R. Zumwalt, Jr.: Hero or Heretic?" in *Quarterdeck and Bridge: Two Centuries of American Naval Leaders*, ed. James C. Bradford (Annapolis, MD: Naval Institute Press, 1997), p. 427.

78. Czarnecki, "Confronting All Enemies," p. 272. The focus of historical effort here is on the period up to approximately 1980—the point at which the case study analyses begin. As a point of observation, the modern Navy still pursues a carrier-centric operational scheme but is less wedded specifically to the carrier itself and is more willing to acknowledge its vulnerabilities.

79. There have been recent challenges to this carrier orthodoxy, most notably by Navy Captain Henry Hendrix, who published a critical paper through the Center for a New American Security. Hendrix's opening line is this: "The queen of the American fleet, and the centerpiece of the most powerful Navy the world has ever seen, the aircraft carrier, is in danger of becoming like the battleships it was originally designed to support: big, expensive, vulnerable—and surprisingly irrelevant to the conflicts of the time." Henry Hendrix, "At What Cost a Carrier?" (March 11, 2013), https://www.cnas.org/publications/reports/at-what-cost-a-carrier (accessed March 22, 2013).

80. The most conspicuous omission is a discussion of the Navy's remarkable battle record in World War II. The Navy's experiences in World War II are in many ways the culminating embodiment of the six beliefs discussed in this chapter. While a World War II tale could have amplified any of the six discussions, I have focused on earlier experiences that helped form the beliefs rather than the major conflict that cemented them.

81. Aaron Wildavsky, "Choosing Preferences by Constructing Institutions: A Cultural Theory of Preference Formation," *American Political Science Review* 81, no. 1 (1987): 4–21.

Chapter 3 · The Few and the Proud

1. Thomas G. Mahnken, *Technology and the American Way of War* (New York: Columbia University Press, 2008), pp. 7–8.

2. Jon T. Hoffman, *Chesty: The Story of Lieutenant General Lewis B. Puller, USMC* (New York: Random House, 2001), p. 217.

3. Victor H. Krulak, *First to Fight: An Inside View of the U.S. Marine Corps* (Annapolis, MD: Naval Institute Press, 1984), p. 155. This more egalitarian social structure contrasts markedly with the Corps' sister service, the US Navy. These differences can cause tension on board Navy ships, as Navy officers enjoy privileges that Marine Corps officers viscerally shun. Navy officers, for example, enjoy "head-of-line" privileges and eat separately from enlisted men and women, whereas the Marine Corps insists that "officers eat last." See Patrick Darcey, "Officers Eat First," *United States Naval Institute Proceedings* 138, no. 5 (2012): 66–67.

4. Thomas Ehrhard, "Unmanned Aerial Vehicles in the United States Armed Services: A Comparative Study of Weapon System Innovation" (PhD diss., Johns Hopkins School of Advanced International Studies, 2000), p. 100; Michael J. Meese and Isaiah Wilson, "The Military: Forging a Joint Warrior Culture," in *The National Security Enterprise: Navigating the Labyrinth*, ed. Roger Z. George and Harvey Rishikof (Washington, DC: Georgetown University Press, 2011), p. 130.

5. Edwin H. Simmons, *The United States Marines: A History* (Annapolis, MD: Naval Institute Press, 1998), p. 1.

6. William Bell Clark, *Naval Documents of the American Revolution* (Washington, DC: Government Printing Office, 1966), 2:972.

7. Robert Heinl, *Soldiers of the Sea: The United States Marine Corps, 1775–1962* (Annapolis, MD: Naval Institute Press, 1962), p. 5.

8. In an example of approved mythology eclipsing the historical record, the official Marine Corps recruiting site's discussion of the historical timeline of the Corps suggests that Congress passed the November 10, 1775, resolution at Tun Tavern. See http://www.marines.com/history -heritage/timeline?articleId=TIMELINE_OVW_1770. Better evidence suggests that Congress approved the resolution in its session at the Pennsylvania State House (Independence Hall), while Tun Tavern was more likely used just for recruiting.

9. Charles R. Smith, *Marines in the Revolution: A History of the Continental Marines in the American Revolution, 1775–1783* (Washington, DC: History and Museums Division, Headquarters, US Marine Corps, 1975).

10. Allan R. Millett, *Semper Fidelis: The History of the United States Marine Corps* (New York: Macmillan, 1980), p. 24.

11. The text of this act is available at https://www.mcu.usmc.mil/historydivision/Pages /Speeches.aspx (accessed August 24, 2012). Even though July 11, 1798, is technically the birthdate of the Marine Corps, Marines energetically celebrate November 10, 1775, as the birthday of the Corps. Marines celebrate their organizational birthday much more passionately than any of the other three services.

12. Merrill L. Bartlett, *Lejeune: A Marine's Life, 1867–1942* (Columbia: University of South Carolina Press, 1991).

13. Thomas C. Linn and C. P. Neimeyer, "Once and Future Marines," *Joint Force Quarterly* 6 (1995).

14. Navy Department, General Order 241, 1933, "The Fleet Marine Force," https://www .usmcu.edu/?q=node/615 (accessed September 1, 2017).

15. Millett, *Semper Fidelis*, p. 451.

16. Krulak, *First to Fight*, p. 227. This core attachment has weakened somewhat among the current crop of junior Marine Corps officers, many of whom have never been on a Navy ship. In recent years, during prolonged land campaigns in Iraq and Afghanistan, the Marine Corps has had to serve more like a second land army—a trend that unsettles Marine Corps leaders. In 2010, Commandant of the Marine Corps General James T. Conway observed: "When I go to meetings and I hear 'Army and Marine Corps' talked about in the same breath, I get uncomfortable. It should be 'Navy and Marine Corps.' One day, again, it will be. But right now, we're simply doing what the Nation asks us to do." Quoted in David H. Gurney and Jeffrey D. Smotherman, "An Interview with James T. Conway," *Joint Force Quarterly* 59 (2010).

17. Clark, *Naval Documents of the American Revolution*, p. 957.

18. Peter Karsten, *The Naval Aristocracy: The Golden Age of Annapolis and the Emergence of Modern American Navalism* (New York: Free Press, 1972), p. 89.

19. Heinl, *Soldiers of the Sea*, p. 33.

20. J. Robert. Moskin, *The U.S. Marine Corps Story*, 3rd rev. ed. (Boston: Little, Brown, 1992), p. 24.

21. Krulak, *First to Fight*, p. 13.

22. Millett, *Semper Fidelis*, p. 122.

23. Ibid., p. 144.

24. Amy B. Zegart, *Flawed by Design: The Evolution of the CIA, JCS, and NSC* (Stanford, CA: Stanford University Press, 1999), p. 57.

25. *Unification of the Armed Forces: Hearings before the Committee on Naval Affairs on S. 2044*, 79th Cong. 118–19 (1946) (statement of General Alexander Vandegrift, Commandant, USMC).

26. Douglas-Mansfield Act, Pub. L. 82-416, 66 Stat. 282 (1952).

27. Millett, *Semper Fidelis*, p. 32.

28. Heinl, *Soldiers of the Sea*, p. 251.

29. Hans Schmidt, *Maverick Marine: General Smedley D. Butler and the Contradictions of American Military History* (Lexington: University Press of Kentucky, 1987), p. 130.

30. Craig M. Cameron, *American Samurai: Myth, Imagination, and the Conduct of Battle in the First Marine Division, 1941–1951* (Cambridge: Cambridge University Press, 1994), p. 100.

31. James A. Warren, *American Spartans: The US Marines: A Combat History from Iwo Jima to Iraq* (New York: Free Press, 2005), p. 9.

32. Krulak, *First to Fight*, p. 176.

33. Thomas E. Ricks, *Making the Corps* (New York: Scribner, 1997), p. 40.

34. Krulak, *First to Fight*, p. 161.

35. Heinl, *Soldiers of the Sea*, p. 13.

36. Ian W. Toll, *Six Frigates: The Epic History of the Founding of the U.S. Navy* (New York: W. W. Norton, 2006), p. 260.

37. Heinl, *Soldiers of the Sea*, p. 15.

38. John C. Fredriksen, *The United States Marine Corps: A Chronology, 1775 to the Present* (Santa Barbara, CA: ABC-CLIO, 2011), p. 14.

39. Moskin, *U.S. Marine Corps Story*, p. 38.

40. Max Boot, *The Savage Wars of Peace: Small Wars and the Rise of American Power* (New York: Basic Books, 2002).

41. Willis J. Abbot, *Soldiers of the Sea: The Story of the United States Marine Corps* (New York: Dodd, Mead, 1918), p. 302.

42. Fredriksen, *United States Marine Corps*, p. 81.

43. Millett, *Semper Fidelis*, p. 301.

44. Edward A. Dieckmann, "Dan Daly Reluctant Hero," *Marine Corps Gazette*, November 1960.

45. Simmons, *United States Marines*, p. 100.

46. Merrill L. Bartlett and Jack Sweetman, *Leathernecks: An Illustrated History of the U.S. Marine Corps* (Annapolis, MD: Naval Institute Press, 2008), p. 291.

47. Warren, *American Spartans*, p. 36.

48. Martin Russ, *Breakout: The Chosin Reservoir Campaign, Korea 1950* (New York: Fromm International, 1999).

49. T. R. Fehrenbach, *This Kind of War* (Washington, DC: Brassey's, 1963), p. 245.

50. Heinl, *Soldiers of the Sea*, pp. 563, 569.

51. Hoffman, *Chesty*, p. 411.

52. Ibid., p. ix.

53. Marion F. Sturkey, *Warrior Culture of the US Marines*, 3rd ed. (Plum Branch, SC: Heritage Press International, 2010), p. 6.

54. Fredriksen, *United States Marine Corps*, p. 124.

55. Warren, *American Spartans*, p. 12.

56. Burke Davis, *Marine! The Life of Lt. Gen. Lewis B. (Chesty) Puller, USMC (Ret.)* (Boston: Little, Brown, 1962).

57. Hoffman, *Chesty*, p. 160.

58. Krulak, *First to Fight*, pp. 141, 143.

59. Ibid., p. 151.

60. *Unification of the Armed Forces: Hearings before the Committee on Naval Affairs on S. 2044*, 79th Cong. 117 (1946) (statement of General Alexander Vandegrift, Commandant, USMC).

61. Quoted in Sturkey, *Warrior Culture of the US Marines*, p. 7.

62. Fehrenbach, *This Kind of War*, p. 290.

63. The full version of the Rifleman's Creed is the first entry on the Marine Corps' public webpage about its heritage and traditions. "Rifleman's Creed," http://www.marines.com/history -heritage/traditions (accessed September 7, 2012).

64. Warren, *American Spartan*, p. 11.

65. Millett, *Semper Fidelis*, p. 611.

66. Alfred A. Cunningham, "Value of Aviation to the Marine Corps," *Marine Corps Gazette* 5 (September 1920): 222.

67. Heinl, *Soldiers of the Sea*, p. 603.

68. J. C. Wylie, *Military Strategy: A General Theory of Power Control* (Annapolis, MD: Naval Institute Press, 1989), p. 72. First published in 1967 by Rutgers University Press. Citation refers to Naval Institute edition.

69. Krulak, *First to Fight*, pp. 225–26.

Chapter 4 · Washington's Own

1. Matthew Moten, *The Army Officers' Professional Ethic—Past, Present, and Future* (Carlisle, PA: US Army War College, Strategic Studies Institute, 2010).

2. Samuel P. Huntington, *The Soldier and the State: The Theory and Politics of Civil-Military Relations* (Cambridge, MA: Harvard University Press, 1957), p. 168.

3. David W. Hogan, *225 Years of Service: The U.S. Army, 1775–2000* (Washington, DC: Center of Military History, US Army, 2000), p. 6.

4. John C. Fitzpatrick, ed., *The Writings of George Washington from the Original Manuscript Sources, 1745–1799* (Washington, DC: Government Printing Office, 1931), 6:112.

5. Jack Marsh quoted in Stephen K. Scroggs, *Army Relations with Congress: Thick Armor, Dull Sword, Slow Horse* (Westport, CT: Praeger, 2000), p. 145.

6. Scroggs, *Army Relations with Congress*, p. 1.

7. Ibid., p. 111.

8. William A. Ganoe, *The History of the United States Army* (New York: D. Appleton-Century, 1942), p. 461.

9. Moten, *Army Officers' Professional Ethic*, p. 14.

10. John Wickham's introduction to John Winthrop Hackett, *The Profession of Arms* (Washington, DC: Center of Military History, US Army, 1986).

11. Don M. Snider, "The U.S. Army as a Profession," in *The Future of the Army Profession*, ed. Don M. Snider and Lloyd J. Matthews (Boston: McGraw-Hill, 2005).

12. Fred C. Weyand and Harry G. Summers, "Vietnam Myths and American Realities," *Commanders Call* 5 (July–August 1976): S4.

13. *Department of Defense Appropriations for 1963: Hearings before the U.S. Senate Committee on Appropriations*, 87th Cong. 762 (1962) (statement of Admiral John S. McCain, Jr.).

14. Scroggs, *Army Relations with Congress*, p. 121.

15. Leonard Wong and Douglas V. Johnson II, "Serving the American People: A Historical View of the Army Profession," in Snider and Matthews, *Future of the Army Profession*, p. 97.

16. Russell F. Weigley, *History of the United States Army* (Bloomington: Indiana University Press, 1984), p. 105.

17. Hogan, *225 Years of Service*, p. 10.

18. "Historical Vignette #107," Headquarters US Army Corps of Engineers, http://www .usace.army.mil/About/History/HistoricalVignettes/CivilEngineering/107PanamaCanal.aspx (accessed November 18, 2012).

19. Hogan, *225 Years of Service*, pp. 3, 20, 23.

20. Huntington, *Soldier and the State*, p. 261.

21. Scroggs, *Army Relations with Congress*, p. 123.

22. Robert M. Utley, "The Contribution of the Frontier to the American Military Tradition," in *The Harmon Memorial Lectures in Military History, 1959–1987*, ed. Harry R. Borowski (Washington, DC: Office of Air Force History, US Air Force, 1988), p. 527.

23. Joshua Chamberlain quoted in Iain Martin, *The Greatest U.S. Army Stories Ever Told: Unforgettable Stories of Courage, Honor and Sacrifice* (Guilford, CT: Lyons Press, 2006), p. 82.

24. Russell F. Weigley, *The American Way of War: A History of United States Military Strategy and Policy* (Bloomington: Indiana University Press, 1977), p. 19.

25. Utley, "Contribution of the Frontier," p. 530.

26. Weigley, *History of the United States Army*, p. 161.

27. Ibid., pp. 252, 253.

28. Carl H. Builder, *The Masks of War: American Military Styles in Strategy and Analysis* (Baltimore: Johns Hopkins University Press, 1989), pp. 37–38.

29. T. R. Fehrenbach, *This Kind of War* (Washington, DC: Brassey's, 1963), p. x.

30. Douglas MacArthur, *Reminiscences* (Annapolis, MD: Naval Institute Press, 1964), p. 386.

31. Andrew F. Krepinevich, *The Army and Vietnam* (Baltimore: Johns Hopkins University Press, 1986), p. 5.

32. Brian M. Jenkins, *The Unchangeable War* (Santa Monica, CA: Rand Corporation, 1970), p. v.

33. John A. Nagl, *Learning to Eat Soup with a Knife: Counterinsurgency Lessons from Malaya and Vietnam* (Chicago: University of Chicago Press, 2005), p. 206.

34. "Army's Branch Listing," http://www.tioh.hqda.pentagon.mil/UniformedServices/us_army _branches.aspx (accessed November 15, 2012).

35. Arthur Twining Hadley, *The Straw Giant: Triumph and Failure, America's Armed Forces: A Report from the Field* (New York: Random House, 1986), p. 67.

36. R. Ernest Dupuy, *The Compact History of the United States Army*, 2nd rev. ed. (New York: Hawthorn Books, 1973), p. 39.

37. Ganoe, *History of the United States Army*, p. 513.

38. J. C. Wylie, *Military Strategy: A General Theory of Power Control* (Annapolis, MD: Naval Institute Press, 1989), p. 46. First published in 1967 by Rutgers University Press.

39. James G. Pierce, *Is the Organizational Culture of the U.S. Army Congruent with the Professional Development of Its Senior Level Officer Corps?* (Carlisle, PA: Strategic Studies Institute, 2010), pp. 101, 80.

40. Snider, "U.S. Army as a Profession," p. 3.

41. Lloyd J. Matthews, "Anti-intellectualism and the Army Profession," in *The Future of the Army Profession*, ed. Don M. Snider and Lloyd J. Matthews (Boston: McGraw-Hill, 2005), p. 73.

42. Leonard Wong, *Stifling Innovation: Developing Tomorrow's Leaders Today* (Carlisle, PA: Strategic Studies Institute, US Army War College, 2002), p. 3.

43. Branch insignia are no longer worn on the Army's latest utility uniform, the Army Combat Uniform (ACU). They are still worn on the jacket of the Army Service Uniform (ASU).

44. Builder, *Masks of War*, p. 33.

45. Michael J. Meese and Isaiah Wilson, "The Military: Forging a Joint Warrior Culture," in *The National Security Enterprise: Navigating the Labyrinth*, ed. Roger Z. George and Harvey Rishikof (Washington, DC: Georgetown University Press, 2011).

46. Scroggs, *Army Relations with Congress*, p. 98.

47. Ibid., p. 104.

48. Weigley, *History of the United States Army*, p. 556.

49. Edgar Raines, Army historian, in discussion with the author, February 2013.

50. United States Army, *American Military History*, Army Historical Series (Washington, DC: Center of Military History, US Army, 1989), p. 14.

51. Ibid., p. 46.

52. Fitzpatrick, *Writings of George Washington*, pp. 107, 110.

53. Cited in John McAuley Palmer, *America in Arms: The Experience of the United States with Military Organization* (New Haven, CT: Yale University Press, 1941), p. 10.

54. Weigley, *History of the United States Army*, p. 80.

55. Ibid., p. 93.

56. Palmer, *America in Arms*, p. 74.

57. Ibid., p. 141.

58. Dupuy, *Compact History of the United States Army*, p. 232.

59. "Army Recruiting Messages Help Keep Army Rolling Along," http://www.army.mil/arti cle/322/Army_recruiting_messages_help_keep_Army_rolling_along (accessed November 20, 2012).

60. Lewis Sorley, *Thunderbolt: General Creighton Abrams and the Army of His Times* (New York: Simon & Schuster, 1992), p. 346.

61. Dupuy, *Compact History of the United States Army*, p. 282.

62. Scroggs, *Army Relations with Congress*; Matthews, "Anti-intellectualism and the Army Profession."

63. Sorley, *Thunderbolt*, p. 346.

64. Edward M. Coffman, *The Regulars: The American Army, 1898–1941* (Cambridge, MA: Belknap Press of Harvard University Press, 2004), p. 401.

65. Palmer, *America in Arms*, p. 79.

66. David S. C. Chu, President, Institute for Defense Analyses, former Undersecretary of Defense for Personnel and Readiness, in discussion with the author, February 2012.

67. Matthews, "Anti-intellectualism and the Army Profession," p. 73.

68. Brian McAllister Linn, *The Echo of Battle: The Army's Way of War* (Cambridge, MA: Harvard University Press, 2007), p. 7.

69. Scroggs, *Army Relations with Congress*, p. 137.

Chapter 5 · Fighting for Air

1. Andrew D. Abbott, *The System of Professions: An Essay on the Division of Expert Labor* (Chicago: University of Chicago Press, 1988), p. 33.

2. Roger G. Miller, "The U.S. Army Air Corps and the Search for Autonomy, 1926–1943," in *Golden Legacy, Boundless Future: Essays on the United States Air Force and the Rise of Aerospace Power*, ed. Rebecca H. Cameron and Barbara Wittig (Washington, DC: Air Force History and Museums Program, 2000), p. 39.

3. Paula G. Thornhill, *"Over Not Through": The Search for a Strong, Unified Culture for America's Airmen* (Santa Monica, CA: RAND, 2012).

4. Herman S. Wolk, *The Struggle for Air Force Independence, 1943–1947*, rev. ed. (Washington, DC: Air Force History and Museums Program, 1997), p. 3.

5. "Air Force History," US Air Force, http://www.airforce.com/learn-about/history/part1 (accessed December 5, 2012).

6. James J. Hudson, *Hostile Skies: A Combat History of the American Air Service in World War I* (Syracuse, NY: Syracuse University Press, 1968), p. 302.

7. John F. Shiner, "The Coming of the GHQ Air Force, 1925–1935," in *Winged Shield, Winged*

Sword: A History of the United States Air Force, ed. Bernard C. Nalty (Washington, DC: Air Force History and Museums Program, 1997).

8. Miller, "Search for Autonomy," p. 50.

9. War Department, *Command and Employment of Air Power*, Field Manual 100-20 (Washington, DC: War Department, 1943), p. 1.

10. William Momyer, *Air Power in Three Wars* (Washington, DC: Department of the Air Force, 1978), p. 10.

11. National Security Act of 1947, Pub. L. 80-253, 61 Stat. 495 (1947), Sec. 208f.

12. Mark Clodfelter, "Molding Airpower Convictions: Development and Legacy of William Mitchell's Strategic Thought," in *The Paths of Heaven: The Evolution of Airpower Theory*, ed. Phillip S. Meilinger (Maxwell AFB, AL: Air University Press, 1997), p. 83.

13. Hudson, *Hostile Skies*, p. 303; Tami Davis Biddle, *Rhetoric and Reality in Air Warfare: The Evolution of British and American Ideas about Strategic Bombing, 1914–1945* (Princeton, NJ: Princeton University Press, 2002), p. 52.

14. According to the terms of the agreement, the aircraft had to pause after each bomb was dropped to allow Navy battle-damage crews to assess the extent of the damage. Robert Frank Futrell, *Ideas, Concepts, Doctrine: Basic Thinking in the United States Air Force, 1907–1960* (Maxwell AFB, AL: Air University Press, 1989), p. 37.

15. John F. Shiner, "From Air Service to Air Corps: The Era of Billy Mitchell," in Nalty, *Winged Shield, Winged Sword*, p. 94.

16. Futrell, *Ideas, Concepts, Doctrine*, p. 37.

17. Alfred F. Hurley, *Billy Mitchell, Crusader for Air Power*, rev. ed. (Bloomington: Indiana University Press, 1975), p. 101.

18. Clodfelter, "Molding Airpower Convictions," p. 79.

19. Charles Dunlap, "Understanding Airmen: A Primer for Soldiers," *Military Review* 87, no. 5 (2007): 128.

20. Perry M. Smith, *The Air Force Plans for Peace, 1943–1945* (Baltimore: Johns Hopkins Press, 1970), p. 35.

21. Futrell, *Ideas, Concepts, Doctrine*, p. 82.

22. Miller, "Search for Autonomy," p. 45; Richard J. Overy, *The Air War, 1939–1945* (Washington, DC: Potomac Books, 2005), p. 82; Donald L. Miller, *Masters of the Air: America's Bomber Boys Who Fought the Air War against Nazi Germany* (New York: Simon & Schuster, 2006), p. 7.

23. David MacIsaac, *Strategic Bombing in World War Two: The Story of the United States Strategic Bombing Survey* (New York: Garland, 1976). The British conducted another strategic bombing survey after World War II. The British proposed an allied survey, but the USAAF insisted on conducting its own.

24. John W. Huston, *American Airpower Comes of Age: General Henry H. "Hap" Arnold's World War II Diaries* (Maxwell AFB, AL: Air University Press, 2002), p. 224.

25. Mark Clodfelter, *The Limits of Air Power: The American Bombing of North Vietnam* (New York: Free Press, 1989), p. 52.

26. Benjamin S. Lambeth, *The Transformation of American Air Power* (Ithaca, NY: Cornell University Press, 2000), p. 32.

27. Stephen P. Randolph, *Powerful and Brutal Weapons: Nixon, Kissinger, and the Easter Offensive* (Cambridge, MA: Harvard University Press, 2007).

28. Clodfelter, *Limits of Air Power*; Robert A. Pape, *Bombing to Win: Air Power and Coercion in War* (Ithaca, NY: Cornell University Press, 1996).

29. Clodfelter, *Limits of Air Power*, p. 205.

30. Kenneth P. Werrell, "Air War Victorious: The Gulf War vs. Vietnam," *Parameters* 22, no. 2 (1992): 45.

31. Clodfelter, *Limits of Air Power*, p. 206.

32. Walter J. Boyne, *Beyond the Wild Blue: A History of the United States Air Force* (New York: St. Martin's Press, 1997), p. 176.

33. Phillip S. Meilinger, *10 Propositions regarding Air Power* (Washington, DC: Air Force History and Museums Program, 1995), p. 3.

34. William Mitchell, *Winged Defense: The Development and Possibilities of Modern Air Power* (Tuscaloosa: University of Alabama Press, 2009), p. 26.

35. Arthur William Tedder, *Air Power in War* (London: Hodder and Stoughton, 1948), pp. 51, 32.

36. War Department, *Command and Employment*, p. 2.

37. Alexander P. de Seversky, *Victory through Air Power* (New York: Simon & Schuster, 1942), p. 10.

38. Biddle, *Rhetoric and Reality*, p. 234.

39. *Department of Armed Forces, Department of Military Security: Hearings before the Committee on Military Affairs on S. 84 and S. 1482*, 97th Cong. 360 (1945) (statement of General of the Army Dwight D. Eisenhower).

40. Meilinger, *10 Propositions*, p. 4.

41. Dunlap, "Understanding Airmen."

42. Almost as common is the wry rejoinder that "indecision is the key to flexibility."

43. William C. Sherman, *Air Warfare* (New York: Ronald Press, 1926), p. 157.

44. Meilinger, *10 Propositions*, p. 49.

45. Hudson, *Hostile Skies*, p. 303; Biddle, *Rhetoric and Reality*, p. 52.

46. Bernard C. Nalty, "The Defeat of Italy and Germany," in Nalty, *Winged Shield, Winged Sword*, pp. 270–73, 276.

47. War Department, *Command and Employment*, p. 2.

48. Department of the Air Force, *Air Force Manual 1-2: United States Air Force Basic Doctrine* (Washington, DC: Department of the Air Force, 1955), p. 4.

49. Ian Horwood, *Interservice Rivalry and Airpower in the Vietnam War* (Fort Leavenworth, KS: Combat Studies Institute Press, 2006).

50. Carl H. Builder, *The Masks of War: American Military Styles in Strategy and Analysis* (Baltimore: Johns Hopkins University Press, 1989), p. 22.

51. While the Air Force has historically tended to favor manned aircraft over any unmanned systems, this preference is not absolute. In his extensive comparison of the four military services' adoption of unmanned aerial vehicles (UAVs), Thomas Ehrhard finds the common myth citing anti-UAV bias among pilots to be overdrawn. Instead, Ehrhard suggests the Air Force's slow adoption of UAVs is more an internal political story than a cultural one. The analysis in this book concurs with Ehrhard's claim and suggests that the enduring belief in the Air Force is a commitment to technology in general, and aircraft more specifically (whether manned or unmanned). See Thomas Ehrhard, "Unmanned Aerial Vehicles in the United States Armed Services: A Comparative Study of Weapon System Innovation" (PhD diss., Johns Hopkins University, 2000).

52. This phrase is part of the first line of the popular poem "High Flight," by John G. Magee, Jr.

53. James Smith, "Air Force Culture and Cohesion: Building an Air and Space Force for the Twenty-First Century," *Airpower Journal* 12, no. 3 (Fall, 1998): 46.

54. Ibid., p. 48. "Occupational" orientation refers to a primary loyalty to the task or occupation, whereas "institutional" orientation gives chief loyalty to the institution itself over the task performed within that institution.

55. Carl H. Builder, *The Icarus Syndrome: The Role of Air Power Theory in the Evolution and Fate of the U.S. Air Force* (New Brunswick, NJ: Transaction Publishers, 1994), p. 35.

56. This statement focuses on the *predominant* Air Force contribution to warfighting: flying aircraft. The Air Force does indeed have many airmen in career specialties that expose them to greater risk in a ground combat zone (combat controllers, air liaison officers, terminal attack controllers, parachute rescue jumpers, security forces, and transportation specialists, to name a few).

57. Miller, *Masters of the Air*, p. 2.

58. This dynamic has recently been under scrutiny with growth of the remotely piloted aircraft (RPA) community. These pilots and sensor operators conduct highly sensitive strike operations by day, then must disengage emotionally to coach their kids' soccer teams an hour later. For more insight on these complex dynamics, see Lt. Col. Joseph Campo, "Distance in War: The Experience of MQ-1 and MQ-9 Aircrew," *Air & Space Power Journal–Spanish* 29, no. 3 (2015): 3–10.

59. Sherman, *Air Warfare*, pp. 11–12.

60. Dunlap, "Understanding Airmen."

61. Department of the Air Force, *Air Force Manual 1-2*, p. 10.

62. Abbott, *System of Professions*, p. 33.

Chapter 6 · Getting There Fast

1. See, for example, Olav Njølstad, "Shifting Priorities: The Persian Gulf in US Strategic Planning in the Carter Years," *Cold War History* 4, no. 3 (2004): 21–55; William E. Odom, "The Cold War Origins of the US Central Command," *Journal of Cold War Studies* 8, no. 2 (2006): 52–82; and Henrik Bliddal, *Reforming Military Command Arrangements: The Case of the Rapid Deployment Joint Task Force* (Carlisle, PA: Strategic Studies Institute, 2011).

2. Odom, "Cold War Origins," p. 58. The names Rapid Deployment Joint Task Force (RDJTF) and Rapid Deployment Force (RDF) were often used interchangeably but were not the same thing. The RDF was the general name for the military's response capability, most often used by civilians in the National Security Council (NSC) and outside the Pentagon. The actual RDJTF was the specific joint task force that fulfilled the general concept of the RDF.

3. Almost without exception, nearly every historical treatment of the RDJTF describes the Army–Marine Corps interaction as one of particularly fractious interservice rivalry. For a representative cross section, see Bliddal, *Reforming Military Command Arrangements*; Odom, "Cold War Origins"; Frank L. Jones, "In Brzezinski's Forge: Fashioning the Carter Doctrine's Military Instrument," in *Imperial Crossroads: The Great Powers and the Persian Gulf*, ed. Jeffrey R. Macris and Saul Kelly (Annapolis, MD: Naval Institute Press, 2012); Dore Gold, *America, the Gulf, and Israel: Centcom (Central Command) and Emerging US Regional Security Policies in the Mideast* (Boulder, CO: Westview Press, 1988); Charles A. Kupchan, *The Persian Gulf and the West: The Dilemmas of Security* (Boston: Allen & Unwin, 1987); Alan Ned Sabrosky and William J. Olson, "USCENTCOM Reconsidered: A Case for Reform," *Journal of Strategic Studies* 10, no. 3 (1987): 310–30; Robert P. Haffa, *The Half War: Planning U.S. Rapid Deployment Forces to Meet a Limited Contingency, 1960–1983* (Boulder, CO: Westview Press, 1984); David A. Quinlan, *The Role of the Marine Corps in Rapid Deployment Forces* (Washington, DC: National Defense University Press, 1983); and Jeffrey Record, "The Military Reform Caucus," *Washington Quarterly* 6, no. 2 (1983): 125–29.

4. Bruce R. Kuniholm, *The Persian Gulf and United States Policy: A Guide to Issues and References* (Claremont, CA: Regina Books, 1984), pp. 15–16; Gold, *America, the Gulf, and Israel*, p. 10.

5. Gold, *America, the Gulf, and Israel*, p. 27.

6. Ibid., p. 10.

7. Ronald H. Cole et al., *The History of the Unified Command Plan, 1946–1999* (Washington, DC: Joint History Office, Office of the Chairman of the Joint Chiefs of Staff, 2003).

8. Ibid., p. 12.

9. The military commanders of specified and unified commands were known as commanders-in-chief (or CINCs) of their respective commands. Today, these commands are called "combatant commands," and as of October 2002 the commanders are called "combatant commanders" instead of CINCs. Secretary of Defense Donald Rumsfeld made this change, insisting that the United States has only one commander-in-chief, the president.

10. Cole et al., *Unified Command Plan*, p. 3.

11. Ibid., p. 37.

12. Haffa, *Half War*, p. 108.

13. Ibid., p. 113.

14. Alexander L. George, "The Causal Nexus between Cognitive Beliefs and Decision-Making Behavior: The 'Operational Code' Belief System," in *Psychological Models in International Politics*, ed. Lawrence S. Falkowski (Boulder, CO: Westview Press, 1979), p. 101.

15. Andrew Moravcsik, "Taking Preferences Seriously: A Liberal Theory of International Politics," *International Organization* 51, no. 4 (1997): 513–53.

16. For examples, see Martin Binkin and Jeffrey Record, "Send in the Marines," *Washington Post*, March 3, 1980; Jeffrey Record, "Why Plan Rapid Deployment of the Wrong Kind of Force?" *Washington Star*, February 3, 1980; Jeffrey Record, "The RDF: Is the Pentagon Kidding?" *Washington Quarterly* 4, no. 3 (1981): 41–51; and Thomas Toch, "Rapid Deployment: A Questionable Trump," *Parameters* 10, no. 3 (1980): 89–91.

17. James R. Schlesinger, "Rapid (?) Deployment (?) Force (?)," *Washington Post*, September 24, 1980.

18. The numbered Army beliefs in figure 6.1, referred to in the text discussion, refer back to chapter 4 (fig. 4.1). Similarly, below, the numbered Marine beliefs in figure 6.2 refer back to chapter 3 (fig. 3.1).

19. "Presidential Review Memorandum 10, Comprehensive Net Assessment and Military Force Posture Review," 18 February 1977, available from Jimmy Carter Library online, http://www.jimmycarterlibrary.gov/documents/prmemorandums/prm10.pdf (accessed March 2, 2013). Huntington took leave from Harvard to serve as the NSC's coordinator of security planning in 1977–78.

20. Quoted in "Comprehensive Net Assessment 1978," p. 7, attached to Memorandum from Brzezinski to Carter, 30 March 1979, "Subj: NSC Weekly Report #92," in "Weekly Reports, 91–101" folder, box 42, Zbigniew Brzezinski collection, Jimmy Carter Presidential Library, Atlanta, GA.

21. Njølstad, "Shifting Priorities," p. 27.

22. "Presidential Directive 18, U.S. National Strategy," 24 August 1977, available from Jimmy Carter Library online, http://www.jimmycarterlibrary.gov/documents/pddirectives/pd18.pdf (accessed March 2, 2013).

23. Ibid.

24. Harold Brown, *Public Statements of Harold Brown, Secretary of Defense, 1977–1981* (Washington, DC: Office of the Secretary of Defense Historical Office, 1977–81), 7:2491.

25. Jimmy Carter, *Public Papers of the Presidents: Jimmy Carter, 1978* (Washington, DC: Government Printing Office, 1978), p. 534.

26. Zbigniew Brzezinski, *Power and Principle: Memoirs of the National Security Adviser, 1977–1981* (New York: Farrar, Straus & Giroux, 1983); Lawrence J. Korb, "The FY 1981–1985 Defense Program: Issues and Trends," *American Enterprise Institute Foreign Policy and Defense Review* 2, no. 2 (1980): 2–63; Steven L. Rearden, *Council of War: A History of the Joint Chiefs of Staff, 1942–1991* (Washington, DC: National Defense University Press, 2012).

27. Robert Murray, former Deputy Assistant Secretary of Defense for International Security

Affairs, in discussion with the author, April 2013; Powell Hutton, Colonel, US Army (Ret.), in discussion with the author, March 2013.

28. "Comprehensive Net Assessment 1978," p. 10, attached to Memorandum from Brzezinski to Carter, 30 March 1979, "Subj: NSC Weekly Report #92," in "Weekly Reports, 91–101" folder, box 42, Brzezinski collection, Carter library.

29. NSC Meeting Minutes, 11 May 1979, "Subj: Middle East Security Issues," in "Southwest Asia/Persian Gulf—[2/79–12/79]" folder, box 15, Brzezinski collection.

30. Memorandum from Ermarth and Sick to Brzezinski, 19 June 1979, "Subj: PRCs on Middle East/Persian Gulf," in "Southwest Asia/Persian Gulf—[2/79–12/79]" folder. This memo was drafted for Brzezinski before the meetings, stating the conclusion that Brzezinski needed to emphasize in the Policy Review Committee the next day.

31. Ibid.

32. Memorandum from Brzezinski to Brown, 9 July 1979, "Subj: Persian Gulf Contingency Forces," in "Southwest Asia/Persian Gulf—[2/79–12/79]" folder.

33. The 3 August 1979 memo is referenced in Brown's reply on 16 August 1979. Memorandum from Brown to Brzezinski, 16 August 1979, "Subj: US Capability to Respond to Limited Contingencies," in "Southwest Asia/Persian Gulf—[2/79–12/79]" folder.

34. David Crist, *The Twilight War: The Secret History of America's Thirty-Year Conflict with Iran* (New York: Penguin Books, 2012), p. 42.

35. This JCS memorandum to the secretary of defense is annotated as a source document for the 10 May 1979 Memorandum from the JCS to the Secretary of Defense, "Subj: US Strategy and Defense Policy for the Middle East and Persian Gulf," RAC Project Number NLC-20-24-2-1-0, Carter library.

36. Michael A. Palmer, *Guardians of the Gulf: A History of America's Expanding Role in the Persian Gulf, 1833–1992* (New York: Free Press, 1992), p. 102.

37. Ibid., p. 103.

38. Crist, *Twilight War*, p. 38.

39. Murray, discussion with author.

40. Don Oberdorfer, "Carter Would Fight for Persian Gulf," *Washington Post*, January 24, 1980.

41. Crist, *Twilight War*, p. 39.

42. Transcript of Rogers's press conference is found in the first appendix to the 1980 Rapid Deployment Joint Task Force (RDJTF) Command History, https://www6.centcom.mil/FOIA_RR_Files/5%20USC%2055(a)(2)(D)Records/Command%20History/1980%20RDJTF%20Command%20History-Fully%20Redacted.pdf (accessed March 5, 2013).

43. Brown, *Public Statements*, 5:1931.

44. Memorandum from Brown to Brzezinski, 16 August 1979, "Subj: US Capability to Respond to Limited Contingencies," in "Southwest Asia/Persian Gulf—[2/79–12/79]" folder.

45. This paper was attached to the 16 August 1979 memo cited in previous note.

46. This prepositioning effort was known as Prepositioning of Material Configured in Unit Sets (POMCUS), which staged most of the Army's heavy equipment across outposts in Germany to expedite the equipping of Army heavy divisions against a Soviet invasion.

47. Odom, "Cold War Origins," pp. 58–59.

48. Maxwell Orme Johnson, *The Military as an Instrument of U.S. Policy in Southwest Asia: The Rapid Deployment Joint Task Force, 1979–1982* (Boulder, CO: Westview Press, 1983), p. 61.

49. Jones, "In Brzezinski's Forge," p. 126.

50. Rearden, *Council of War*, p. 404.

51. Erwin C. Hargrove, *Jimmy Carter as President: Leadership and the Politics of the Public Good* (Baton Rouge: Louisiana State University Press, 1988), p. 148.

52. Paul Starobin and Robert Leavitt, "Shaping the National Military Command Structure: Command Responsibilities for the Persian Gulf," Case 85-628 (Kennedy School of Government Case Program, Harvard University, 1985), p. 18. This case study was commissioned by Robert Murray, who was personally involved in much of the RDJTF action as deputy assistant secretary of defense for international security affairs.

53. *U.S. Security Interests and Policies in Southwest Asia: Hearings before the Committee on Foreign Relations, United States Senate*, 96th Cong. 306 (1980) (statement of Walter Slocombe, Deputy Undersecretary of Defense for Policy Planning). Two days later, on March 6, 1980, Secretary of Defense Harold Brown used exactly the same line in a speech to the Council on Foreign Relations in New York.

54. Cole et al., *Unified Command Plan*, p. 56.

55. Starobin and Leavitt, "Military Command Structure," p. 22.

56. Cole et al, *Unified Command Plan*, p. 56.

57. Starobin and Leavitt, "Military Command Structure," p. 23.

58. Murray, discussion with author.

59. Cole et al., *Unified Command Plan*, p. 57.

60. General (Ret.) Volney F. Warner, interview by Colonel Dean M. Owen, 2 February 1983, US Army Military History Institute Senior Officer Oral History Program, Project #83-3, p. 192, in General Volney F. Warner papers, US Army Heritage and Education Center, Carlisle, PA.

61. Starobin and Leavitt, "Military Command Structure," p. 20.

62. See n. 2 on the use of the names Rapid Deployment Joint Task Force (RDJTF) and Rapid Deployment Force (RDF).

63. Revised Briefing Sheet for the CJCS, 6 November 1979, "Subj: JCS 2147/627–Identification of Forces for the Rapid Deployment Joint Task Force," in "Presidential Directives re Defense Policy Development, JCS papers, 1980" folder (1 of 3), box 36, William Odom papers, Library of Congress Manuscript Division, Washington, DC. The Navy and Marine Corps had favored creating a JTF in the August 1979 memo; apparently, this concern in November 1979 was over giving the JTF too much formal recognition and status as opposed to creating an ad hoc JTF as needed for specific crises.

64. Memorandum for Service Chiefs and CINCs from JCS, 29 November 1979, "Subj: Rapid Deployment Joint Task Force Headquarters," in "Presidential Directives re Defense Policy Development, JCS Papers, 1980" folder (3 of 3), box 36, Odom papers.

65. Murray, discussion with author.

66. George C. Wilson, "Marines to Form Rapid Reaction Force," *Washington Post*, December 6, 1979.

67. Fred S. Hoffman, "Marines to Be Made Strike Force," *Philadelphia Inquirer*, December 6, 1979.

68. Crist, *Twilight War*, p. 34.

69. Starobin and Leavitt, "Military Command Structure," p. 26.

70. General (Ret.) Robert Barrow, interview by Brigadier General (Ret.) Edwin Simmons, 17 December 1991, Oral History, Session #14, pp. 67–68, Marine Corps Archives, Quantico, VA.

71. Capitol Hill Press release, 7 December 1979, in "Rapid Deployment Force (RDF): Inception" folder, Marine Corps Historical Division, Quantico, VA. The letter appears to merge political discussions about the RDF and a potential rescue of the recently taken American hostages at the embassy in Tehran.

72. 126 Cong. Rec. 4942–43 (1980).

73. General (Ret.) Carl Stiner, in discussion with the author, April 2013.

74. *Hearings on Military Posture and H.R. 6495, Part 5 of 6 Parts, Military Personnel, before the House Committee on Armed Services*, 96th Cong. 3 (1980) (statement of Lt. Gen. P. X. Kelley). "CONUS" refers to the 48 contiguous US states.

75. General (Ret.) Volney Warner, in discussion with the author, March 2013.

76. Memo from Warner to Brown, 21 April 1980, "Subj: USREDCOM/RDJTF Planning and Command Relationships," in "Presidential Directives re Defense Policy Development, JCS Papers, 1980" folder (1 of 3).

77. Memo from Warner to the Chairman of the JCS, 12 June 1980, "Subj: USREDCOM/ RDJTF Issues," in "Presidential Directives re Defense Policy Development, JCS Papers, 1980" folder (1 of 3).

78. Warner, interview by Owen, p. 193.

79. Memo from Warner to the Chairman of the JCS, 12 June 1980, "Subj: USREDCOM/ RDJTF Issues," in "Presidential Directives re Defense Policy Development, JCS Papers, 1980" folder (1 of 3).

80. Within the US military, the National Command Authority refers to the source of lawful authority for military action, and specifically to the president and the secretary of defense (or their designated representatives).

81. Memo from Kelley to Warner, 6 June 1980, "Subj: Comments on REDCOM Proposed Changes to the RDJTF Terms of Reference," in "Presidential Directives re Defense Policy Development, JCS Papers, 1980" folder (1 of 3).

82. Lieutenant General (Ret.) Dale Vesser, in discussion with the author, March 2013.

83. "U.S. Army Chief Denies Competition with Marines," *Jacksonville Daily News*, December 17, 1980.

84. General Edward C. Meyer, interview by Colonel Keith Nightingale, 1988, Senior Officer Oral History, Project 1988-4, transcript, p. 2, in General Edward C. Meyer papers, US Army Heritage and Education Center, Carlisle, PA.

85. Ibid., p. 283.

86. Jessica Deighan Blankshain, "Essays on Interservice Rivalry and American Civil-Military Relations" (PhD diss., Harvard University, 2014).

87. For more on this interesting side story, see James Kitfield, *Prodigal Soldiers* (New York: Brassey's, Simon & Schuster, 1995), p. 238.

88. When General Kelley was the commander of the RDJTF, he departed from this prevailing Marine view. In nearly every speech and congressional testimony, Kelley insisted that the contribution of all four services was critical to the success of the RDJTF.

89. NSC Meeting Minutes, 17 December 1980, in "Presidential Developments re Defense Policy Development, White House 1977–1982" folder (2 of 2), Odom papers.

90. Odom's consistent advocacy for a new unified command for the Middle East was evidently a source of some amusement within the NSC. Odom's parting gift from Brzezinski was a signed photo with a handwritten comment saying, "No, we cannot yet set up the Indian Ocean command. As ever, Zbig." Cited in Starobin and Leavitt, "Military Command Structure," p. 38.

91. Memo from Odom to Brzezinski, 4 November 1980, "Subj: Security Framework for the Persian Gulf: Next Steps," in "Presidential Developments re Defense Policy Development, White House 1977–1982" folder (2 of 2).

92. Memo from Odom to Allen, 11 February 1981, "Subj: Persian Gulf Security Framework," in "Presidential Developments re Defense Policy Development, White House 1977–1982" folder (2 of 2).

93. *Department of Defense Authorization for Appropriations for Fiscal Year 1982: Hearings before the Senate Committee on Armed Services, First Session on S. 815, Part 2*, 97th Cong. 623 (1981) (statement of General Edward Meyer).

94. Ibid., p. 649.

95. Ibid., p. 733.

96. An Army staff paper dated 15 December 1980 maps out how such a transition to EUCOM

and then to a full unified command might occur, in "Presidential Directives re Defense Policy Development, JCS Papers, 1980" folder (3 of 3).

97. *Department of Defense Authorization for Appropriations for Fiscal Year 1982: Hearings before the Senate Committee on Armed Services, First Session on S. 815, Part 2*, 97th Cong. 731 (1981) (statement of General Robert Barrow).

98. Ibid., p. 908.

99. *Department of Defense Authorization for Appropriations for Fiscal Year 1982: Hearings before a Subcommittee of the Senate Committee on Appropriations, Part 1*, 97th Cong. 454 (1981) (statement of General Robert Barrow).

100. Letter from Warner to Weinberger, 21 January 1981, in Warner papers.

101. Later, Warner regretted delivering the letter so early in Weinberger's tenure, before his new boss had a chance to familiarize himself with the issues. See Warner, interview by Owen, pp. 176–77.

102. Letter from Warner to Weinberger, 6 March 1981, in Warner papers.

103. *Department of Defense Authorization for Appropriations for Fiscal Year 1982: Hearings before the Senate Committee on Armed Services, First Session on S. 815, Part 4*, 97th Cong. 1729–30 (1981) (statement of Lt. Gen. P. X. Kelley).

104. Caspar Weinberger, *Public Statements of Caspar Weinberger, Secretary of Defense* (Washington, DC: Office of the Secretary of Defense Historical Office, 1981), 3:2051.

105. Ibid.

106. In his 1983 oral history interview, Warner stated: "I think that the RDJTF . . . reflects that the chance of failure to make programs work outside of the existing unified command plan is 100 percent. There are five reasons for their failure, and collectively, they're referred to as the Joint Chiefs of Staff." Warner, interview by Owen, p. 168.

107. Cole et al., *Unified Command Plan*, p. 63.

108. A major issue was whether to include Israel, Syria, and Lebanon in the new command or leave them in EUCOM. Another slightly humorous issue arose over what to name the new command. See Crist, *Twilight War*, pp. 54–57.

109. The RDJTF's sparring partner met the same fate not long thereafter. Readiness Command was disestablished in 1987. See Cole et al., *Unified Command Plan*, p. 118.

110. Joint Staff background paper, 19 January 1981, "Rapid Deployment Force: Subject of Pentagon Battle," in "Presidential Directives re Defense Policy Development, JCS papers, 1981" folder.

111. *Department of Defense Authorization for Appropriations for Fiscal Year 1982: Hearings before the Senate Committee on Armed Services, First Session on S. 815, Part 2*, 97th Cong. 625 (1981) (statement of General Robert Barrow).

112. In General Warner's explanations for his retirement, he essentially shifts blame for Weinberger's decision to the JCS. His parting shot was intramilitary, not civil-military, in orientation.

113. Odom, "Cold War Origins," p. 64.

114. Murray, discussion with author.

115. Cited in John Fialka, "Doubt Rises on Force to Protect Gulf," *Washington Star*, January 11, 1981.

116. Starobin and Leavitt, "Military Command Structure," p. 33.

Chapter 7 · Getting to Yes

1. HASC News Release, 11 September 1986, in "020 DA Reorganization Misc Documents" folder, HRC-2, Army Center of Military History, Fort McNair, Washington, DC.

2. The most thorough history is James R. Locher, *Victory on the Potomac: The Goldwater-Nichols Act Unifies the Pentagon* (College Station: Texas A&M University Press, 2002). Locher was a staff member on the Senate Armed Services Committee and was instrumental in shep-

herding reform ideas through the bureaucratic maze. His account is the most complete, and while he certainly pursues objectivity, his deep personal investment in passage of the act should be considered in reading this work.

3. Demetrios Caraley, *The Politics of Military Unification: A Study of Conflict and the Policy Process* (New York: Columbia University Press, 1966), p. 6.

4. Joint History Office, *Organizational Development of the Joint Chiefs of Staff, 1942–2010* (Washington, DC: Office of the Chairman of the Joint Chiefs of Staff, 2011), p. 1.

5. Ibid., p. 2.

6. Caraley, *Military Unification*, p. 17.

7. Lawrence J. Korb, *The Joint Chiefs of Staff: The First Twenty-Five Years* (Bloomington: Indiana University Press, 1976), p. 14.

8. Caraley, *Military Unification*, p. ix.

9. Ibid., p. 4.

10. Unified commands are organized geographically or functionally, consisting of forces from multiple military services. Specified commands operate similarly, but with forces from only one service. The military commanders of these commands were formerly known as commanders-in-chief. Today, these commands are called "combatant commands," and as of October 2002, their commanders are called "combatant commanders." Secretary of Defense Donald Rumsfeld made this change to emphasize that the United States has only one commander-in-chief, the president. Because the title "CINC" was in use during the period of this case study, I refer to these commanders as CINCs in the text.

11. Harry S. Truman, *Public Papers of the Presidents: Harry S. Truman, 1945* (Washington, DC: Government Printing Office, 1945), p. 556.

12. The law was signed on July 26, 1947, but most of the provisions did not take effect until September 18, 1947. Office of the Secretary of Defense (OSD) Historical Office, *The Department of Defense: Documents on Establishment and Organization, 1944–1978* (Washington, DC: Government Printing Office, 1978).

13. Amy B. Zegart, *Flawed by Design: The Evolution of the CIA, JCS, and NSC* (Stanford, CA: Stanford University Press, 1999), p. 110.

14. National Security Act of 1947, Pub. L. 80-253, 61 Stat. 495. Quotes in this paragraph are from §§ 202, 211, and 212.

15. OSD Historical Office, *Department of Defense*, p. 63.

16. Even though the JCS did not operate as a voting organization, this stipulation was inserted to constrain (in spirit) the chairman's power over the corporate JCS.

17. William J. Lynn, "The Wars Within: The Joint Military Structure and Its Critics," in *Reorganizing America's Defense: Leadership in War and Peace*, ed. Robert J. Art et al. (Washington, DC: Pergamon-Brassey's, 1985), p. 175.

18. Pub. L. 85-599, 72 Stat. 514. Quotes in this paragraph are from § 5.

19. Richard C. Steadman, *Report to the Secretary of Defense on the National Military Command Structure* (Washington, DC: Government Printing Office, 1978).

20. Henry Kissinger, *White House Years* (Boston: Little, Brown, 1979), p. 398.

21. Steadman, *Report to the Secretary*, p. 52.

22. William K. Brehm, "The Organization and Functions of the JCS" (report for the Chairman, Joint Chiefs of Staff, by the Chairman's Special Study Group, April 1982), p. 46.

23. Jeffrey Smith, interview by James Locher, 16 June 1998, transcript, p. 3, in box 59, James Locher papers, National Defense University Library, Fort McNair, Washington, DC.

24. Department of Defense Directive 1320.5, "Assignment to Duty with Joint, Combined, Allied and Office of the Secretary of Defense Staffs," 2 December 1959, copy obtained by the author from OSD Historical Office.

25. The Steadman report found that "the positions defined as joint duty were defined too

broadly and . . . frequent exceptions were allowed by the Services." Steadman, *Report to the Secretary*, p. 63.

26. Ibid., p. 35.

27. Alexander L. George, "The Causal Nexus between Cognitive Beliefs and Decision-Making Behavior: The 'Operational Code' Belief System," in *Psychological Models in International Politics*, ed. Lawrence S. Falkowski (Boulder, CO: Westview Press, 1979), p. 106.

28. Ibid., p. 101.

29. The numbered Navy beliefs in figure 7.2 (and, later, fig. 7.5), also referred to in the text discussion, refer back to chapter 2 (fig. 2.1). Similarly, below, the numbered Army beliefs in figure 7.3 (and fig. 7.6) refer back to chapter 3 (fig. 3.1).

30. Even though the chairman did not—and does not—formally command US forces, the principle applies to the nature of the chairman's duties.

31. David C. Jones, "What's Wrong with the Defense Establishment," in *The Defense Reform Debate: Issues and Analysis*, ed. Asa A. Clark IV et al. (Baltimore: Johns Hopkins University Press, 1984), p. 273.

32. David C. Jones, "Why the Joint Chiefs of Staff Must Change," *Presidential Studies Quarterly* 12, no. 2 (1982): 138–49.

33. David C. Jones, "Reform: The Beginnings," in *The Goldwater-Nichols DOD Reorganization Act: A Ten-Year Retrospective*, ed. Dennis J. Quinn (Washington, DC: National Defense University Press, 1999), p. 5.

34. Brehm, "Organization and Functions," p. 3.

35. Jones, "Joint Chiefs of Staff Must Change," p. 147.

36. *Hearings on Military Posture and H.R. 5968 (H.R. 6030), Department of Defense Authorization for Appropriations for FY83, before the House Committee on Armed Services*, 97th Cong. 338 (1982) (statement of General David Jones, Chairman of the Joint Chiefs of Staff).

37. Ibid., p. 339.

38. Archie D. Barrett, Colonel (Ret.), USAF, in discussion with the author, February 2013. Barrett had just completed writing a book on defense reform. That Barrett was there to seize on Jones's statements was quite remarkable and unforeseen.

39. Ibid.

40. *Reorganization Proposals for the Joint Chiefs of Staff, Hearings before the Investigations Subcommittee of the House Committee on Armed Services*, 97th Cong. 46 (1982) (statement of General David Jones).

41. Edward C. Meyer, "The JCS—How Much Reform Is Needed?" *Armed Forces Journal International* 119, no. 8 (1982): 82–90.

42. Ibid., p. 82.

43. *Reorganization Proposals*, 97th Cong. 5 (1982) (statement of General Edward Meyer).

44. *Reorganization Proposals*, 97th Cong. 101 (1982) (statement of Admiral Thomas B. Hayward).

45. Ibid., p. 253.

46. *Reorganization Proposals*, 97th Cong. 159 (1982) (statement of Admiral [Ret.] Thomas Moorer).

47. Ibid., p. 161.

48. James L. Holloway III, "The Quality of Military Advice," *American Enterprise Institute Foreign Policy and Defense Review* 2, no. 1 (1980): 34.

49. *Reorganization Proposals*, 97th Cong. 211 (1982) (statement of Admiral James Holloway).

50. Ibid., p. 213.

51. *Reorganization Proposals*, 97th Cong. 572 (1982) (statement of R. James Woolsey, former Undersecretary of the Navy).

52. *Reorganization Proposals*, 97th Cong. 260 (1982) (statement of General [Ret.] Harold

Johnson). Note how this reverses the expression of Admiral Ernest King in 1945 (as quoted in chapter 2): "any step that is not good for the Navy is not good for the Nation."

53. Memorandum, 15 January 1981, "Subj: Joint Chiefs of Staff," in "Weinberger–1982" folder, box 36, Locher papers.

54. Admiral Thomas Hayward, "Improving the Effectiveness of the Joint Chiefs of Staff," concept paper, p. 13, in "Weinberger–1982" folder.

55. Hittle had been involved in the Marine Corps' advocacy effort during the 1947 unification debates and had published works on military staff organization. See, for example, J. D. Hittle, *The Military Staff: Its History and Development* (Harrisburg, PA: Military Service Publishing, 1944).

56. Memorandum for the Secretary of the Navy, 22 October 1981, Personnel Issues–Hittle Memos, in box 7A, John F. Lehman Papers, Naval History and Heritage Command (NHHC) Archive, Washington Navy Yard, Washington, DC (copy in box 33, Locher papers).

57. The memorandum is undated and unsigned, but Lehman's handwriting across the top reads "Excellent!" Memorandum in "OI–JCS Reorg 1982" folder (2 of 3), box 4, Lehman papers (copy in box 33, Locher papers).

58. The engagement strategy with Senator Tower is discussed in memoranda from Hittle to Lehman, dated 1 March 1982 and 1 September 1982 (copies in box 33, Locher papers).

59. Under Representative Richard White's leadership, the House passed a modest reform bill by voice vote on August 16, 1982. See Cong. Rec. H5947–53 (daily ed., Aug. 16, 1982).

60. Senators Tower, Denton, Warner, and Nunn attended. Tower was in the Navy reserves, Denton was a retired admiral, and Warner had been secretary of the Navy. Nunn, however, was pro-reform.

61. Daniel Kaufman, Brigadier General (Ret.), USA, in discussion with the author, February 2013.

62. See Clark et al., *Defense Reform Debate*.

63. "020 Reform of the Joint Chief of Staff (JCS)" binder 1 of 2, HRC-2, Army Center of Military History. All quotes in the paragraph are from this document.

64. "An Exclusive AFJ Interview with General John W. Vessey, Jr., Chairman, Joint Chiefs of Staff," *Armed Forces Journal International* 120, no. 10 (1983): 45. A common refrain from numerous witnesses, including senior Navy officers, during the 1982 HASC hearings was a plea to wait and let General Vessey have a turn as CJCS.

65. Ibid., p. 49.

66. General John W. Vessey, interview by OSD Historical Office, 21 March 1990, transcript, p. 15, in box 63, Locher papers.

67. Ibid., p. 18.

68. General Edward Meyer, interview by James Locher, 25 June 1998, transcript, p. 21, in box 61, Locher papers.

69. Ibid.

70. Ibid., p. 16.

71. "Memorandum for Secretary of Defense," 22 November 1982, accession number 330 84 0002, in "020 JCS (Oct–Dec)" folder, box 20, Weinberger personal papers (copy in box 36, Locher papers).

72. Caspar Weinberger, interview by James Locher, 27 October 1998, transcript, p. 3, in box 63, Locher papers.

73. *Reorganization Proposals for the Joint Chiefs of Staff, Hearings before the Investigations Subcommittee of the House Committee on Armed Services*, 98th Cong. 61 (1983) (statement of General John Vessey).

74. Meyer, in fact, had been on record in support of JCS reform as recently as the previous February (1983), just four months before this collective JCS testimony. In his testimony to the

House budget committee on February 17, 1983, Meyer quipped, "I am to the right of Genghis Khan on everything as far as issues like [defense organization] are concerned and very positive in my views."

75. *Reorganization Proposals*, 98th Cong. 54 (1983) (statement of Representative Ike Skelton).

76. *Reorganization Proposals*, 98th Cong. 78 (1983) (statement of General Edward Meyer).

77. Benis M. Frank, *U.S. Marines in Lebanon, 1982–1984* (Washington, DC: History and Museums Division, Headquarters, US Marine Corps, 1987), p. 3.

78. Zegart, *Flawed by Design*, p. 144.

79. Ronald H. Cole, *Operation Urgent Fury: The Planning and Execution of Joint Operations in Grenada, 12 October–2 November 1983* (Washington, DC: Joint History Office, Office of the Chairman of the Joint Chiefs of Staff, 1997).

80. *Organization, Structure and Decisionmaking Procedures of the Department of Defense, Hearings before the Senate Committee on Armed Services, Part 5*, 98th Cong. 187 (1983) (statement of James Schlesinger, former Secretary of Defense).

81. *Organization, Structure and Decisionmaking Procedures of the Department of Defense, Hearings before the Senate Committee on Armed Services, Part 6*, 98th Cong. 217, 223 (1983) (statement of John Lehman, Secretary of the Navy).

82. *Organization, Structure and Decisionmaking Procedures of the Department of Defense, Hearings before the Senate Committee on Armed Services, Part 8*, 98th Cong. 318, 322, 326 (1983) (statements of the JCS).

83. Joint Chiefs of Staff Memorandum, 21 February 1984, "Subject: Improving the Quality and Timeliness of JCS Advice/Responses," in "OP-60" files, box 10, NHHC (copy in box 34, Locher papers).

84. Army Field Manual (FM) 100-5, *Operations*, 20 August 1982, available from https://archive.org/details/FM100-5Operations1982 (accessed September 5, 2017).

85. Raoul Alcala, Colonel (Ret.), USA, in discussion with the author, February 2013. Colonel Alcala was the lead Army action officer involved in this joint effort with the Air Force.

86. Copy of memorandum in Richard G. Davis, *The 31 Initiatives: A Study in Air Force–Army Cooperation* (Washington, DC: Office of Air Force History, US Air Force, 1987), pp. 91–92.

87. Generals Wickham and Gabriel were classmates at West Point and good friends. According to the Army action officer closest to the process—Colonel Raoul Alcala—their personal friendship unquestionably helped the process of interservice cooperation move forward.

88. Alcala, discussion with author.

89. James Stefan, Colonel (Ret.), USA, in discussion with the author, February 2013.

90. Ibid.

91. General John Wickham, interview by James Locher, 9 May 1995, transcript, p. 23, in box 63, Locher papers.

92. Jack Wood, Colonel (Ret.), USA, in discussion with the author, February 2013.

93. "Memorandum for the Secretary of the Navy," 1 February 1983, in "OI-JCS Reorg–1983" folder (1 of 2), box 4, Lehman papers (copy in box 33, Locher papers).

94. Locher, *Victory on the Potomac*, pp. 172–76.

95. "Navy Secretary Strafes Bureaucrats," *Washington Post*, March 5, 1983.

96. Quoted from draft letter from CNO to various members of Congress, in Navy staff files, box 34, Locher papers.

97. Report of the Chief of Naval Operations Select Panel, Reorganization of the National Security Organization, March 1985, p. I-5, in "OP-60" folder, box 34, Locher papers.

98. Ibid., p. I-6.

99. Locher, *Victory on the Potomac*.

100. Colonel Barry M. Goldwater, "A Concept for the Future Organization of the United States Armed Forces" (Air War College, Maxwell AFB, AL, 1958), pp. 1–2.

101. *Defense Organization: The Need for Change, Staff Report to the Committee on Armed Services, United States Senate* (Washington, DC: Government Printing Office, 1985).

102. Ibid., p. 3.

103. Ibid., p. 11.

104. "Memorandum for Vice Chief of Staff, Army. Subject: Review of Nunn/Goldwater Study," 24 October 1985, in "Department of Defense Reorganization, 1984–1991, Chief of Staff DOD Reorganization Oct-Nov-1985" folder, John A. Wickham, Jr., papers, Army Military History Institute, Carlisle, PA (copy in box 34, Locher papers).

105. Ibid.

106. Edgar Raines, "Memorandum for Record," 11 December 1985, p. 3, in "HRC 321 Special Review Committee, Goldwater-Nunn" folder, Army Center of Military History. Dr. Raines served as part of the Special Review Committee, and his memo serves as the best after-action report of the committee's proceedings.

107. "Proposed Charter for DOD Organization Special Review Committee," in "HRC 321 Special Review Committee, Goldwater-Nunn" folder.

108. Ibid.

109. Raines, "Memorandum for Record," 11 December 1985, p. 3.

110. Special Review Committee (SRC) briefing slides, slide 6, in "HRC 321 Special Review Committee, Goldwater-Nunn" folder.

111. After much research, the SRC's final briefing stands out as one of the very few balanced treatments of the key issues.

112. Seth Cropsey, former Deputy Undersecretary of the Navy, in discussion with the author, January 2013.

113. "Memorandum for the Secretary of the Navy, Subj: Draft SASC Staff Report on Defense Reorganization," 20 September 1985, in "OI-JCS Reorg–1985" folder (5 of 8), box 5, Lehman papers (copy in box 33, Locher papers).

114. Document copy in "OP-60" folder, box 34, Locher papers.

115. *Reorganization of the Department of Defense, Hearings before the Committee on Armed Services, United States Senate,* 99th Cong. 155 (1985).

116. Ibid., p. 283.

117. Kaufman, discussion with author.

118. *Reorganization of the Department of Defense,* 99th Cong. 507, 595.

119. Archie D. Barrett, *Goldwater-Nichols Act Readings: Legislative Activities and Documents Leading to the Passage of the Goldwater-Nichols Department of Reorganization Act of 1986* (Monterey, CA: Naval Postgraduate School, 2001), p. 5:57.

120. "Memorandum for the Secretary of the Navy, Subj: Packard Commission Strategy: Action Memorandum," 21 August 1985, in "OI–Packard Commission" folder, box 7, Lehman papers (copy in box 33, Locher papers).

121. "Memorandum for the Record, Subj: Status of the Defense Reorganization Issue," 9 December 1985, in "OI-JCS Reorg–1985" folder (7 of 8), box 5, Lehman papers (copy in box 33, Locher papers).

122. Letter from John Lehman to Secretary of Defense Weinberger, 31 January 1986, in "OI-JCS Reorg–1986" folder (1 of 8), box 6, Lehman papers (copy in box 33, Locher papers).

123. Letter from John Lehman to Vice President George Bush, 31 January 1986, in "OI-JCS Reorg–1986" folder (1 of 8), box 6, Lehman papers (copy in box 33, Locher papers).

124. Michael Ganley, "Senate Armed Services Resolves Most Issues in DOD Reorganization Bill," *Armed Forces Journal International* 123, no. 9 (1986): 18.

125. James Kitfield, *Prodigal Soldiers* (New York: Brassey's, Simon & Schuster, 1995), p. 293.

126. Michael Ganley, "Reorganization Bill Almost Certain to Reach President's Desk This Year," *Armed Forces Journal International* 123, no. 10 (1986): 16.

127. William Cohen, Captain (Ret.), USN, in discussion with the author, February 2013.

128. Ibid. Weinberger forwarded the letter to Lehman for the secretary of the Navy to take appropriate action. Lehman did not take any action against Cohen.

129. "An Interim Report to the President by the President's Blue Ribbon Commission on Defense Management," February 1986, available from https://digitalndulibrary.ndu.edu/cdm/compoundobject/collection/nduldpub/id/2523/rec/3 (accessed September 7, 2017).

130. "Summary of a Directive Implementing the Recommendations of the Blue Ribbon Commission on Defense Management," unclassified White House Summary, in David Packard, *Appendix to a Quest for Excellence: Final Report to the President by the President's Blue Ribbon Commission on Defense Management* (Washington, DC: White House, 1986), pp. 34–37.

131. "Message to Congress Outlining Proposals for Improvement to the Defense Establishment," in Packard, *Appendix*, pp. 43–50.

132. Letter from Goldwater and Nunn to Weinberger, 5 May 1986, in box 33, Locher papers.

133. Locher, *Victory on the Potomac*, p. 419.

134. Michael Ganley, "Lehman Chastised by His Mother over Dispute with Goldwater on DOD Reform," *Armed Forces Journal International* 123, no. 10 (1986): 18.

135. Letter to the Honorable Ronald W. Reagan, undated, unsigned, in "OI-JCS Reorg–1986" folder (8 of 8), box 6, Lehman papers (copy in box 33, Locher papers).

136. Pub. L. 99-433, 100 Stat. 992.

137. SRC Briefing Slides, slide 28, in "HRC 321 Special Review Committee, Goldwater-Nunn" folder, Army Center of Military History.

138. Ibid., slide 34.

139. Powell Hutton, Colonel (Ret.), USA, in discussion with the author, February 2013.

140. Edgar Raines, US Army historian, in discussion with the author, February 2013.

141. John Lehman, former Secretary of the Navy, in discussion with the author, February 2013.

142. US Const., art. I, § 8.

143. Letter from Rear Admiral George Miller to Secretary of the Navy John Lehman, 9 May 1986, in "OI-JCS Reorg–1986," folder (3 of 8), box 6, Lehman papers (copy in box 33, Locher papers).

144. Lehman, discussion with author.

145. John F. Lehman, *Command of the Seas* (New York: Scribner, 1988), p. 112.

146. Self-attributed quote in Admiral Moorer's notes from a two-day retreat held at Fort A. P. Hill in October 1985, notes dated 7 October 1985, in "OI-JCS Reorg–1985" folder (5 of 8), box 5, Lehman papers (copy in box 33 of Locher papers).

147. Pub. L. 99433, 100 Stat. 992.

148. Barrett, discussion with author.

149. Ibid.

150. Association of the United States Army, 1987, "Fact Sheet: Department of Defense Reorganization Act of 1986—A Primer," p. 38, in "020 DA Reorganization, Miscellaneous Documents," HRC-2, Army Center of Military History.

Conclusion

1. Plato, *The Republic*, trans. Richard W. Sterling and William C. Scott (New York: Norton, 1985), 71.

2. Peter Feaver, *Armed Servants: Agency, Oversight, and Civil-Military Relations* (Cambridge, MA: Harvard University Press, 2003), p. 6.

3. For a video presentation of Peter Feaver describing the empathy gap, see "Power Struggle—Peter Feaver," https://www.youtube.com/watch?v=WIU8rIOkkVo (accessed December 4, 2016).

4. See, for example, Eliot Cohen, *Supreme Command: Soldiers, Statesmen, and Leadership in*

Wartime (New York: Free Press, 2002); Richard H. Kohn, "How Democracies Control the Military," *Journal of Democracy* 8, no. 4 (1997): 140–53; Marybeth Peterson Ulrich, "Infusing Normative Civil-Military Relations Principles in the Officer Corps," in *The Future of the Army Profession*, ed. Don M. Snider, and Lloyd J. Matthews (Boston: McGraw-Hill, 2005).

5. Eliot Cohen, "The Unequal Dialogue: The Theory and Reality of Civil-Military Relations and the Use of Force," in *Soldiers and Civilians: The Civil-Military Gap and American National Security*, ed. Peter Feaver, and Richard H. Kohn (Cambridge, MA: MIT Press, 2001).

6. Robert Work, "Remarks to the Air Force Association" (National Harbor, MD, September 21, 2016), https://www.defense.gov/News/Speeches/Speech-View/Article/973907/remarks-to-the-air-force-association (accessed January 1, 2017).

7. Robert Work, "Remarks by Deputy Secretary Work on Third Offset Strategy" (Brussels, Belgium, April 28, 2016), https://www.defense.gov/News/Speeches/Speech-View/Article/753482/remarks-by-deputy-secretary-work-on-third-offset-strategy (accessed January 1, 2017).

8. The author learned of this term through various conversations with Pentagon personnel.

9. Robert Work, "Remarks to the Association of the U.S. Army Annual Convention" (Washington, DC, October 4, 2016), https://www.defense.gov/News/Speeches/Speech-View/Article/974075/remarks-to-the-association-of-the-us-army-annual-convention (accessed January 1, 2017).

10. Paula G. Thornhill, *"Over Not Through": The Search for a Strong, Unified Culture for America's Airmen* (Santa Monica, CA: RAND, 2012).

11. Memorandum, "Forging Two New Links to the Force of the Future," 1 November 2016, https://www.defense.gov/Portals/1/Documents/pubs/Forging-Two-New-Links-Force-of-the-Future-1-Nov-16.pdf (accessed January 1, 2017).

12. For a useful summary of current defense reform issues, see Kathleen J. McInnis, "Goldwater-Nichols at 30: Defense Reform and Issues for Congress" (Congressional Research Service, report no. 44474, June 2, 2016), https://fas.org/sgp/crs/natsec/R44474.pdf (accessed January 1, 2017).

13. "Fact Sheet: Building the First Link to the Force of the Future," https://www.defense.gov/Portals/1/features/2015/0315_force-of-the-future/documents/FotF_Fact_Sheet_-_FINAL_11.18.pdf (accessed January 1, 2017).

14. "Forging Two New Links."

15. Memorandum, "The Next Two Links to the Force of the Future," 9 June 2016, https://www.defense.gov/Portals/1/features/2015/0315_force-of-the-future/documents/FotF_Fact_Sheet_-_FINAL_11.18.pdf (accessed January 1, 2017).

16. McInnis, "Goldwater-Nichols at 30," pp. 24, 28.